Please don't let me go, Papa!

Please don't let me go, Papa!

A true story

Ricaardoe Di Done

Published by
Theo Done & Associates Ltd.,
Montreal, Canada

Commentaries

This book recounts the remarkable saga of a father in search of his son. The father's entanglement with the legal system almost ruins his life. However, his courage and endurance enable him to triumph and he is finally reunited with his son".

Attorney Ramrao Adik an educationist & futurist is Former Deputy Chief Minister and Finance Minister of Maharashtra, India.

"Please don't let me go, Papa! chronicles a fascinating journey of legal twists and turns through a system that failed to understand the awesome motivational power of one man's irreversible love for his son".

Chief MacLeod is Chief of Police for the Cape Breton Regional Service in Nova Scotia, Canada, Vice President of the Canadian Association of Chiefs of Police and Chairperson of the Crime Prevention /Community Policing Committee.

Edgar A. MacLeod

"Please don't let me go, Papa! is a powerful indictment of a legal system that fails, totally, to meet its obligation to work "in the best interests" of children of separated and divorced parents. It illustrates, on behalf of the countless children and parents who are caught in similar situations, why changes need to be made to our legal and social structures, to ensure that children do not become the tool of animosity between adults/parents who no longer live together".

Eugenia Repetur Moreno

Mrs. Moreno is Executive Director of the Canadian Association of Social Workers (CASW), and was a professor at the School of Social Work, University of Chile, Santiago for several years prior to coming to Canada.

"There are few areas of family law that have been more thoroughly studied and have produced fewer useful changes for children and their parents than that of child custody and access. *Please don't let me go, Papa!* provides concrete and achievable recommendations to our legal and social structures that have children as their central concern, and that promise more positive outcomes than what happens currently".

John Mould

Mr. Mould, a children's advocate, is currently the President of the Canadian Association of Social Workers and the North American Vice-President of the International Federation of Social Workers

"A heartbreaking account of a father's love for his son bedeviled by the legal system. Their reunion after sixteen years testifies to the author's unyielding determination to prevail in spite of formidable odds".

Judge Marx is former professor of law and former Minister of Justice and Attorney General of Quebec, Canada.

Hon. Justice Herbert Marx

Dedication

To my son Rick,
and all other children of this world.

I was the prize, but I did not feel like one

When I was young I thought that my life was a mistake – that everyone I knew would have been better off if I had never been born. I believed that my life only caused harm to those around me. In my eyes, my two families despised each other, and I felt the need to suppress my true feelings because they only made my parents angry.

I have lived through many name changes and have always gone by two different names with my two families. Each side disliked the name chosen by the other. I was torn between two families I loved, leaving me with no sense of real identity. Lost in life and full of anger, grief and insecurity, I am incapable of relaxing and enjoying myself. It is my nature not to trust and I have no confidence in my ability to succeed. I rarely smile. Sometimes the hate I feel is turned towards myself, sometimes towards my parents, and sometimes towards society as a whole. Almost every morning that I can remember, I have awakened angry at life – some days worse than others. Then everyone around me gets a taste of it, and at age 22, I have still to pull myself out of my self-made prison.

The more conflict and anger there is at home and during the course of a separation, the harder it is for the children and the worse they may turn out. Children feel as though they are at fault for everything, and many seek out drugs, liquor, crime and street life as a means of escaping reality.

For so much of my life, I was the prize, but I did not feel like one. I hope this book will open society's eyes to the butchery caused by unpleasant family separations. I also hope that laws will be changed to ease the process and treat children like actual people instead of objects. This could make all the difference in their ability to succeed in life.

Ricaardoe Branden Di Done

© **Theo Done & Associates Ltd., 2001.**
2175, Mountain Street
Montreal, Quebec
H3G 1Z8
Canada

First Published September 2001

National Library of Canada cataloguing in publication

Di Done, Riccardo, 1950-

Please don't let me go Papa!

Canadian ed. Rev. and corr.

Includes bibliographical references.

ISBN No. 2-923161-00-9

1.Di Done, Riccardo, 1950- 2.Custody of children – Canada. 3.Children rights – Canada 4.Domestic relations – Canada 5.Fathers and sons – Canada. 6.Divorced parents – Canada   I. Organization for the Protection of Children Rights. II. Title.

HQ759.915D52 2003   **306.874'2**   **C2003-941141-9**

CONTENTS

ACKNOWLEDGEMENTS

I would like to thank the following people who have in some way strongly supported my cause and helped to ensure that my son had the opportunity to know both his parents. Amongst this group of people are those who have enabled me to make this book possible and those who have helped Ricaardoe Jr. during his teenage years: Mikea Allard, Helen Amoriggi, Josette Béland, Rando Biasini, Michel Bissonet, Frank Carbone, Charles and Sylvana Caruana, Frantisek Cikanek, Marcel Corbeil, Dominic D'Abate, Domenic D'Alessandro, Vincent Della Noce, Garry Romulus Dieuveil, Senator Sheila Finestone, Claire Harting, Cheryl Hass, Joseph Lalla, Denis Landry, Réjean Leblanc, Dr. Sami Mohanna, Joe Papa, Senator Lucie Pépin, Gilles Proulx, Philip Shaposnick, Robert Roy, Don Solcitto, Howard Starkman, Jacob Vanderschaaf, André Verret, Vile'm Weber, Marilyn Weston.

A special thank you to the following members of my family who have continually supported, encouraged and loved me throughout the years and who have given me the strength to pursue and achieve my goals: Françoise Di Done, Theodore Di Done, Antonietta Di Done Colmano, Riccardo Colmano, Brigitte Jalbert, Ricaardoe Jr. Di Done, Alexandra Nancy Di Done, Antoni Vito Di Done, Marina Manoushka Di Done, Samantha Chiarina Di Done.

Many thanks to Laurene Bennett, a gifted writer and editor. Her ability to help me thread together my ideas and recollections – from the contents of several filing cabinets filled with court transcriptions, affidavits, judgments, letters, media coverage, and other miscellaneous documents – turned my real life experience into a readable story.

We express our deep appreciation to Ms. Carol Andrade for extensive editing of the final manuscript.

PREFACE

Ricaardoe Di Done has put into the harsh light of print what so many parents, both men and women, express only to friends and confidants. Sometimes the stories are longer, at other times they are short outbursts of confusion, outrage and bewilderment at a system that has lost touch with the ability to humanely deal with the needs and the desires of the rights of children and

William Rowe

parents in the midst of separation, divorce, custody and access.

Few have the financial or emotional resources to maintain their quest to stay in their children's lives in an appropriate, loving, supportive role, while the legal/judicial child welfare system presents an ever changing miasma of bureaucratic confusion, partial truths and other unwarranted biases. Most people simply walk away in guilt and despair and possibly turn to alcohol or other forms of self-medication, while others simply cut their losses and live the rest of their lives with a missing piece in their soul.

Sometimes, it is hard to hear these stories without wallowing recriminations. Many observers desperate to retreat to the fragile safety of their own relationships and families merely want a clear culprit to blame.

Ricaardoe Di Done is exceptional in his insistence on finding another way, and against all odds, he succeeds in remaining a strong presence in his son's life. His continued campaign to seek alternatives such as mediation and family counseling to routinely replace litigation as a means of resolving custody and access disputes, has led to numerous recommendations, some of which have already come to pass.

This is Ricaardoe Di Done's story, but clearly readers will find resonance in the very human drama it portrays.

Dr Rowe has held professorships at McGill, Memorial University and the University of Western Ontario and has authored/edited numerous books, articles and research reports. His research activities include family violence, AIDS prevention, care and curriculum development and health care outcomes.

Preface

I became involved with Ricaardoe Di Done in the latter part of 1987. The Legal Services Society of British Columbia appointed me as his lawyer in a contested adoption proceeding that was to be heard in the Kamloops Registry of the Supreme Court of British Columbia. At first, this seemed like a relatively normal case where two parents had different views regarding their child. But after reading through the large stack of papers I received, it became apparent that this was anything but a normal case.

*Peter
Allik-Petersenn*

The child in the case had previously been the subject of four different lawsuits in three provinces, including a previous adoption in British Columbia that had been set aside. The contested adoption proceeding that I was to be involved in as Ricaardoe Di Done's lawyer, was the fifth! Ironically, Ricaardoe Jr. was just under 12 years old when the trial took place in March of 1989 and his consent to the adoption was therefore not needed. Had Ricaardoe Jr. been 12 years or older, his consent would, in fact have been needed. Even more ironic is the fact that just before he turned 19, his adoption was set-aside by the same Supreme Court of British Columbia in the Kamloops Registry that originally made the Order. Ricaardoe Jr. is now again legally the child of both his natural parents.

What if there had been compulsory mediation when Ricaardoe Jr's parents separated? What if both parents had been required to seriously consider whether, in his best interests, they should attempt to arrive at an agreement regarding their son, instead of starting down a long legal path which would lead to five lawsuits in three provinces.

It is my hope that everyone who reads this book will seriously consider doing their part, however small that may be, in influencing major changes in the laws relating to families. Such laws should require and emphasize mediation as a first step and leave lawsuits only as the last step in disagreements by parents regarding their children. Laws relating to families should further replace the current language, which treats children as possessions with wording that emphasizes responsibility and care for them instead.

Mr. Allik-Petersenn was in business for 12 years before he decided to pursue a career in law. He has practiced primarily family law since 1976 and has been involved in family mediation since 1993. His understanding of the shortcomings of the legal system has made him a strong crusader for alternative dispute resolution methods. He is the Director of the O.P.C.R. in British Columbia.

Preface

In poignant and compelling language, the author describes his turbulent 16-year-journey through an almost unbelievable maze of legal chicanery as he struggles to maintain a vital relationship with his natural son. Overcoming obstacle after obstacle, he strives to provide a consistent source of identity for his maturing boy, and to allow him what all of us take as self-evident: that a child be nurtured and loved by those that are dear to him and be permitted to flourish within his extended family.

Arthur Neuman

The experiences encountered in his personal life spurred Ricaardoe Di Done to establish the Organization for the Protection of Children's Rights, which devotes itself to making the voices of the children of families in difficulty heard. The author's successful efforts in bringing this national organization to life are interwoven with his personal narrative. And the singularly compelling child in this real-life drama, a son like any other, but a casualty in an adult conflict, emerges as the raison d'être for discarding the current adversarial legal system in favor of more humane methods of resolving family conflicts involving children.

Dr. Neumann is a clinical psychologist consulting to child welfare agencies in Alberta, Canada. He specializes in the assessment and treatment of traumatic disorders. He is Director of the O.P.C.R.. in Alberta.

Preface

You are a man who leaves nobody indifferent!

By your side, we feel animated by your flame, your will to create the impossible.

Visionary, gregarious, stimulating, A righteous man, thus a fighting man!

Aldo Morrone

What Mahatma Gandhi did to free a people, What Martin Luther King did to free a race,

You want to do to free our families from the yoke of obscurantism in our culture

and force us to abandon our intimate games and abuse.

A fellow road companion salutes you

Mr. Morrone is a clinical psychologist, family mediator and professor teaching mediation in the School of Social Work Continuing Education Program, at McGill University and various institutions in Europe.

FOREWORD

*"**Please don't let me go, Papa !** "* is the lifetime story of one man fighting to be united with his son, a struggle born out of his love and concern, which is so naturally given to fathers every where as it is to mothers.

Rashmi Mayur

However, we do not live in a natural or normal world, but an industrial-technological one, different from everything we have known through history. With all our so-called "Progress", we live in a world of social nightmare – broken families, separated parents and children, outdated and unjust laws, cruelty, callousness and unconcern. The symptoms are evident everywhere and the consequences are experienced starkly by children deprived of one or both parents and living in social oppression, loneliness and depression.

Ricaardoe Di Done's is one such story. For almost 16 years, he was deprived of a normal relationship with his son. His legal struggle to right this injustice caused him intense emotional pain and drove him to poverty, even imprisonment. All this happened in wealthy, civilized Canada, widely recognized as being among the best countries in the world.

Yet, his is not an isolated example. It is symptomatic of the ubiquitous breakdown of the family and the community that is too often the common experience of people in the modern world. The greatest victims are children, so vulnerable in their need for love, security and stability.

Never in history have so many children been victims of violence as they are today. And that is true regardless of whether they live in advanced countries like Canada – or whether they are suffering a different form of violence in the hunger, disease, toxic factories and sex trade of the developing world.

Please don't let me go, Papa ! should be read by everyone who cares for children and their families, for in spite of its painful subject matter, it is ultimately a book of hope. It envisages the fostering of a warm and humane society, founded on values of love, kindness, cooperation, respect and friendship. Its thoughtful recommendations call for major legal reforms that will help the children of separation and divorce benefit from the love and guidance of both their parents and extended families. Children everywhere are crying for such a world. A world of tomorrow. A world that, with goodwill and effort, is possible today.

Let all the children of the world advance towards the rising sun.

Rashmi Mayur, Ph.D., is Director, International Institute for Sustainable Future, Mumbai, India and President of the Global Futures Network, New York, USA. He is an advisor to the UN and several governments in the developing world on issues of sustainable development, social welfare and technology application. He is the Chairman of the Global People's Assembly to be held in India in August 2002.

Prologue *

This is the story of Ricaardoe Di Done's extraordinary struggle to maintain an active, loving relationship with his young son subsequent to his break up with the child's mother. It is the story of psychological and emotional conflict and looks at how the legal process can be systematically manipulated to serve the ends of those whose goal is vindictiveness or to serve their own personal needs.

In 1980, Ricaardoe and Peggy Token had lived together for eight years, were engaged to be married and were planning to buy a home together in Edmonton. Then, everything went awry. She disappeared to marry another man, taking their two-year-old son, Ricaardoe Branden, with her.

Only after months of searching was Ricaardoe able to discover their whereabouts and renew his close bond with his son. A four-day court hearing resulted in Peggy obtaining custody of their child with Ricaardoe receiving visiting rights. Peggy attempted to do everything in her power, however, to block those rights from being exercised.

In an attempt to regain contact with his son, Ricaardoe Di Done entered a nightmare world of petitions, counter petitions, affidavits and expert reports that, over a 16-year period, took the family through the courts of three provinces, landed Ricaardoe in jail for contempt of court, saw him charged with kidnapping (and subsequently discharged), imposed on him a two-and-a-half-year separation from his son, and subjected the boy to two unwanted adoptions and seven name changes.

As a result of this terrible experience the author grew to realize that the problems of family breakdown are only aggravated by a legal system that pits parent against parent, traps children in the middle, and exacts a huge social cost. Emotionally, physically and financially drained, he also discovered that the nightmare he was living was shared by countless other couples and their children, whose family tragedies might have been avoided had there been a system in place that encouraged them to resolve their differences outside the adversarial territory of the courtroom.

Consequently, Ricaardoe began a crusade for widespread change in an effort to see education and mediation routinely replace lawsuits and lawyers' letters in the resolution of family conflict. In the process, he gave up a lucrative career and endured poverty and a hunger strike, while founding a national organization dedicated to children's rights.

But even as many of the author's recommendations are on the verge of being implemented, much work remains to be done if we are to safeguard our children's basic need to know and enjoy the love and security of both their parents and the extended families, and to grow up in an environment of security and peace.

* The names of some individuals were changed in order to maintain anonymity

INTRODUCTION

On a hot and humid July afternoon in 1996, my then 18-year-old-son, Ricaardoe Branden Di Done, Jr., sat in the small, cluttered office of the Organization for the Protection of Children's Rights in Montreal, (founded by me in 1983) staring at two pieces of documentation. Several minutes passed before he picked up a pen and signed the letter and affidavit to the British Columbia Supreme Court that would finally put an end to the 16 years of legal wrangling that had engulfed most of his childhood and all of his adolescent years.

The two documents confirmed that he did, indeed, wish to overturn the ruling that, seven years earlier in that same court, had allowed him to be adopted against his will by his mother and her husband. They also established beyond question that he wanted me, his biological father, to be officially recognized as such – legally as well as in *every* other sense of the word.

It was an extraordinary action for him to take. And it was a decision that he should never have had to face.

Fortunately, he signed the documents before his nineteenth birthday, the legal age of majority in British Columbia where he stayed. Overturning the adoption, as an adult, would have required a decision of the Supreme Court of Canada, which would have been under no obligation to hear the case.

Nevertheless, he agonized over his decision to sign. Though it was what he wanted, he knew his action would catapult him back into a situation, with his heart torn between two homes, two cultures, two families and two natural parents – his mother, Peggy, and myself.

* * * * *

Rick (as he now prefers to be called) was only 26 months old when the common-law relationship his mother and I had shared for almost a decade came to an end. Peggy left to secretly marry the man who would, much later, be permitted to adopt our son – not once, but twice — against the wishes of both my son and myself. This book is the story of how those adoptions were allowed to happen and how, against great odds, they were eventually overturned.

It is also the story of a tangled journey through the legal maze of child custody and a struggle over many years and across a continent to maintain a loving relationship with my son after the courts gave custody to his mother. During those years, I was represented by ten different lawyers in a non-stop battery of court actions and counter actions that took place in three Canadian provinces – sometimes simultaneously. I was charged with kidnapping and jailed for 11 days for contempt of court. Following that episode, I was unable to see or contact my son for almost three years. I have appeared before many Parliamentary committees and endured a 38-day hunger strike, even as I relinquished a lucrative business career to campaign full-time for the rights of children caught in the middle of their parents' divorce. As a result, I faced financial disaster, accumulating debts that included more than $200,000 in legal fees, expert reports and other court-related costs.

This is a simplified personal accounting of what happened when Peggy and I found ourselves incapable of coming to an agreement on how we could both continue to share in the parenting of our son, following our own separation. What it doesn't reveal is the emotional toll all this has taken – on our son, ourselves, our parents, families and friends. What is worrisome is the extent to which this legal warfare has affected – and will continue to affect – our son. Even the fundamental stability of having one's own name was denied him. In less than 10 years, his name was changed seven times.

Even if Rick's situation is extreme, he is certainly not alone. Recent figures show that almost half the total number of divorces granted involved a custody order for dependent children.[1] Moreover, not only has separation and divorce among parents increased in frequency over the past few decades, it is occurring earlier and earlier in the lives of children, according to Canada's National

Longitudinal Survey of Children and Youth (1998). In the early 1970s, one in five children had seen their parents separate by the age of 11; by the late 1980s, the same proportion of children were just under five years old when their parents separated. According to the Canadian Council of Social Development, one in six Canadian children under the age of 12 have seen his or her parents split up. Imagine how staggering that figure would be if calculated on a worldwide basis. And the more intense the conflict between the parents, the more negative the impact will be upon the children.

This is a sad reflection of just how inadequate existing legal systems can be in dealing with the problems of family breakdown and child custody, even in advanced democratic societies. Frustratingly, the system itself can end up hurting the very children it is supposed to protect.

I speak from my own experience and from that of many others I have met in similar situations. Too many lives are in shambles because of the constraints of a system that has not kept up with social needs. Hardly a week goes by without a news report of how a bitter custody dispute erupted into senseless and tragic violence.

Only recently are we beginning to question the very term "child custody," which harks back to a notion of children as possessions who could be awarded like livestock or property to the successful claimant. Thankfully, our society has evolved. Children are no longer "possessions"; they are now being perceived as individuals with rights and needs.

But we continue to use such words, which address more the rights of parents than of their children. Words shape our thinking. Substitute the term "parental responsibility" for "custody" – and all of a sudden we open the window on a new perspective. Out of the realm of ownership and possession and into a world where the focus is now on the needs and rights of children and the *responsibility* of both parents to love, care for and guide their offspring to maturity – whether they happen to form an intact family unit or not.

Since its founding, the Organization for the Protection of Children's Rights (OPCR) has worked to increase public awareness of the impact of family breakdown on children. It has collaborated with parents, social workers, psychologists, lawyers, judges, educators, law enforcement officers and politicians to advocate widespread change in the way the courts routinely deal with family breakdown and to promote ways of equipping parents with the professional support and tools they need to act in their children's best interests.

OPCR's own research – together with its compilation of other studies shows that the risk of drug and alcohol abuse, school dropout, delinquency, mental and physical health problems and suicide is significantly higher among children from broken families than from intact families. It is not likely that the rate of divorce and family breakdown will plummet in the near future. The question is how can we lessen its trauma for all concerned.

I am not a psychologist, social worker or legal expert. But in working closely with those who are experts in the field of human relations, I have discovered that my conclusions are backed up by internationally recognized research.

My experience is that of a father who very narrowly escaped losing his son forever and who had to struggle ceaselessly to keep the lines of communication open. I have watched my son torn apart by a conflict totally beyond his youthful control. As a human being I have not only felt the pain of family breakdown deeply and directly, but have seen how, cancer-like, it also strikes at grandparents, family members and friends.

Children don't make the decision to split up, their parents do. When this happens, no child should be put in a position where he or she feels forced to choose between them. There are obvious exceptions – but they are not the focus of this book. I am referring to more or less "normal" families where both parents are decent people who love their children but cannot, for whatever reason, see themselves spending the rest of their lives together.

But even when it comes to divorce, the children's needs should remain paramount. They are different from our own. They need the constant love and reassuring presence of both parents, whether or not they live under the same roof.

To arrive at such an arrangement requires an enormous amount of effort and goodwill on the part of both parents – at a time when each is reeling from the anger, confusion, distrust and hurt that accompany the breakdown of a relationship. Yet our traditional legal system – to which divorcing parents naturally turn – is, by nature, adversarial. Rather than encouraging this goodwill, it pits parent against parent in a kind of twisted winner-takes-all emotional sweepstakes.

To obtain custody each party, represented by legal counsel, has to do their utmost to show why he or she is the "better" parent and why the other person is not. Then when that particular bit of messiness is over and a court decision reached, the same two people who have been verbally at each other's throats are expected to start cooperating on issues as delicate as access rights and financial support.

Obviously the courts are not responsible for the problems of two individuals who have fallen out of love. Yet ironically, the current legal system can encourage and contribute to the further breakdown of human relationships. Here there are no winners.

However, it doesn't have to be this way. Some jurisdictions in both Canada and the U.S. have created special courts that deal only with these family-related disputes. These courts encourage – and in some cases require – couples contemplating divorce to first see if they can resolve their dispute through mediation, which unlike litigation, does not assign blame.

Mediation recognizes that both parents have an important role to play in the nurturing of their children, encouraging them to work together to reach an agreement that takes both children's and parents' needs into consideration. It is hard work, true enough, but the results are in its favor. Evidence shows that mediated settlements are respected by both parents to a much higher degree than court-imposed settlements, and are also attained faster, at less cost and with greater satisfaction for all concerned.[2]

Should parents be unable to reach a mediated settlement – or should one or both of the spouses prove uncooperative, the option of going to trial remains. Except that in a specialized court where judges deal exclusively with family law cases, they are particularly sensitized to the effects of divorce on children and other family members and will take these critical factors into account in their decisions.

Mediation was almost unheard of at the time Rick's mother and I could have benefited from it. I have no way of knowing what effect the chance to sit down with a mediator and discuss our differences in an informal and non-confrontational setting would have had on the eventual outcome. What I do know is that the litigation route we took brought only heartache, misery, stress and a mountain of legal bills.

The biggest irony is that after 16 years, 13 major lawsuits and a multitude of smaller legal actions, Peggy and I went full circle. We started out as Rick's natural and legal parents and we remain his natural and legal parents today.

Peter Allik-Petersenn is the British Columbia lawyer who represented Rick and I when the second adoption was finally overturned. From a professional point of view, he says it was one of the most fascinating cases in which he was ever involved. He also describes it as "a colossal waste of time and money that produced tremendous ill will." Worst of all, he says, are the emotional scars it has left on Rick.

Parenthood is the greatest responsibility that most people will ever undertake. Its joys, sorrows, frustrations and delights cross cultural, linguistic and geographic lines. Its legacy is the ultimate bottom line – survival of the species. Yet, how seriously do we prepare for it?

Both need and opportunity exist to educate people – starting in childhood – on the responsibilities they will one day shoulder as parents. And when relationships start to falter, there is an urgent requirement to sensitize people about how their actions can affect their kids.

This is not to suggest that couples should stay together simply "for the sake of their children." But a better understanding of the repercussions of family breakdown on children might at least cause parents to think seriously about how they manage their relationship. Should their life as a couple eventually dissolve, it would also better prepare them to share parenting responsibilities in a way that puts the interests of their children before their own hurt and pride.

My story is a classic illustration of the harmful effects of litigation on a family splitting apart. There is no intention of apportioning blame. What happened, happened, and in my recounting of events, I have tried to be as objective as possible. Certainly, Peggy and I had our share of human failings, but my point is that there was no process or mechanism in place that required – or even helped us – to put aside our escalating conflicts in a manner acceptable to everyone – most importantly our son.

Sixteen years is too long a period to debate a child's future. By then, the child is well on the way to making his or her own decisions. The time lost can never be regained.

Today, I share my life with an extraordinary woman, Brigitte Jalbert, and our five children: Alexandra, Antoni, Marina, Samantha and Rick, for which I am continually thankful.

The rest of this book will chronicle how, against great odds, Rick became an integral part of our family in Montreal. He also maintains strong ties with his mother and his other family in B.C. But the journey that got Rick to this point was anything but happy – and all of us continue to live with its consequences.

Many people have wondered if the price I paid to maintain a relationship with Rick wasn't too high for both him and me. They ask me why I didn't simply let go at a certain point. I had a new family on which to lavish my attention and I could have withdrawn from Rick's life and freed him from the perpetual tug-of-war he was living.

On the surface, this may have seemed an acceptable, even a noble, solution. But before me was always the image of Rick—two, five, maybe ten years down the road, wondering why one day the father who claimed he loved him suddenly walked out of his life and never returned. Perhaps blaming himself and doubtless hating me.

The constant strife that his mother and I lived both inside and outside the court room was a horrendous drain of emotion, energy and life that has left permanent scars on us, our families and our son. Yet, in my mind, there was never any choice. The bond that held me was my love for Rick. I could not abandon him.

MEETING PEGGY

I first met Peggy Token in Montreal in the autumn of 1971. I was 21 and she was 20. She and her younger sister, Lydia had moved there from Edmonton the previous year, and the two of them did secretarial and bookkeeping work for a contractor named Monte on a construction site in the city's east end.

Monte and my father were long-time acquaintances. My father owned a small plumbing business and Monte occasionally sub-contracted work to him. On this particular occasion, my father was to install all the plumbing for several low-rise apartments that Monte was building.

I had been working with my dad more or less steadily since high school. The first morning we arrived on the site, my enthusiasm for the job rose significantly the moment we entered the basement suite that served as the contractor's office and came face-to-face with the two smiling Token sisters.

My father could read me like an open book. "Don't get involved," he warned under his breath, well aware that Monte liked to surround himself with young, attractive women and didn't appreciate competition. Despite his words of caution, I found some excuse to drop by the office several times a day. Within a short time, it became obvious that both Peggy and Lydia looked forward to my visits as much as I enjoyed seeing them.

Peggy was five foot four, with blue eyes, shoulder-length blond hair, a gentle personality and a winning smile. Lydia was slightly taller with long brown hair and a wild streak that made my head spin. One day I worked up the courage to invite both of them to go horseback riding the next weekend. To my delight they agreed.

At 21, I was shy, innocent and eager to please, Anything but wild, I was fascinated by these two young women who lived alone in a strange city far removed from their family and friends. Their lifestyle seemed daring – even exotic – compared to my own sheltered and very traditional Italian upbringing.

Ever since I could remember, my father had been my hero; as a child, his friends called me his shadow because wherever he went, I would tag along, holding his hand. His own father had migrated to Canada from northern Italy in 1901 and settled in a proudly Italian neighborhood populated by other recent immigrants. To this day, the area is known as Little Italy. In 1950, the year I was born, we were still a very tightly knit community where family was everything and children treasured.

My mother came from a very different background. Her family were long-standing Quebecois who could trace their roots in this province back some three hundred years. She was a beautiful woman and well educated, unlike my father who had little formal education. My mother had studied at the École des Beaux Arts in Montreal and other family members often remarked on her talent at drawing and painting.

Although their divergent backgrounds were often a source of tension, my parents clearly loved each other throughout the 44 years of their marriage. When my mother lay dying of cancer in the early 1990s, my dad would arrive at the hospital early every morning and stay by her side until late in the evening. After she died, he was like a lost soul.

Yet, from my perspective as a child, my mother always seemed a distant figure whom I could reach for, but never really touch. She was never a demonstrative person and must have kept all her feelings bottled up inside. It was only after she died, when I was going through her belongings, that I discovered that the drawer of her night-table was crammed full of photos of my son and myself, as well as a whole series of newspaper clippings about my struggle for her grandson. Only then did I realize to what extent she must have cared and been pained by my difficulties.

My mother's cool restraint was all the more glaring when contrasted with the boisterous warmth and open caring and affection of the Italian side of the family. I was also very close to my paternal grandfather who lived with us until his death when I was 11 years old. An excellent chef, he did most of the cooking for the family, and my mouth still waters at the thought of his polenta, risotto and wonderful apple and blueberry pies.

There were always friends and family around our house. We were the first ones on our street to own a television set and most evenings there was a visitor or two sitting in our living room, drawn by its novelty. On Saturday evenings and Sundays after church, our kitchen would be crowded with family, friends and neighbors. My dad and his father would strap on their accordions and the singing, dancing and laughter would go on for hours.

My father was well known throughout the community and liked and respected for his honesty and generosity. Families struggling to make ends meet, remember plumbing jobs done free or at a much lower rate than the work was worth. That was his way. If he thought you needed something, he would give it to you. As long as we had the essentials, he didn't worry. His popularity finally drew him into politics as an organizer for the local Liberal party.

My father's two sisters – Toni and Ida –were also very important figures in my young life. Toni had no children of her own and perhaps that's why she always seemed to have extra time for me. Throughout my childhood and even into adulthood, I have often turned to her for guidance; a deep affection exists between us to this day. Knowing she was always there for me compensated for the lack of closeness I felt with my own mother.

My father and his family ingrained in me a deep sense of belonging and self-worth – values that I have in turn tried to pass on to my own children.

One of my earliest memories is of my father trudging through the heavy underbrush along the bank of one of his favorite trout streams, with me – not much more than six – riding high on his shoulders. He was an exceptionally strong man, but even so, it couldn't have been easy for him to carry me and his fishing gear over wet, uneven ground. Yet he never considered leaving me behind at home. We belonged together.

Such simple and ordinary gestures accumulate over time into the absolute knowledge that one is loved unconditionally. Without that knowledge, it is so easy for children to falter. With it, they can go on to move mountains.

My father believed in moving mountains for his family. Even when business was bad and he fell on hard times, he somehow always managed to produce gifts for everyone at Christmas or birthdays.

One summer, when my sister and I were small, he rigged up a large screen on the roof of our back shed, rented an old projector and showed movies to the neighborhood. It was quite a sight as families from several houses around sat out on their balconies for this early version of home entertainment. This went on for many weeks, until someone, fed up with all the noise, called the police. That put an end to the otherwise popular event, but as a result, I became fascinated with theatre, acting, music and singing. When I left high school, my dream was to pursue a career in entertainment.

That was the first time I would have a difference of opinion with my father, who held strongly traditional views about what was best for me and my future. An honest, sensible trade such as plumbing was, in his estimation, the only type of career worth considering.

Crawling about in dark, confined spaces fitting pieces of pipe together, never particularly appealed to me. Yet, my relationship with my father was so close that going against his wishes was almost unthinkable. I couldn't imagine doing anything that might cause him pain. In any case, circumstances intervened and made up my mind for me.

My parents, my sister and I had been visiting some cousins who lived across the city and we were driving home on a Sunday evening in winter, shortly after my seventeenth birthday. Tall snow banks had further narrowed the winding road that followed the river's shoreline when an oncoming car, driven by two young kids, went out of control and hit us head-on.

My mother and sister, seated beside my father in the front, were extremely fortunate to escape with relatively minor injuries. My dad's right arm, instinctively outstretched to cushion the impact, prevented them from hurtling through the windshield. I was in the back seat and emerged with only a few scratches. But my father was laid up for months. His leg was broken in several places and his mouth badly gashed along the base of the gum where he slammed into the steering wheel.

To make matters worse, the leg was set badly and had to be re-broken and set a second time after its initial healing. Then, shortly after the second cast was removed and he was finally able to get up and around after months of inactivity, he encountered another major setback. He had gone to the lumberyard to pick up some material for some minor renovations he had been planning around the house. He was standing near a tall stack of 12-foot-long planks, when suddenly one of them came loose and crashed down on the foot of his newly healed leg. He was back in a cast for several weeks.

This latest misfortune started a chain reaction of depression, painkillers and alcohol that took my father many years to overcome. To help support our family, I set aside my youthful aspirations and took courses in plumbing, heating and blueprint reading. By the age of 21, I was a master plumber and gas fitter. When my father was finally able to resume his plumbing business, I worked alongside him. However, the lingering pain took its toll and he was never quite the same man.

My plan had long been to put my salary aside and buy a house a year with my father for 10 years. I had seen so many of my grandfather's and father's friends get very wealthy doing just that. Eventually I hoped to marry and have several children, always envisioning my future wife coming from a similar Italian background.

Then Peggy Token caught my eye and my heart. At first I would flirt with both her and Lydia in Monte's construction office, but over time, Peggy and I paired off. The first Christmas after we had met, her parents came to visit from Edmonton. With them was a young man from Fort St. John, B.C. His name was Jack Roaff, and Peggy introduced him simply as a family friend who had originally come to her parents' naturopathy clinic in Edmonton for training and had stayed to work for them.

Peggy's parents Allen and Bertha, were interested in building a health spa in B.C. in a town called Osoyoos. Her father was a licensed naturopath who already operated his Vina Clinic out of the family's Edmonton home. He and Bertha planned to run the new spa, but they needed a financing partner. Peggy thought of her boss, Monte, since he had access to investment capital and could oversee construction. She arranged for her parents to meet him.

As my own relationship with Peggy intensified, it was also obvious that Monte, although some 30 years her senior, had an interest in her that went far beyond her secretarial abilities. My father had been right. At first, she played along – partly because of her parent's spa project, and partly, I think, because she initially found his interest flattering and his flamboyant lifestyle exciting. But as time progressed, she grew increasingly distressed with Monte's now unwanted attentions, and in the spring of 1972, she and Lydia decided to move back to Edmonton. She asked me to follow her.

Up until then I had never traveled beyond a 200-kilometre radius of Montreal. Now, all at once, a number of reasons combined to make up my mind.

Like so many other eastern Canadians, I had always dreamed of seeing the Rockies. And I missed Peggy. But I was also having a hard time dealing with my father's drinking and recurring bouts of depression. For the first and only time in our relationship, we were fighting constantly. A few years earlier we had bought a triplex together and I had now moved into the second floor flat. But even that was too close.

When the job with Monte ended, my father had invested in a small grocery store with the insurance money he had finally received from his accident. But his illness and the resulting change in his disposition were chasing customers away. Finally, my aunt Toni's husband, Richard stepped in to take over. I couldn't stand to see my father deteriorate this way, but if I said or suggested anything, he would just get angrier. When, shortly after Peggy's departure, one of my best friends was getting married in Calgary, I made up my mind to go.

In late June, with a small insurance policy as collateral, I borrowed $200, bought a one-way ticket and with $88 in my pocket boarded a plane west. It was my first flight. I didn't have a clue what to expect at the other end and I had no idea whether I was leaving for two weeks or two years. All at once, my life had become a blank sheet. But with the insecurity also came a new sense of freedom and 30,000 feet above the earth, I could really believe the world was opening up before me.

When we touched down in Edmonton, I was amazed by the flatness of the surrounding landscape and the wide-open space that continued as far as I could see. I waited anxiously for Peggy who had promised to come and pick me up. I was to stay with her family until I had a chance to look around and get my bearings.

The Token household came as an even greater culture shock. Their large stucco and wood six-bedroom cottage sat on a nicely landscaped lot in an older, and what used to be very residential section of the city. Over time, businesses had moved in and they were now just at the beginning of a commercial zone. Vina Clinic occupied the entire first floor of their home.

They had a beautiful Chrysler convertible, and moved on a social plane populated with lawyers, doctors and other well-educated professionals – so different from my working-class parents in their comfortable, but modest neighborhood with its narrow, brick, multi-family homes. To a kid used to consuming platefuls of steaming pasta, meals at the Tokens – when they weren't dining out in nice restaurants – consisted of endless variations of salads and cottage cheese.

Shortly after we entered the house, Peggy suggested I put my bag upstairs in her room. I looked at her curiously, having fully expected to sleep by myself in a spare room in the basement. She assured me there was no problem. From the very beginning, her whole family accepted that we would share a room and live as a couple. I didn't know what to think. I was still quite shy about our sexual relations, and with my strict 1950s Italian Roman Catholic upbringing, I could only imagine what my parents would say.

The Tokens were very polite, but restrained in their dealings with me. With no money, little experience and only a high-school education, willingness to work and an affable personality in my favor, I was hardly the son-in-law they dreamed of. They didn't have to spell out the obvious, that they one day hoped to see Peggy married to a well educated professional or business person with a promising future.

But, at least initially, they didn't discourage our relationship. Peggy was now working in her parents' clinic as a therapist, and after recently experiencing problems keeping staff, they didn't want to risk having her run away with me.

There were good reasons for their caution. I later discovered that Peggy had previously been involved with Jack Roaff, the young man who had accompanied her parents to Montreal. He had recently quit his job at the clinic and returned to British Columbia, and her parents may well have feared that Peggy would be tempted to take up with him again and follow him. From their point of view, my arrival was probably a timely diversion.

Peggy and her family introduced me to a style of life I had previously only dreamed of. Shortly after my arrival, Peggy accompanied me to my friend's wedding in Calgary. Then we joined the rest of her family for a weekend at an elegant hotel in Waterton Lakes National Park – south of Calgary on the Alberta-Montana border. There were seven of us altogether – Peggy's parents, her youngest sister Tania, Lydia and her new boyfriend, Curtis, Peggy and myself.

It was a wonderful place and I was awestruck with each new view of the spectacular surrounding mountains. Yet my enjoyment was tinged with the knowledge that I could never afford this on my own and that I was totally dependent on the Tokens' goodwill.

Naive, alone and away from my family for the first time in my life, I was already insecure, so I compensated in the only way I knew. I went out of my way to be pleasant and polite and I was soon tackling whatever small maintenance jobs I could around the Token house. I also found a job at a health club called The European Spa that was close by downtown Edmonton. The hours were long, the pay lousy and the commute by bus from the Tokens took over an hour each way. But it kept me busy and gave me a little bit of income – as well as the courage to stay on in Edmonton.

Not long after I started working, the Tokens got a call from Monte, asking if he could send his two young teenage sons for some treatment at the clinic. The partnership deal was still under discussion and an investment of several million dollars was at stake. For the duration of the sons' visit, the Tokens asked me to move out of Peggy's room and into the basement. Neither Peggy nor I were overjoyed about this arrangement, but given my precarious position I could hardly make a fuss.

After the sons left, Monte himself arrived. He and Peggy's parents arranged to travel to Osoyoos together to check out the site of the proposed spa. As long as Monte was visiting, the Tokens insisted that I would have to move out and stay in a motel. They also pressured Peggy to accompany them and Monte to Osoyoos.

The day before his arrival, Peggy was in tears. She didn't want to go; she kept telling her parents she wanted nothing further to do with the man. I had also tried to caution them against getting too involved with the contractor based on my father's recent experience – he was never fully paid for the work he had done. Peggy's parents made it clear they could handle their own business dealings. And they let their daughter know that her refusal to accompany them could jeopardize the entire family's future.

I had never seen Peggy so unhappy – caught between her dislike of Monte and her desire to please her parents. I tried to convince her that she didn't have to go – that we could take off somewhere together. But in the end she went with her parents and Monte. That was the first time I understood to what extent her parents, and especially her mother, could manipulate and control her.

With little money and no family or friends of my own in the city, I was way out of my depth. Part of me wanted to flee back to Montreal, but my pride wouldn't let me. I also knew I'd just end up fighting again with my father and I loved him too much to risk any further damage to our relationship.

The incident with Monte marked a turning point in my feelings towards Peggy. Up until then, I had been totally infatuated with her – I won't say "in love" because I believe that real love develops over time after careful nurturing and many shared experiences. Now, to the attraction I felt for her was added a deep sense of sympathy and loyalty.

Peggy never discussed what happened in Osoyoos, but soon after her return, we began to talk about getting out on our own and starting afresh in Calgary as soon as we had some savings to fall back on. In September, I saw a newspaper ad for a plumber to work on a housing development in Fox Creek, north of Edmonton. I applied and got the job. During the short time I was there, I lived on the site and only returned to Edmonton on weekends.

After the Fox Creek job ended, I took another construction job for the same company – this time in the Yukon. After a few weeks I had managed to put enough money aside to feel confident that we could strike out on our own.

When I returned to Edmonton around the end of November, Peggy and I decided to drive to Vancouver with Lydia and her boyfriend Curtis. I never liked Curtis who had a nasty, coarse streak that emerged whenever he drank too much – which was often. After a few days in Vancouver, we parted company and Peggy and I took an eastbound train across the Rockies to Calgary, where we intended to look for work.

I no longer recall whether Peggy told her parents we were just going for a short vacation or if she let them in on our real plans. In any case, by the time we returned to Edmonton for a short visit at Christmas, they realized we would be going back to Calgary.

During our first few weeks in Calgary, we stayed with my friend Denis and his wife, and visited with Peggy's older half-brother, from her father's first marriage. Like his father, Bob Token had trained as a naturopath and operated a clinic in Calgary, where he lived with his wife and children. We got along well with Bob and his family and, within a short time, Peggy started working in his clinic. In January 1973, I found a job with a construction company and began training to become a project manager.

Those were the beginning of exciting times in Alberta. With the discovery of a large oil deposit that came to be known as the tar sands, the province was on the verge of a major boom and people were arriving from all across the country seeking jobs and a better future. It was a good time to be in construction as municipalities acted to keep up with the housing shortage. Peggy and I rented a furnished apartment and bought a second-hand car. We began to create a life for ourselves and to meet new friends.

Then, early in the spring, we received a call from Bertha Token. She was very upset and in a tearful voice described how busy they were at the clinic and how her husband's health was failing. Allen Token was considerably older than his wife and was then already into his sixties. Bertha went on to complain that I had taken their daughter away at a time when they needed her support more than ever.

Allen Token's health was an ongoing family concern. If one listened to Bertha, he was regularly on the verge of dying, and yet friends of mine who worked at Vina Clinic a few years later, said they never saw any signs of serious illness. They believed he was simply exhausted. The man was highly regarded for his groundbreaking naturopathic treatments and was obsessed with his work. Patients would often arrive at the clinic well into the evening.

Bertha's call struck just the right chord, and within days, Peggy had left for Edmonton, duty-bound to help her parents. I couldn't leave my work, but with Easter only a couple of weeks away, we agreed that I would drive up to Edmonton then to see how things were working out.

While in Edmonton, I happened to drop by a grocery store I had discovered that imported a wide variety of Italian food. The owner and I often chatted and he knew everyone there was to know in the city's Italian community. When he learned I had been working in Calgary and was just back to visit Peggy, he said, "Why are you working there? I want you to go see Peter Battoni and tell him I said to hire you and offer you a better job!"

Peter Battoni owned one of the largest construction companies in Edmonton, involved in building many of the new high-rise apartments and office buildings that were quickly transforming the city's skyline. He went on to build the Edmonton Coliseum.

By now Peggy had told me she couldn't return to Calgary. She was back working in her parents' clinic and didn't feel she could leave them.

With nothing to lose, I called Battoni. He was overseas, but I was put in touch with several other managers, and to my amazement, was hired. I just had time to go back to Calgary, resign from my job there and move our few belongings back to Edmonton before I started at Battoni.

I loved that job. Although it didn't pay much, the opportunity to advance was there for someone who was eager to learn and had the reputation as a hard worker. Moreover, the scope of the projects the company was involved in, exposed me to many influential people and helped me create my own circle of friends both within the city's Italian population and in the community at large. My experience and confidence grew and I dreamt of being a successful general contractor myself one day.

Once again Peggy and I were living with her parents. Peggy wouldn't hear of moving elsewhere and I followed her lead. All my life, I had seen my family and neighbors scrimp here and cut corners there to build the hard-earned nest egg that led to property and a better standard of living. It was commonplace for members of an extended Italian family to live together to support each other and save money. I viewed the time Peggy and I lived in her parents' home exactly in that light.

Nevertheless, the incident with Monte continued to gnaw at us. As the months passed, I found it ever more difficult to get along with Bertha whose relationship with people varied according to how useful they could be to her. I also had frequent clashes with Lydia's boyfriend, Curtis.

About this time, the Tokens, together with Lydia and Curtis, had invested in a coffee-shop style restaurant in one of the new high-rises Battoni had built. Through my sources there, I learned that Curtis was causing problems with other tenants in the building and the owners wanted him out. They had nothing against the Tokens' continued interest in the restaurant – they just didn't want Curtis managing it.

I shared this information with Peggy's parents and within a couple of days I was summoned to a family meeting, where Lydia and Curtis claimed I was interfering strictly out of jealousy. The Tokens ignored my warning. Shortly afterwards, a second coffee shop opened in the building and severely undercut Lydia and Curtis' prices. They were forced to close and the Tokens lost their investment.

That did nothing to alleviate the friction I already felt in that house, and as much as I cared for Peggy, it spilled over into our relationship. By late summer, homesick for Montreal and my own family, I asked for some vacation time and hopped a flight home.

The visit did me a world of good and when the time came to leave, I decided to drive back with a friend who wanted to see the West. I bought a second-hand red Mercury and we made the trip in just a few days. Back in Edmonton, nothing had changed. Peggy and I were at a stalemate. I had no intention of staying with the Tokens and she refused to leave.

The snow and cold arrived early that year, and by October it had already settled in with a ferocity that mirrored the chill I felt inside me. I told Peggy, her family and my boss at Battoni that I had to return to Montreal to arrange some family business and I couldn't be sure when I'd be back. I promised to keep in touch. Then I climbed into the red Mercury and drove. The day I arrived in Montreal, the motor died. That was all the omen I needed. I would stay at least until Christmas – and take it one day at a time.

Through some friends, I heard that a paper mill in Port Cartier was looking for pipe fitters and I applied and got a job. Port Cartier is an isolated town more than 800 kilometers from Montreal on the north shore of the Gulf of St. Lawrence. The snow there lasted till June, but the pay was fantastic. I reported for work in January 1974. During the five months I lived in Port Cartier, I made as much as $1000 a week with overtime. For a 23-year-old, that was an incredible amount of money.

In late spring, a strike shut the mill down. Then we got hit with a huge snowstorm. I took the first flight south to Montreal where the city was bathed in sunshine and enjoying an early heat wave. Right then and there, I knew I had seen enough ice and snow for one season.

Throughout my stay in Port Cartier, Peggy and I kept in frequent touch by letter and phone. She would send me photographs of herself inscribed, "To my dearest Ricaardoe from your loving Peggy." I missed her, and without the thorny presence of her family always coming between us, the problems we had experienced the previous year, seemed to simply evaporate. After a short visit with my own family, I was once again on a flight headed for Edmonton.

For the Tokens, my arrival was very timely. They had recently bought a large house next door, which they planned to renovate and convert into apartments, but they had had problems keeping workers on the site and their finances were running out. They had already lost a substantial sum of money in the coffee-shop venture of the previous year and were on the verge of losing this investment, too. We struck a deal: they would pay me $5 an hour and I would get a crew together and finish the work. They were also to give Peggy a share of the profits.

It was a big comedown from my Port Cartier salary, but for Peggy's sake, I agreed and within a couple of months, the renovations were completed and the Tokens' investment salvaged.

Over the next few months I did a lot of work around the Tokens' home and also helped out in their clinic. Peggy's parents began to look at me with new respect. The months in Port Cartier had toughened me – I was also training regularly in karate – and I was no longer the shy kid that had arrived on their doorstep three years before. I had some money behind me and was working to start my own business.

By now, Peggy and I had also formed a close circle of friends that included Stagen Warness (a newly graduated medical doctor who was related to Bob Token's wife), Stagen's wife, Shazene, and Shazene's cousin, Crystal, and her husband, Wayne Kading. We went on camping trips, organized barbeques, and partied at each other's houses. We also spent a lot of time dreaming up investment schemes that we hoped would one day make us all wealthy.

On one particular occasion, Stagen and I approached Allen Token with an idea to create a combination health center/spa where Stagen and Allen could combine their medical expertise and I would run the business end. Stagen and I understood we would be equal partners, but as our planning evolved, Allen insisted on having the major interest. The deal fell apart, opening old wounds between me and the Tokens.

Peggy and I also started to bicker – again about her family. I felt her parents were taking advantage of her and wondered openly why she had never received her share of the profits of the renovation project. But while she would occasionally grumble behind their backs, her loyalty remained firmly with them. It was the same old impasse. As much as we cared for each other, we could never clear the hurdle that inevitably rose between me and her parents.

That's when I became interested in someone else. Her name was Cheryl and we had met at a party at the Tokens a couple of years before. At the time, she had been employed by Lydia and Curtis in their restaurant, and initially it was our mutual dislike of Curtis that drew us together. Our attraction deepened and by the spring of 1975, I made arrangements to move back to Montreal. Cheryl planned to follow me later.

I never told Peggy about Cheryl. I just said I missed my family and wanted to go back home for a while. Somehow I thought this was the least painful way to end our strained relationship. If I simply drifted away, I reasoned that time would take care of the rest, and we would both reach the inevitable conclusion that it just wasn't meant to be.

Things didn't work out quite that way. Cheryl never followed me to Montreal because Peggy did. Barely a week had passed since my arrival when Peggy called with the news that she was flying in the next day. I tried to convince her to wait – that I'd return to Edmonton soon. But she insisted on coming.

Her sudden appearance in Montreal changed everything. Away from the negative influences that always overtook us in Edmonton, the old attraction resurfaced. Before we knew it, we had spent almost two happy years together in Montreal.

Peggy got along well with my family. She especially liked my aunt Toni and the feeling was mutual. Over time, Toni came to look at her as the daughter she never had. My relations with my father were also on the mend. I had matured and was better able to cope with his mood swings. His drinking was at last under control and he accepted that I was now an adult and had proven my ability to survive on my own. But it was the unspoken knowledge that we had missed each other more than we dared to admit that brought us together once again.

I found a job at one of the big oil refineries in the east end and Peggy worked at the same company's downtown office. We were earning good money, had our own apartment and a lifestyle that included nice clothes, frequent nights-out at the city's best hotels and, what since the age of 10 had always represented for me the pinnacle of success, a Lincoln Continental.

The memory is still vivid. I was walking along the street with my aunt Toni, when a Lincoln sped past us. I couldn't help noticing its sleek, luxurious lines. "That's the car your uncle would like to have one day," commented my aunt, aware of my interest. "Some day I'll have one," I replied.

It was Peggy who finally convinced me to buy the Lincoln. The day I drove that car home, I was on top of the world.

By now I had accumulated several thousand dollars, which in 1976 was a respectable sum. I wanted to get into real estate development full time and, with two of my father's acquaintances, began looking for available land on the outskirts of the city. One of my prospective partners was a well-known notary and the other had been behind the successful development of an entire city district in the 1950's.

Montreal, in the summer of 1976, was in a festive mood as the city prepared to host the Olympic games. The future looked optimistic and we were just at the point of buying up a large number of lots when labor problems erupted in the construction industry. We put our plans on hold, waiting for the dispute to be settled. Then in November, the province plunged into political uncertainty with the election of its first separatist government. As property values fell in response, Peggy and I decided it was time to look elsewhere and we set our sights on Florida where we had heard the real estate market was really starting to move. We planned to leave early in the New Year.

In the meantime, we invited Stagen and Shazene Warness to spend Christmas with us in Montreal. We enjoyed a wonderful week together and by the end of it, their glowing descriptions of the investment opportunities in a now-booming Alberta turned the tide in favor of Calgary. Stagen now had his own medical practice and was doing very well. He suggested that I could manage his investments for him.

By January, Peggy and I had packed up and said goodbye to family and friends in Montreal. From a purely business point of view, our decision to return to Alberta made perfect sense. If only our relationship could also have prospered.

In Calgary, we moved in with the Warnesses until we could set up on our own. They had a large house and assured us there was plenty of room for the four of us, but living with them at close quarters soon wore Peggy down. Stagen's sense of humor consisted of putting people on the spot just to see how they'd react. To get Peggy going, he would tell her I had been flirting with other women and claimed there was one woman in particular I was interested in.

It wasn't true, but Peggy wasn't amused, and not long after, announced she was leaving for Edmonton to resume working with her parents.

We continued to see each other on weekends, traveling back and forth between the two cities. I couldn't leave Calgary for more than a day or two at a time because I was in the midst of negotiating a major development deal that had started out as a modest housing project and had grown to include an industrial park. The local town council had endorsed the project and were highly supportive, but in the end I couldn't put together sufficient finances.

I joined Peggy in Edmonton and that's when we discovered she was pregnant. At 27, I was delighted at the prospect of starting our own family, but Peggy wasn't nearly as convinced. We weren't children anymore, I argued; it was time to make a commitment. After much coaxing and assurances that I really wanted this child, she decided to go through with the pregnancy.

I couldn't have been happier. Peggy and I were together, we were eagerly anticipating the birth of our first child, and my career was really starting to take off. Alberta was booming, and as the Warnesses had promised, there was plenty of opportunity for astute property developers. In both Edmonton and Calgary, what was once farmland was being annexed to accommodate new housing for a swelling population. For some time, I had been expanding my circle of business contacts and associates. I was also gaining a reputation for being adept at securing deals that would yield healthy profits within a very short time.

I had so much energy in those days that several friends were trying to convince me to enter provincial politics. Even my relationship with Peggy's parents had improved.

Through all this, Peggy and I still had our dream of opening up our own health spa and in the fall of 1977, we traveled together to Germany for two weeks of specialized training in the use of cosmetics. Peggy already had considerable knowledge in this area through her training at Vina Clinic.

On the return trip, we stopped in Montreal for a few days and announced our engagement to my family and friends. My father was delighted. "It's about time you get married and raise a family," he said, slapping me on the back. "You're always saying how much you love kids. Now you've finally decided. That's good."

Peggy and I planned to marry in the New Year, but she would never set a date. She kept delaying, making excuses about her father's health and how much her help was needed at the clinic.

I had always believed her parents were behind her continual stalling. Perhaps they believed they would lose her completely if we got married. Peggy herself later maintained that in spite of our love for each other, we were never really compatible. She claimed that when she decided to have our son it was with the full expectation that she would raise him alone and take full responsibility for him.

How different the perceptions and recollections of two people living in apparently the same situation, can be! I recall only a period of joyful expectation. I truly thought we were happy together.

Now I look back and wonder if it was just my imagination or did we ever share the same values and goals. Did we understand the other person's innermost hopes and fears? Did we really talk to each other, and more importantly, did we listen to what the other person had to say?

Had we been able to answer those questions, I suspect our story would have had an entirely different outcome. Certainly, our son would have been a far happier child.

"I LOVE YOU THIS MUCH ALL THE WAY AROUND!"

Peggy went into labor on a cold mid-winter day in late January 1978. Together we drove to the Edmonton General Hospital, both nervous and excited about the imminent birth of our child. Throughout the hours of labor, I remained at the hospital, deeply moved by the emotional and physical strength Peggy displayed in bringing that new life forth. Finally, the contractions intensified to the point that she was wheeled into the delivery room.

I had never seen any kind of birth before, never mind a human one; indeed in the late '70s, it wasn't yet commonplace for men to assist at the birth of their children and Peggy's doctor was a traditionalist who automatically assumed I would wait outside. When I mentioned that I really wanted to attend, he seemed surprised. It took polite but stubborn insistence before he finally agreed.

The little details surrounding even the most meaningful occasions in one's life have a way, over time, of fading from memory, yet the feelings and emotions endure. I remember very little about the precise sequence of events that day. Only that when it was all over, a very happy Peggy was smiling at our tiny, perfect son cradled in her arms and tears of joy were escaping down my cheeks as we marveled at this new life that was so much a part of us.

Ricaardoe Branden Collin Theodore Di Done was born on January 29, 1978. His name had been the source of much discussion in the weeks leading up to his birth. Unlike today, when parents often learn the sex of their unborn child in the early stages of pregnancy, we didn't know if Peggy was carrying a boy or a girl. When we couldn't agree on names that we both liked, I suggested a compromise: if it was a boy I would choose the name; if it was a girl, she would have the final say. Peggy had a habit of never saying yes or no outright. She would simply smile and give me the impression she was in agreement.

Based on this assumed understanding, I named our son Ricaardoe. His original birth certificate also bore the name Branden (Peggy's preference), as well as the names of his two grandfathers. In my family, naming a child after close relatives was a time-honored tradition that spoke of pride, history and continuity through time.

From the very beginning, I called him Ricaardoe or else "Junior," while Peggy, for months after his birth, used the simple endearment "Plum." Later on, once our relationship had fallen apart, she insisted that she had never agreed to the name Ricaardoe. To this day, he is still known as Branden Token by his relatives and friends in Alberta and B.C.

Right until our son's birth, Peggy had found one reason after another to delay our marriage. Even so, at the hospital, she called herself Mrs. Di Done in a nod to the social conventions of the day. Hence our son's earliest records show his surname as Di Done. I was thrilled. Though countless generations had come and gone since our family could count itself among a long-dead aristocracy, our pride in our name and our heritage persisted. As an Italian, giving my son the same name my grandfather and I carried was the strongest symbol I could offer of my boundless commitment to him.

When we brought Rick home, we were still living with Peggy's parents. The only difference was that we had now moved downstairs to a large, furnished suite in the basement. Throughout her pregnancy, Peggy had continued to help out at the clinic. Once she regained her strength and Rick had settled into a routine, she intended to resume her duties as much as possible. Since the clinic was also part of the house, she could manage to nurse the baby and keep a watchful eye on him.

Early in the spring, my father's younger sister, Ida, came to visit us. She was the first of my relatives to see the baby, and I was touched that she would travel all the way to Alberta to be with us. To mark the occasion, we opened a bottle of wine that my uncle Richard had made 23 years before in 1955.

Ida taught both Peggy and I a lot about caring for our child. One day, Peggy noticed that she spoke to the baby in full sentences – the way one would address an older child or adult. She asked Ida why she was doing this, believing it pointless because the baby was far too young to understand. Ida explained that you have to talk to babies. "That's how they learn," she said. "You'll see how eventually they'll answer you."

We were all learning quickly and, as far as I was concerned, we were blessed with our son, our health, and the promise of a good future. Never one to shrink from opportunity, I firmly believed, "The sky's not the limit, it's just the beginning." Thinking big was where my father and I had always differed. He never thought we could be more than what we were born to and would call me a dreamer when I would confide my plans to him. It's true I am a dreamer – but I refuse to stop at dreams.

At that point in our lives, I was dreaming of becoming a millionaire, of banking our money and reinvesting it in the right deals, so we would eventually be able to live off the income. We would have been well on our way to achieving the goal, if our relationship hadn't collapsed.

I had no reason to believe Peggy didn't share my dreams. A few months after Rick's birth, we were visiting Bob Token and his family in Calgary, when Peggy noticed a "for sale" sign on a beautiful apartment building in one of the nicer areas of the city. She even took down the phone number, encouraging me to look into it.

The very next day, I called Stagen Warness and the two of us went to see it. We liked what we saw and I promised Stagen that once I had finished with the renovations, we'd be able to sell out and double our money within six months. We went in on the deal, completed the project and doubled our money in three months time. About the same time, we invested in a second property in another part of the city, with a third partner, an influential lawyer named Howard Starkman, who was a long-time acquaintance of the Tokens. He had also handled some of my own legal transactions.

Negotiating these deals and managing the subsequent renovations kept me in Calgary for at least half of Rick's first year. But there was no way I would go for long periods without seeing my son. Sometimes Peggy and the baby would come to stay with me in Calgary for a few days; otherwise I would return to Edmonton every couple of weekends. I looked forward to those times and the smiles and gurgles I would get when I bathed or changed our son. Each time I returned to Edmonton, the trunk of my car would contain a new outfit and a couple of boxes of diapers, as well as the blueprints, survey maps and other documents I always seemed to be carrying.

Peggy and I didn't always agree on childcare and we often had minor arguments about how Rick was being fed or dressed. Sometimes they were more serious – like the day I came home from Calgary just in time to see my son, alone in his walker in the kitchen just off the clinic, reaching for a full box of acupuncture needles that someone had carelessly left on a shelf within his reach.

During Rick's first summer, Peggy and I, along with the baby, got together for frequent camping trips in the Rockies with friends. In my family, children were always included in any festivity or family outing, and on a couple of occasions, he even stayed with us at the beautiful old Banff Springs Hotel. In August, my younger cousin, Nancy, came to visit and we spent several days with her, playing tourist and enjoying the summer sun.

As my son grew and made his first attempts to walk, he and I developed our own special game. After any absence, I would make a point of looking for him immediately upon my return. As soon as we made eye contact, I would spread my arms out as wide as I possibly could and say, "I love you t-h-i-s m-u-c-h a-l-l t-h-e w-a-y a-r-o-u-n-d!" His face would break into a huge smile as he tried to imitate me and eagerly stretch out his own little hands. Then I would scoop him up and give him a big hug, and he would shriek with pleasure.

It was a simple game that made us both laugh. But in the years to come, confronted by countless sleepless nights and Peggy's claims in court that I never lived with her after our son was born, or showed the slightest interest in his care, its memory would be one of the few things that would continue to nourish my spirit.

The nightmarish years would come soon enough, but at that point, we still had good times to look forward to. In December 1978, Peggy and I arranged to spend the Christmas holidays in Hawaii with Stagen, his wife, and Stagen's 80-year-old but extremely energetic grandmother. A business contact had turned over some properties in Hawaii to some associates and me in repayment of a debt. Stagen and I left for Honolulu a week or so ahead of our families to check out these properties and look into other possible investments. Peggy, the baby and Stagen's wife and grandmother joined us in Hawaii just before Christmas.

The photos I took on that trip show a smiling family playing in the waves and building sand castles on the beach. Rick's first Christmas under the palm trees was a happy one – and the only one he would share with both his mother and his father.

After Hawaii, I was so optimistic. Peggy and I seemed at last to be on solid footing and we began talking about buying our own home. The timing was perfect, as the Tokens themselves had just purchased a new home and would be moving shortly. They planned to continue operating Vina Clinic out of the old house and hoped to expand their business by renting surplus space to other professionals. Their new home, located in a quiet, treed, neighborhood, was only a few minutes away.

Around this time, I got a call from Howard Starkman. He, Stagen and I had cleared over $150,000 from our recent investments and we were looking for a new venture. Howard and his brother Ben had recruited several other potential partners. Prices were rising all over Alberta, whereas in B.C and Quebec, they were still relatively low. We eventually settled on Quebec, based on Starkman's reasoning that I had family there. "Italians stick together," he said. "If we should run into difficulties, Ricaardoe has family and friends in Montreal who can help us out." As the only Quebecer, I was elected to scout out potential properties and handle any negotiations.

I must say the idea appealed to me. I liked the thought of spreading our investments between the two provinces and having the means to make frequent trips back and forth between Edmonton and Montreal. Peggy, too, was favorable and we began to think about how we could divide our time between the two cities so that Rick could grow up enjoying the love and affection of both his extended families. Several years remained before we would have to concern ourselves with schooling arrangements and settle more permanently in one given location. For now, the situation was ideal.

In the first few months of 1979, I made several trips to Montreal to look for real estate projects. I found several, including one that I thought was a terrific deal on Sherbrooke Street right near Lafontaine Park. There were other offers on the building, and I wanted to move quickly, but a call to Howard Starkman gave me the impression it would take at least a couple of weeks before he and his other partners would decide.

The asking price for this particular property was more than $3 million, but I had negotiated it down to $1.8 million. Unfortunately, there was no way Stagen and I could raise that kind of money on our own. Instead, we put a down payment on a 60-unit apartment building on Lajeunesse Street, figuring we had lost our chance at the other one. When Starkman called me back the next day to give me the go-ahead on the Sherbrooke Street deal, it was too late.

The Lajeunesse apartment building was a dump – but I was confident that hard work, good management, time and careful renovations would turn it into a worthwhile investment. When I told Peggy about it, we agreed to move to Montreal to handle the project. I would oversee renovations and regular maintenance contracts, and she would handle the bookkeeping. All the while, I would continue to keep an eye open for other properties for our friends in Alberta, and on several occasions, hosted groups of potential Western investors.

We arrived in Montreal just as the full beauty of summer was making its annual pilgrimage to the city. Toni and Richard had a comfortable basement apartment that could easily accommodate Peggy, Rick and me and we lived there for several happy months during which Peggy and Toni grew even closer.

My aunt has such a kind-hearted, warm and generous personality that it would take an exceptionally difficult individual not to like her. She was the one who always fussed over me when I was a child and took me on special outings. Every year at Christmas, she would bundle me onto the streetcar for the trip downtown to see Santa Claus, and she was the one you could always turn to for a hug and a kind word. Richard was not only my uncle, but my godfather and namesake, and I was also very fond of him. Their door had always been open wide for me, and living with them now seemed the most natural and pleasing arrangement thinkable.

Peggy also got along well with my father. Like my aunt and uncle, he was protective of her and wanted to be sure she was happy in Montreal. He used to ask her regularly, "Is Ricaardoe treating you all right? Because if he doesn't, I'll take his ears off!" Invariably she would respond that everything was fine and he was not to worry about us.

It had been several years since my father had operated his own business, but he kept busy doing estimating work for other plumbers he knew. His health was much improved, to the point that he was building a cottage for my mother and himself in the Laurentians, about an hour's drive north of the city.

When he wasn't working on the cottage, he made a habit of dropping by his sister's every morning for coffee and a small talk before he went about the rest of his day. He had done this for years. He and Toni had always been very close and the two of them looked forward to this morning ritual.

Those early morning visits also gave him a chance to spend some time with his grandson, on whom he clearly doted. Rick would climb onto his lap as soon as he saw him, and call out, "Again! again!" when my father sang for him.

I, too, enjoyed those pleasant moments in my aunt's kitchen that brought together three generations of Di Dones. Peggy would often sleep in, so together with my aunt and my father, I was the one who would change Rick and feed him, before leaving for my day's appointments.

As the summer progressed, we also took time out for picnics, visits with family and friends, and frequent trips to my parents' cottage. Before we knew it, the days grew shorter and the first tinges of frost could be seen on the remaining flowers and vegetables in my aunt and uncle's garden.

One evening around the beginning of October, we were lingering at the dinner table after one of my aunt's hearty meals. Rick was playing on the floor nearby and my uncle was in the midst of one of his many jokes that could keep us entertained for hours. Everyone was relaxed, and both the laughter and the homemade wine were flowing freely.

Then the phone rang. It was Bertha Token. To this day, my aunt remarks on the dramatic transformation that overtook Peggy as soon as she took the phone. Her face paled and her expression, full of life and laughter just moments before, suddenly glazed over.

When she returned to the table, her voice sounded hollow and distant. "I have to go back to Edmonton," she said. "There are problems at home. My father's not well and my mom's really upset. She said they can't manage any longer without me."

I had my doubts, but there was no point trying to interfere. If Peggy believed her parents needed her, she would be on the next plane home. I just found it curious that these major crises in the Tokens' lives only seemed to surface whenever Peggy left Edmonton and we started to create a life for ourselves. The passing years had only fuelled my cynicism. I could never figure out whether Bertha, counting on Peggy's inexpensive labor to get Vina Clinic over one more financial hurdle, took advantage of her daughter's emotions and seeming inability to say no, or whether her intent was simply to get her away from me.

I wasn't the only one who had difficulties with the Tokens – particularly Bertha. Jack Roaff was one of many who left their employment because he couldn't get along with her. The Tokens had frequent problems retaining competent people and, as a result, Vina Clinic was chronically short-staffed.

Within a day of Bertha's phone call, Peggy had packed clothes for herself and Rick, and the two of them flew to Edmonton. We talked by phone almost every day. She said her father was very tired and at his age, he couldn't possibly keep up the same hectic pace he had maintained for years. The family's financial security was at stake. She thought it best if she stayed in Edmonton and worked full-time at the clinic. "If that's what you want, we'll all move back to Edmonton," I assured her. "I'll work out something with my dad – I'm sure he'll be able to take over the administration of Lajeunesse – and I'll just travel back and forth as needed."

October 22 that year marked Peggy's twenty-eighth birthday and I had been planning a surprise celebration for her with family and friends at a classy downtown restaurant. A few days before the event, I phoned her, saying: "If you can get away, there are two tickets waiting for you and Ricaardoe Jr. to fly to Montreal. I have a nice surprise for you. After that, we'll all go back to Edmonton."

Peggy loved dressing up and going out for dinner in elegant restaurants and, to all appearances, her birthday was a great success. It was also our farewell party. A day or so after the party, I drove Peggy and our son to the airport for the return flight to Edmonton and then set out myself for the long drive west with our belongings.

Upon my arrival in Edmonton several days later, I was taken aback to learn that Jack Roaff was once again living in the Token home and working at Vina Clinic. Peggy had mentioned nothing about this in our phone calls or during her short trip back to Montreal for her birthday.

When I asked about his sudden re-appearance in Edmonton, she made light of it. It was no big deal, she said. Her parents had simply asked him to come and help out at the clinic after her father got sick.

Given what I had heard about his past relationship with the Tokens, I was very surprised, but took her at her word. Before long, however, it became abundantly apparent that his presence was far more than a matter of mutual convenience revolving around work. Every morning, after he caught a glimpse of Peggy and I together, his departure for the clinic was signaled by the sound of a door slamming in anger, followed by the squeal of his pick-up's tires as he screeched away from the curb. Whenever our paths crossed, the tension in the house shot up like a hand that has carelessly brushed against a hot burner.

When I confronted Peggy, she insisted that Jack was just a good friend who was going through a rough time and needed her help. "But he's still in love with you," I protested.

There was nothing to be concerned about, Peggy assured me. I was the only one she loved. When Jack moved out a few days later, I let the matter temporarily drop.

Until the day I came home to find both Peggy and our son gone. Bertha told me Jack had shown up at their home pleading with Peggy to go away with him. Peggy had been so concerned about his emotional well being that she had finally agreed. She had said she owed it to Jack to try to help him and she intended to return just as soon as she was sure he was all right!

I didn't know what to think. Peggy had a way of getting involved in other people's problems and being unable to extricate herself. On one level, I sympathized with her desire to help a suffering friend. But that didn't erase my own growing confusion and hurt. What was she trying to prove? Only a few days before, we had been looking at a nice home facing a park – just like she had always wanted. We were talking about buying it. And now this? How could she jeopardize our son's safety by taking him along with Jack in such a state? Whom did she really love – me or Jack?

Three or four days passed before she and Rick returned. Repeatedly, she apologized for causing me worry, but insisted she had only gone to try to help Jack. " He has no one to live for," she pleaded. "He's not like you. You're smart at business, you're a good dancer, you've got lots of friends – you've got everything going for you. I was just so worried about him."

"Let's just forget about it," I said, and our lives settled down to what once more seemed a normal pattern. Then a few weeks later she and Rick disappeared again. This time when they returned, she ran to me, and before I could say a word, collapsed at my feet, and clung to my leg with a vice-like grip. I literally had to hobble across the length of a large room, with her still attached, before I finally got her to release my leg. Through a flood of tears, she kept repeating how sorry she was to have left again. She begged for my forgiveness, saying I was the only one she really loved.

I desperately wanted to believe her. What else could I do? Walk out on her and my son for a moment's lack of judgment? That wasn't my way. As baffled as I was by her strange behavior, I was also convinced that the anguish she was feeling was real. And what's the point of saying you love someone, I told myself, if you turn away from them when their pain is greatest? "Everyone makes mistakes," I said finally, hugging her to me. "We have to put this behind us; we have a child to think of."

The very next day, she was gone again. I couldn't believe this was happening and went about in a complete daze. I couldn't concentrate – all I could think about was where my son was and would I ever see him again. My dreams of a happy family life were shattered. Worse still, since Peggy and I had never married, I had no idea of my legal status as the father of my child.

At night, exhausted but unable to sleep, my fears would magnify tenfold. Often I would end up at my friend Joe's place. He would find me in the morning, fully dressed on his couch, with the TV still going from the night before.

Then just as suddenly as she had left, Peggy returned with our son. I have no idea how long she was gone, just that she swore she had never planned to leave with Jack. She said he had arrived unexpectedly at the house and begged her to go for coffee. She was convinced he just wanted to talk things through. She had bundled Rick up and climbed into Jack's truck and before she realized what had happened, they were on the highway heading for B.C. He refused to stop or turn around, and she was frightened to do anything that might further upset him. She said it had taken several days to calm him down to the point that he agreed to drive her back.

She seemed so confused and her story so authentic that, even today, I believe she was telling the truth. I also began to wonder if she hadn't become a victim of her mother's meddling. It seemed more and more likely to me that Jack had only agreed to answer the Tokens' emergency call for help at their clinic on the condition that Peggy be there too. That might explain the strange phone call we had received that night at my aunt and uncle's house back in October, and Peggy's almost hypnotized reaction.

For the sake of our son, we agreed to give our relationship another try and began living together once more. One morning in late March, just before daybreak, we were all awakened by the doorbell, followed quickly by a loud banging. It was Jack. With him was his cousin, a huge barrel of a man who must have weighed over 300 pounds. Jack himself was a good height and physically strong from recent jobs in heavy construction. That morning, however, he was a broken man. He was sobbing that he needed Peggy – that he wanted to marry her – and he had to know her decision. He kept repeating that his life wasn't worth living without her. He even asked me to forgive him and said what a gentleman I had been so far to handle the situation so graciously.

The man was in such a state, it was almost impossible not to feel sorry for him. Like a scene from a soap opera, the drama went on for at least a couple of hours. Peggy was in tears as she claimed she wanted to stay with me. Jack was persistent: "If it doesn't work out," he told her, "we can always get a divorce." His cousin was even less subtle: he told her it was time she stopped playing with people's feelings and made up her mind. I will never understand what was going through her mind that morning. Did she suspect that Jack was so distraught he might even contemplate suicide? Did she believe that she could prevent such a thing from happening? Or did she really love him? And if that was the case, why was her decision so agonizingly difficult?

Whatever her reasons, she eventually said she would go. I was beyond caring – like Jack's cousin, I just wanted her to make up her mind. "Go if you want, but you leave our son with me," I finally said in complete exasperation. She was ready to agree, but Jack quickly intervened: "You wouldn't take a child away from his mother," he said, looking directly at me. He knew that Peggy would never stay with him if she was separated from her son.

Whatever happened, I knew at that moment that my relationship with Peggy was over. She promised she would bring Rick back and that I shouldn't worry about not seeing him. How did I know if I could trust her? As frantic as I felt about her leaving with our son, I just kept telling myself over and over: "Stay calm. You have to play their game. You have to stay calm."

Physically preventing her from taking Rick would have led to violence. Calling the police would have been futile. It wasn't my home and they were more likely to believe the child's mother in her own house surrounded by her family rather than me, the unmarried natural father.

The last thing I wanted was for Peggy to view me as a threat. Based on her past behavior, I was positive that my only chance of seeing my son again rested on my ability to keep a cool head. Otherwise, she and Jack might simply disappear forever, taking Rick with them.

It was a desperate gamble and I stood back as Peggy hastily packed a suitcase and gathered our still sleepy son into her arms.

As I watched them drive off together in Jack's truck, I was amazed at how little I really knew about the woman with whom I had shared almost nine years of my life. I could only hope against hope that my gamble would pay off and she would keep her promise to return with our son.

REVELSTOKE (MARCH 1980-JANUARY 1981)

A day or so after Peggy's departure, I moved out of the Token's home and took my own apartment. Several times a day I would telephone her parents to see if they had any news, and for the first time, they acted truly sympathetic towards me.

Eventually I confided to them that I was thinking of applying for custody of Rick. Now I wonder at my own naïveté, but the shock of recent events had stirred up such turmoil inside me that I needed to know their reaction. I was intent on protecting my relationship with my son, but I was also terrified that any move on my part might just push Peggy deeper into hiding.

The Tokens convinced me not to proceed with a custody application. "Peggy is so mixed up and she has so many problems," they told me. "If, on top of that, you make her believe she could lose Rick, you'll completely demolish her."

Instead they encouraged me to wait until Peggy came back with Rick. "Then you can tell her you want to take him to Montreal for a couple of weeks to visit your family. There's still a chance you two could reconcile. If you go to Montreal with the child, she may well follow you. That's what she's done in the past."

Within a few days, Peggy called from Calgary. She said she had talked things over with her parents and it was all right with her if I took Rick to Montreal. She also insisted she wanted some kind of agreement in writing before she would turn him over to my care.

We arranged to meet in downtown Calgary the next day. When I arrived at the meeting spot, Peggy was already there. She was holding Rick's hand and Jack stood beside them.

"Hello, Ricaardoe," she said. "How are you?"

"I'm always fine. You know that, Peggy," I answered neutrally. "And how's my big boy?"

"Papa!" Rick cried out, with a smile and ran over to give me a hug.

Peggy handed me two documents, both in her handwriting, that she had already signed. The first one, dated a few days earlier, noted that she was leaving our son under her mother's guardianship for a one-month period and that she agreed with his having a two-week holiday in Montreal during that time. "I declare that I am by no means deserting him irresponsibly," it concluded with her signature.

The second one, dated that day – April 4 – read, "I, Ricaardoe Di Done, hereby agree to return Ricaardoe Branden Jr. to his mother in Calgary (or Edmonton) no later than April 30, 1980. This trip to Montreal is to be viewed strictly as a temporary visit, fully approved by Peggy as such."

She asked me if I would sign both documents. I went along and signed them, knowing that she would never leave Rick with me unless I did. Seeming compliance was my only defense against her unpredictability. What I wouldn't learn for many months to come was that she and Jack had been married two days before. The two of them were actually leaving on their honeymoon!

Rick stayed with me at my apartment in Edmonton. We would drop by the Tokens almost every day and they encouraged me to go ahead with my trip to Montreal. I was really looking forward to that visit. I hadn't seen my family since the fall and so much had happened. I knew they were anxious, too, to see how Rick was adjusting to all the change about him.

Our trip was also planned to coincide with a major business deal. In partnership with Howard and Ben Starkman and some other investors, I was about to close the purchase of a 336-unit apartment complex on Robert Street in Montreal. We were all set to leave when our departure was delayed by urgent business in Edmonton.

It was the end of April before Rick and I finally got away to Montreal. Peggy herself was late in returning to Edmonton and we missed each other by a couple of days, but the Tokens knew they could easily reach me at my aunt Toni's. The day before I left, I received notification that Peggy was applying for custody of Rick in family court in Edmonton and a preliminary hearing was scheduled for May 22.

I immediately called a friend of mine who was a lawyer and nervously explained what had happened. He said to go ahead with my trip – that he'd respond on my behalf and ask for the hearing to be postponed until June. He also cautioned me that if Peggy went ahead with her application for custody, I didn't stand a chance against her.

Through my real estate dealings, I now counted several lawyers among my circle of friends who were quite aware of the situation between Peggy and me and who also knew how close my son and I were. More than one pulled me quietly aside with this advice: "Ricaardoe, if this goes to court, you have to understand that the court invariably decides in favor of the mother. A woman has to be shown to be totally unfit as a mother, for the father to get custody."

They suggested that if I wanted to gain custody, the only real course open to me was to leave Alberta with Rick and lay low for a couple of years in Montreal, Ottawa or some other city. "After a couple of years, you will have established a residence and no judge will dispute your relationship with your son," they said. "Then you have a good chance of getting custody."

"That would mean separating my son from his mother," I responded. "That's not what I want to do and I don't think it's what's best for him. I would much rather see us come to some arrangement where we could share in his upbringing."

"That's all very well," my friends said. "But the system doesn't work that way. Just think about it."

In the days and weeks that followed, I thought about little else. My son was my world and I couldn't imagine living without him. Only when Rick and I touched down at Montreal's Dorval Airport on an early May afternoon did some of the tension that had permanently installed itself in my shoulders begin to ease.

My father and aunt Toni were waiting for us at the arrival gate, and as we drove home through the city still fresh with the full burst of spring green, I relaxed for the first time in months. The emotional distance between Montreal and Edmonton seemed even greater than the physical miles that separated the two cities and the very different worlds they represented for my son and me. Here we could laugh, play in the park, and feel secure in each other's company. We were inseparable.

At the end of May, my son – now almost two and a half – was baptized in the beautiful Madonna Della Difesa church. Built in 1918, this church, with its magnificent stained glass windows and white marble altar, forms the heart of Montreal's Italian community. It had been the setting of every major event in my father's family from the time both grandparents emigrated from Italy. Here they were married, and my father and his sisters baptized. From here, too, my grandparents were buried, my parents were married and my sister and I baptized. Now it was Rick's turn.

Peggy had never had any desire to have him christened and it had been a sore point between us. After all the months of uncertainty, I no longer cared much about what Peggy wanted. I wanted what I believed was best for my son. Baptizing him in this church that was so much a part of my family was a tangible way of connecting him to the traditions, roots and values that were his birthright.

The child in each of us needs these occasions to remind us that every individual is special. I am still touched by the memory of my father and Toni standing beside Rick in that big church, holding his hands. With the exception of my son, no two people meant more to me than they, and you could feel the bond of affection that was growing ever stronger between Rick and his godparents.

Since our arrival, we had been staying with Toni and Richard. Rick was gaining back the weight he had lost over the winter and his cheeks, set against the sunny blondness of his hair, were once again full of color. He was learning his ABCs and starting to count in English, French and Italian. When I had to leave for a few hours to take care of business, he would stay with my aunt.

I often discussed with my father and my aunt whether I should go ahead and apply for custody in Montreal where I had a network of family and friends who knew me and could vouch for my good intentions. "A lot of lawyers have told me this is the only way to prevent Peggy from taking off with him again. It's not that I want to stop her from seeing Rick, it's just that I want to make sure she doesn't try to cut me out of his life."

"Peggy would never do that!" my aunt exclaimed. "The child belongs with both his parents and if you ever try to keep her away, I'll have nothing more to do with you. And if she ever tries to do that to you, I'll personally go and find your son and bring him back to you."

My father was less insistent, but he too still hoped that Peggy and I would come to some agreement – maybe even reconcile our differences. But as I hesitated over whose advice to follow, I was sure of one thing: I was in no hurry to return Rick to Edmonton.

We had been in Montreal just over a month, when Peggy phoned. The date for the court hearing was quickly approaching and I had been expecting her call. What caught me off guard was her manner. Instead of being angry that I had not yet returned with Rick, she said she regretted what had happened over the past few months and missed us both terribly. She wanted to join us – to be a family again.

After all we had been through, I was highly suspicious of her motives. How could I tell if she was sincere or only acting? Only when she agreed to cancel the custody hearing as a sign of good faith did I feel sufficiently reassured to tell her to come. At the very least, we needed to talk. A few days later, Rick had a big grin on his face as he waited with me at the airport where her plane was about to land.

Perhaps the mind really has little influence in affairs of the heart. Or we believe what we need to believe. My nervous system was emitting distant early warnings sufficient to protect the continent and yet I agreed to give our relationship one more try.

Peggy was certainly convincing about her desire to get back together and I still felt that much of our current predicament was due to her mother's constant manipulation of her daughter's feelings to her own ends. Yet, all Peggy's arguments and even the deep sympathy I felt for her would not have been sufficient cause for reconciliation, had it not been for our son. It was normal for a child to grow up with his mom and dad and I didn't want to deprive him of this basic right. I was also looking forward to having more children one day and my great desire was for a big family.

When I was growing up, I often watched my father forgive and forget, even when he knew a business contact had tried to cheat him. He would always give people a second and even a third chance. It was both his strength and his weakness, and I had exactly the same tendency. "You'll have to give me six months to a year," I finally said to Peggy. "It's going to take a while to adjust and make things right once more between us, but for Rick's sake, we have to try."

We moved into an apartment in the building on Lajeunesse Street in which I still had part ownership. My family was delighted. Despite all our problems, they were still very fond of Peggy. On one particular occasion, my father sat us down and told us what we had done wasn't fair to our son. That day he asked Peggy to swear to him that she was not having a relationship with Jack. She told him she really wanted to get back together with me.

I won't pretend everything was rosy for the three weeks we lived together. One of my conditions was that Peggy put a stop to all communication with Jack. Her ambiguous relationship with him was a source of frequent arguments. During one of these "discussions," she let slip that Jack had told her she could always come back to him if things didn't work out with me. That really set me off. "What are you saying?" I said, my voice rising. "I thought we were trying to find a solution here – so that our son can grow up with the love of his mom and dad and his grandparents and the benefit of both our families. Now you're telling me with a little grin that you can go back to Jack any time. Are you crazy? Either you turn the page or you leave!"

* * * * *

The next day it happened. The arrival home on a muggy hot July afternoon to an apartment that was far too quiet. Empty drawers and clothes closets. And a long letter on the kitchen table, penned in Peggy's neat, flowing handwriting, confiding that, once again, she was leaving me. "I recognize the step I'm taking will create a permanent rift between us and heaven knows when we'll speak again," she wrote. "The fact is that we can't live together... The unhappiness is that we can't split the little person in half to each enjoy a portion." Had she stayed, she wrote, it was inevitable that I would have eventually driven her to the airport and put her on a plane, keeping Rick with me. "I am forced to leave this way because Baby needs his mother," she added. "The little fella will be happy and well cared for – I'll send you progress reports. Farewell."

I was still standing motionless holding that letter when my father rang the doorbell. He had come to take Peggy shopping for the new stroller he had promised her the day before.

I honestly don't recall much of what happened in the days that followed. I know only that I had never felt such emptiness and was constantly tortured by the thought that I might never see my son again. Through the Tokens, I learned that Peggy had traveled by bus to Toronto and then flown back West. Apparently she had arrived safely and Rick was fine, but she had gone into hiding and didn't want anyone to know where they were.

I lingered in Montreal for another few weeks – not knowing where to turn. I went through the motions of carrying on my business, but my mind was far more occupied with unearthing some clue as to Peggy and Rick's whereabouts. At the end of August, I flew to Edmonton.

The day I arrived, I went to the Tokens to see if they had any news. Just as I was walking up to their door, a courier truck pulled up and the driver approached with a letter addressed to Bertha Token. After a few pleasantries, he asked me if I lived there and would I sign for the letter. As I glanced at the envelope he handed me, shivers moved up and down my spine. The handwriting was Peggy's.

Once inside, I showed the letter to Bertha and we opened it together. Its contents threw me for a loop. In it, Peggy wrote to her mother, "Letting go of Ricaardoe is not easy for me, for I'm not sure if it's the right thing." For six pages, she went on to discuss our relationship, but there was no indication of where she or Rick were. Strangely, she never mentioned Jack once, even though they had already been married for four months.

Each day in Edmonton, I went through the motions of carrying on my business. I still practiced karate and made a point of working out for a couple of hours daily. It helped me retain my sanity. At night I couldn't stand to be alone. Though never a big drinker, I would go out every evening and party with friends, consuming many glasses of wine in a desperate attempt to silence the dread that lurked within. As long as other people surrounded me, I felt I could keep up the pretence that I was somehow managing.

A lot of people held my hand during that period. Josette Gauthier was one of them. She was an ex-Quebecer living in Edmonton, who, for a time, had been going out with my friend Joe. She, Peggy and I had become good friends.

All that autumn, I camped in with Josette and her two teenage boys, trying desperately to maintain some kind of routine. Often I would play soccer with her boys or take them to a movie. Josette had been divorced for some time and she seemed to appreciate that her sons once again had a male presence in their lives. There was never anything but friendship between us and we remain good friends today.

I called or dropped in on the Tokens every other day. One night, not too long after my arrival, I was there when the phone rang. I picked it up only to hear Peggy's voice at the other end. "Peggy," I said, "it's Ricaardoe. Where are you?"

She wouldn't tell me; she only said she was sorry about how she had left with Rick, but that, at least for the present, it was how things had to be. "We can't get along as a couple," she said, "and you made it very clear that if I wanted to go, there was no way you'd let me leave with our son."

"What about me and Rick?" I responded. "How can you keep us apart all this time and say you care about him? You know how much we love each other."

She said she'd think about bringing him to Edmonton for a visit. A few days later, she called back to say they would be coming, but then cancelled out the day before they were to arrive. This cat-and-mouse game continued for several weeks.

Each disappointment was harder to take. Soon some of my friends were advising me to back off for a while. "By pushing so hard to get your son, you're scaring Peggy even farther away," they said. "Pretending you no longer care may be the only way to bring her – and your son – back."

The prospect left me numb. I had miscalculated Peggy so many times already. What if she accused me instead of abandoning my son? Or what if she and Jack disappeared across the U.S. border in a tangle of new identities that would slowly erase me from my son's young memory? I had to find them.

Out of sheer frustration, I, too, became devious. One day I called the Alberta Government Telephone company. "How do you do," I said. "My name is Dr. Allen Token. I have a small problem. I'm in the midst of preparing some income tax statements and I've misplaced several of my telephone bills. Would it be possible to get copies of my last few months' statements?" When the agent replied that this wouldn't be a problem, I said, "Wonderful. I'll be sending a certain Ricaardoe Di Done to your office to pick them up."

That is how I learned that the Tokens had received collect calls from several different numbers in British Columbia. Sometimes the calls originated from Kamloops, sometimes from Revelstoke. I made up my mind to drive to Revelstoke to try to find Rick and Peggy. If that didn't work, I would continue on to Kamloops. Revelstoke was a good 10-hour drive from Edmonton on the other side of the Rockies. Kamloops was approximately 200 kilometers further west into B.C. along the Trans-Canada Highway.

By now we were well into November and weather conditions in the mountains could change at a moment's notice, particularly around the Rogers Pass. I had no idea what awaited me in Revelstoke and asked Josette if she could accompany me on the long drive, but she couldn't afford the time off as she was just returning to work after several weeks' sick leave.

When my father heard I was planning to make the trip on my own, he insisted on sending someone to travel with me. "I don't need anyone," I told him.

— "It's winter," he said. "It's not safe; anything could happen in the mountains." He was also concerned with what might happen should I meet up with Jack.

This is how I came to know Leon Côté. He was a contractor and painter who had been working with my father for several months and had earned his trust. My father liked him and felt he could be counted on in an emergency. My dad paid Leon's airfare and he flew to Edmonton from Montreal on November 21. We set out very early the next morning.

Much of that drive remains a blur of swirling snow and wet pavement, climbing steadily into that awesome ridge of mountains that unfolds in never-ending peaks along the spine of a continent. I drove fast—too fast—for the conditions and I talked incessantly, unburdening myself to Leon. He was a good listener. About my age, with two young sons of his own, he could relate to my plight. Quiet and shy by nature, he was also an imposing figure—over six-feet tall with a thick black moustache. My father wasn't taking any chances.

I remember the snow, the steady swish of wiper against windshield, and the sensation of urgent speed as the car hurtled forward. We were making good time when, well into the Rockies, some deep instinct told me to brake just as we were rounding the top of a very steep incline. What we saw next was sobering to the extreme. Emergency vehicles were stopped near an overturned van that had lost control on black ice. Had I not heeded that strange feeling, we would have smashed right into the other cars – or gone careening over the side of the mountain.

About half an hour further down the highway, we encountered another close call. Once again I got the same strong urge to slow the car and managed to bring it to a stop just before we reached a fallen tree that lay stretched across the road. From then on, I trusted my intuition. It wouldn't be the last time it warned me of impending danger.

By the time we reached Revelstoke, darkness had fallen. Although it was cold, there was no snow on the ground; we had left the bad weather behind. Leon and I found a motel for the night. Pulling the now-worn copy of the Tokens' phone bill out of my jacket, I dialed the operator.

— "Good evening," I said into the phone. "I've just arrived in Revelstoke and am trying to locate some friends. It's their 25th anniversary and there's a surprise party for them, but I only have their phone number. Would you be able to tell me their address?"

— "Why don't you just call and get the address," the voice on the other end inquired.

— "But I've come all this way to surprise them and that would spoil everything," I protested.

But the attempt failed. A second attempt with another operator yielded similar results. The third time, I must have sounded sufficiently convincing or so desperate that the person finally broke down and gave me the address, listed under a name I didn't recognize.

Revelstoke isn't a big town and Leon and I drove up and down several streets until we eventually found the address the operator had given me. The house was a white stucco bungalow and beyond it was a trailer court. Across the street was a small grocery store with a phone booth outside. We parked in the shadows near the store and watched the house for several minutes. The lights were on, but the curtains were drawn and it was impossible to see inside. Outside, there were no signs of anything familiar.

After a while, I told Leon I was going to use the pay phone to call my dad and let him know we had arrived. As I picked up the receiver, the number on the phone caught my eye. "I don't believe it," I said out loud. "We've found them!" I hurried back to the car to give Leon the news. The pay phone's number matched one of the numbers on the Tokens' bill.

"That's got to be their house," I said excitedly. "Peggy must have come across the street to use this phone." Now if only the string of good luck and coincidences that had brought me here would last until I found my son, I thought. Leon and I sat in the car watching for a few more minutes. When nothing further developed, we decided to leave for the night and take our chances in the morning.

All night I tossed and turned, falling in and out of restless sleep. What would happen? Would Peggy make a scene? Call the police? What would I say? How would Rick react after months of separation? There was no way to predict how things would unfold – I only knew that I hadn't come all this way to leave without my son.

With the first light of morning, Leon and I rose, had breakfast, and drove back to the house. This time, I recognized Jack's truck parked out front. He must have just recently come down out of the mountains because there was still snow on the roof and hood. Neither Leon nor I were anxious for an encounter with Jack if we could avoid it, so we decided to return a while later, hoping by then he would have left for work.

Then we remembered the small airstrip at the edge of the town that we had noticed the previous day. We drove over and started talking with the pilot of a small propeller plane. He was a friendly type and when we inquired about whether it would be possible to charter his plane to Calgary later that day, he said, "No problem. Just give me an hour or so notice." We shook hands and Leon and I left, promising to contact him later.

At worst, we reasoned, I could find a way to get Rick away from Peggy and make a dash for the airport, while Leon drove the car back over the mountains. Even if Peggy called the police, I figured they wouldn't intervene once they learned I was the child's father. We had never gone to court to determine custody, so on what legal grounds could they stop me? However, I hoped it wouldn't come to this, but I was preparing myself for anything. Until you actually live through an experience like this, it's difficult to imagine what extreme measures a parent can be driven to in order to be reunited with a much loved child.

Just before lunch, Leon and I returned to the house, hoping to catch Peggy and Rick at home. Once again we parked across the street, a little way back from the small grocery store. This time Jack's truck was gone. "It's now or never," I thought, taking a deep breath and forcing myself to get out of the car, cross the road and walk up the path to the door of the bungalow. Leon waited in the car, keeping a lookout.

As the door swung open in answer to my knock, I was astonished to see Peggy's face break into a lovely smile. I had rehearsed many scenarios over and over in my mind, but a warm welcome wasn't one of them.

"Ricaardoe," she said, looking truly pleased to see me. "What a surprise! Come in. What are you doing here?" "I've come for Rick," I answered, stepping just inside the door into the kitchen. "I'm here to take him back to Edmonton. You can come if you want, it's up to you."

Before she could answer, our son, who had seen me the moment I entered, dashed from the living room where he had been playing and flew into my arms. "Papa," he shouted, wrapping his arms around my neck and hugging me. "I love you this much all the way around. Where've you been, Papa? I missed you, Papa!"

"I love you, too, and I've missed you so much," I answered, trying hard to control the lump in my throat.

I told Peggy I couldn't go on being separated from Rick. "The child needs both his parents. We have to come to some agreement once and for all, but no matter what, I'm taking him back to Edmonton. That's his home and that's where he belongs."

There was no way anyone could deny my son's happiness at seeing me, and Peggy knew she couldn't pry him away. She said she had actually been thinking of going to Edmonton for a visit. Her parents could always use her help and Jack was doing much better. He was working regularly as a foreman on the construction of a nearby dam and was also busy managing the trailer court that he now owned next door.

I lingered for a few more minutes while she quickly packed a bag for herself and Rick and turned off whatever she had been cooking. She included a small bag of diapers, surprising, since Rick had been completely toilet trained when I had last seen him in July. Peggy had even remarked what good care we had taken of him when she arrived in Montreal.

Peggy held out Rick's jacket. "We're going for a long car ride with Papa to visit Grandma and Grandpa in Edmonton," she told him. I swung him up onto my shoulders and carried him to the car where Leon waited. Peggy locked the door and joined us.

Some four months later in court, Peggy gave an entirely different account of my arrival in Revelstoke. She testified that she and Rick had been already dressed in their winter coats, and were just preparing to leave the house, when I arrived out of the blue and "grabbed the child off the doorstep." She claimed the only hope she had of getting Rick back was to accompany us all the way to Edmonton.

Yet, what I recall is a relatively calm trip with Rick sitting on my knee, happily chatting away and playing. Leon drove most of the way, while I discussed with Peggy how we could arrange our lives so that we could both be part of our son's future. "We could each rent a place in the same neighborhood," I volunteered. "That way Rick could go back and forth between us."

We drove straight through, stopping only to pick up some sandwiches to eat in the car. All the way back to Edmonton, Peggy's words and actions gave me the distinct impression that she might seriously consider, even welcome, a reconciliation.

But regardless of how pleasant she was being, I was really scared and knew I'd only feel safe once we crossed the border into Alberta and familiar territory.

By the time we reached Edmonton, it was close to 10:00 p.m. I intended to check into the Edmonton Plaza Hotel with Rick and Leon until Peggy and I had a chance to figure out where our relationship was headed. When I offered to drive her to her parents, she said no, she preferred to stay with us at the hotel.

Looking back, I feel only sadness at how little either of us trusted the other. We both feared the other person would disappear with Rick, as if he were a favorite possession that could be moved and hidden away at will. Peggy, Rick and I ended up sharing a room.

The next day, we took a long walk in the park. I did my best to reassure Peggy that no matter what happened between us, I had no intention of ever depriving her of her son. All I wanted was to ensure that I, too, remained a part of his life. "But there's no damn way I'm going to stand by and let you take him back to B.C.," I told her. "You're not going to disappear with him again – he needs both of us."

Peggy listened quietly and said she wanted to talk things over with her parents. At the Tokens, we agreed it would be best if she remained with them for a few days, while Rick and I stayed with Josette Gauthier. Peggy got along well with Josette and led her to believe she intended to remain in Edmonton. They even made plans to attend an opera together in the coming weeks.

When I called my dad to let him know I had found Rick and we were together in Edmonton, his reaction was swift: "What are you waiting for? Get on a plane and get yourselves back to Montreal. We'll get you a good lawyer and you can apply for custody here where you have the support of all your family."

— "Dad," I said. "If I'm going to apply for custody, it will be right here in Edmonton. This is where Rick was born and it makes sense that he stay here where we can both be close to him. And there's still a small chance we could even get back together. You were the one who said I should give her the benefit of the doubt."

— "That was before she took off with the child and hid him from you," he shot back. "For God's sake, wake up. Or they're going to fool you again."

— "I don't want to do to her what she did to me," I responded. "That's not what's best for Rick. Believe me, I'm being careful. She's not going to take off with him again."

In preparation for my custody application, I took Rick to be examined by Ron Harshman, an Edmonton psychologist that we had visited back at the beginning of the year, when I was first contemplating it. Every lawyer I knew had advised me that, if I were to proceed, I would need the backing of an expert attesting to my abilities as a parent and the close bond that existed between my son and myself. I was also concerned about any deep-seated effects the upheaval of the previous months might be having on Rick.

When he was with me in Montreal back in May, he had been fully toilet trained and could count to 10 in English, French and Italian. Now he was back in diapers, could no longer remember his numbers and wasn't speaking as well as he had before.

Naively, I still thought there was a chance that with enough good will, Peggy and I could come to some arrangement without going to court. What never occurred to me was that she could have already obtained an order from the Supreme Court of British Columbia the previous August granting her interim custody of Rick. I knew little about the workings of the legal system when it came to family matters. I certainly didn't think it possible that she could have been granted custody without due notification time. Furthermore, she had only been living in B.C. a matter of months. How could she have applied for custody there in such a short time?

I was in for a very rude awakening. She could and did obtain an interim custody order – on an *ex-parte* basis – in other words, without my being present. She also had a restraining order issued to prevent me "from making contact or endeavoring to make contact or otherwise interfering" with either herself or Rick.

At the time, B.C. law stated that when a child was born to a common-law relationship, as long as the father's name appeared on the birth certificate, the father was to be served notice of a custody proceeding. I had never received any such notice, despite the fact that I was in constant touch with Peggy's parents and they knew where I could be reached. Peggy had also written to my aunt Toni at least once over the previous months and could have relayed a message to me through her anytime.

To obtain the interim order, she claimed that I had threatened her with violence, and that she lived in constant fear that I would "steal" our son away. She must also have convinced someone within the legal system that she had no knowledge of how to contact me.

The details of that B.C. order would become known to me soon enough: Peggy wasted no time after her arrival in having it registered in Alberta's Court of Queen's Bench. From my point of view, the order wasn't the only thing I remained ignorant about. I still hadn't the slightest inkling that she and Jack were married, and neither anything she said nor did, led me to believe that she intended to spend the rest of her life with him.

We had been in Edmonton only a week when the Tokens invited me to dinner on December 2 to celebrate the eighteenth birthday of their youngest daughter, Tania. All that day I was on edge. I couldn't shake the feeling that something bad was going to happen that night. I asked Josette if she would come with me to the Tokens.

It was a cold, snowy night and driving conditions were terrible. I wanted to cancel, but Peggy kept insisting that Rick and I be part of the celebration. Because of the icy roads, Josette, Rick and I arrived late, part way through dinner. The whole family was gathered around the dining room table and everyone was in a good mood.

The Tokens had gone all out. The best china was on the table, and the food was appetizing and plentiful. But I couldn't dispel my sense of unease. I did my best to hide my nervousness and made pretence of enjoying my dinner. Josette, too, had a bad feeling about the evening and barely touched her food.

After an hour or so, Tania, Lydia and another friend excused themselves as they had made plans to go out and we said our good-byes. The rest of us moved into the living room. A short while later, the doorbell rang, and before I knew what was happening, two uniformed Edmonton police officers had entered the house—one by the front door, one by the back. I froze as one of the officers approached, asking: "Are you Mr. Ricaardoe Di Done?" When I nodded, he handed me a document.

"What's this?" I said, staring blankly at the paper.

"It's a custody and restraining order, sir," he answered.

"What do you mean custody order?"

"I'm sorry, Mr. Di Done, but the court has granted custody of the boy to his mother. We're here to see that it's enforced. There's also a restraining order against you – if you do anything to try to prevent them from leaving, you will be arrested."

I began to read the paper, desperately trying to absorb its meaning. The only thing I really understood was that my son was going to be taken away from me. It took several seconds before I noticed that the name on the custody order was Peggy Roaff. "How naive could I have been?" I thought, realizing at last that she and Jack were married. But when I confronted her outright, she didn't answer yes or no. Just the trace of a smile confirmed that she had outsmarted me.

"This is impossible," I told the police. "We never went to court – no one ever advised me of anything – how can this be happening? Can I at least call my lawyer?"

"Go ahead," they said. "We'll wait."

I called Howard Starkman and every other lawyer friend I knew – asking them, pleading with them, to do something to stop this. But each one gave me the same answer: "You have no choice, Ricaardoe, you have to let your son go. You'll have to go to court to try to get him back".

I will never forget the rest of that night. When I returned to the living room, Peggy had gathered her things together and was asking the police if they would escort Rick and her to the airport. They said that was beyond their responsibility and she should call a cab, but that they would wait to make sure the two of them got away safely.

"How could you do this?" I said, turning to Peggy. "I thought we were trying to find some middle ground – so that our son could be with both of us. If I had been in bad faith, I could have fled with him and gone into hiding. But I didn't – I stayed here because I wanted to find a solution for our son's sake. Instead you slap me in the face. How can you do this to your own son?"

When Rick realized that his mother was taking him away and that I wasn't coming, he began to shriek: "I want Papa! I want Papa!" He lodged himself in my arms and clung to me with every bit of his strength. "No!" he shouted every time someone tried to remove him. "No, Papa. Don't let me go no more. Don't let me go. I don't want to go back."

Peggy couldn't get near him to dress him – he kept pushing her away. Finally he was so hysterical, he threw himself down on the floor. After several minutes of our trying everything to comfort him, his shrieks of anger relented at last into sporadic sobs. Exhausted, he collapsed in a heap.

I was the only one he would allow to touch him. Embarrassed, the two police officers asked me if I could get him into his snowsuit. They looked as if they wished they were anywhere but in that living room. They could see I was no criminal and were clearly touched by my predicament; they said the court order gave them no choice but to turn Rick over to Peggy's care. Under the strain of so much emotion, he had fallen fast asleep and I managed at last to zip him into his winter coat and fasten up his boots. I gave him one more kiss as I placed his now relaxed form into Peggy's arms. By the time she and Rick got into the taxi and drove off, I was sobbing uncontrollably.

Josette, too, was in tears and the Tokens were pale and quiet. "You know how much my son loves me," I said to Bertha, wiping my eyes. "How could you invite me over like this, knowing this was going to happen?" She swore she had nothing to do with it and was completely ignorant of Peggy's plan. She and Allen also said this was the first they had heard of Peggy's marriage to Jack.

Josette and I remained at the Tokens for another half hour, trying to collect ourselves and figure out what to do. I felt like someone had ripped my heart out. I didn't know where to turn or who to believe. All day, I had expected trouble. I had been prepared for an argument. But never did I imagine that Peggy would set me up and serve me with a custody order in that way. Finally, Josette called a mutual friend who lived a few minutes away and asked if we could come over to have some tea and calm down. We sat in the car outside the Tokens for several minutes until I was able to pull myself together enough to drive.

Coleen Christy made us welcome and listened to my sad story in disbelief. She was among the first of many people, who, through both large and small gestures and sometimes-substantial inconvenience to themselves, would be there when I most needed help. When I asked if I could call Montreal, she showed me the phone unquestioningly.

I called my father. As I poured out my story, he swore softly in Italian on the other end of the line. It took a while before I got out all the details. I was still stunned by all that had just happened and I was also frantic about Rick. "What if she disappears for good this time?" I asked in desperation. "What can I do?"

My dad didn't say much. He had made his opinion known as soon as I had arrived in Edmonton with my son. He told me simply that he would support me in whatever I had to do to get my son back.

My aunt Toni couldn't believe what I was telling her. She had trusted Peggy even more than I. All along she had told me not to worry, that Peggy was part of the family and would eventually come back to me. "Now what do you think of Peggy?" I asked bitterly. "Are you still going to come out here and find Rick and bring him back to us yourself?" That was the only time in my life I remember making my aunt cry.

I hung up the phone and rejoined Josette and Coleen. "This can't be happening," I said, pacing back and forth. "It took so long to find him." I was too restless to sit still and we decided to go to a small café nearby called the Bistro Praha where we knew the owner. It was a friendly, comfortable place that I often visited with friends.

Just before 11:00 p.m., Josette and Coleen said they had to leave, as they both had work the next morning. As I was driving them home, I suddenly decided to take a detour past the municipal airport. I stopped the car in front of the terminal building, asked Josette and Coleen to wait a couple of minutes, and approached the entrance. "If there's a God, there's no way she's going to leave with our son. She must still be inside with him," I murmured to myself. Through the glass doors, to my great relief, I saw Peggy and Rick seated in the lounge waiting for the last flight to Calgary that night. I returned to the car, told Josette and Coleen they should go, and asked Coleen if she could keep my car overnight. Then I went inside the terminal.

When Rick saw me, he ran into my arms and hugged me. Peggy was right behind him. "You must really hate me," I said to her, as our eyes met.

"I could never hate you, Ricaardoe. I care for you too much," she replied simply.

"You have a strange way of showing it," I answered.

I tried to convince her not to go, but she insisted they were leaving. "In that case, I'm going to buy a ticket, too," I said, still holding my son in my arms, and moving towards the counter. The police had warned me not to interfere with her or follow her, but I was beyond caring. "If you don't want me around, you'd better call a security guard now. There's one right over there. Otherwise, I'm getting on the same flight as you." Softening my tone, I added, "We have to talk. We can call a priest or a psychologist. You know the Italian priest, Father Alessandrini. He knows me – I could call him right now and I'm sure he'd meet with us."

Eventually, Peggy called her parents. After she hung up, she agreed to go somewhere to talk. The airport coffee shop was closed, but the Edmonton Inn was just across the street. The three of us sat down at a table, and we must have remained there at least another hour. Once again, I tried to convince her how important it was for both of us to share in our son's upbringing. "You saw him tonight." I said, "He became hysterical when he knew we were going to be separated again. We have to think about him." She said she couldn't stay in Edmonton. Her home was with Jack and his work was in B.C. They were making a life together there. She was Rick's mother and he belonged with her.

That's when I made up my mind. I excused myself to use the telephone and called Margaret Turfus, a family law specialist and a partner in the firm of lawyers with whom I regularly did business. It was after midnight when I woke her. I explained that it was an emergency – that there was no way I was going to let my son be taken away again and that I was temporarily leaving the city with him. "But I want to be very clear that I'm not kidnapping him," I insisted. "I'm doing this to protect him so that we can have a fair hearing in an Alberta court with everyone who should be there, present so that they won't disappear with him anymore." I asked her to begin proceedings for joint custody on my behalf first thing the next morning. I gave her my word I would return with Rick once a court date had been set.

Then I called Coleen Christy, and asked if she could come to meet me with my car, in spite of the late hour. Thankfully, she agreed.

When I returned to the table, Peggy and I talked for a few more minutes, while Rick dozed on my lap. I didn't yet have a plan and I was extremely worried. If Peggy wanted, all she had to do was call the hotel security and I could be arrested. Before long, Coleen entered the coffee shop and joined us at the table. After a few moments of small talk, Peggy excused herself and went to the washroom with Rick to change his diaper.

When they got back to the table, Rick immediately climbed into my arms and I wrapped my fur coat around him. Before Peggy realized what I was doing, I had gotten up and with Rick still in my arms, was hurrying out of the coffee shop. My heart was pounding as I stepped over the small railing that separated the coffee shop from the hotel lobby, and made my way out of the main door and into the front seat of a waiting taxi. I locked the back door on the passenger side, but Peggy, trailing with Rick's snowsuit and mitts, was right behind. She ran around the car and managed to get in the back on the other side. Coleen, who had followed us out of the hotel, stood, bewildered. I shouted for her to follow us in my car.

The taxi driver was just as confused. I asked him to take us to a certain street corner that I knew was within walking distance to Josette's. I had no intention of returning there that night, but I wanted Peggy to think that's where I'd be. Meanwhile, Peggy was yelling to the driver, "No, take me to the nearest police station. He's going to have me beaten up."

"This is my cab," I answered. "No one is forcing you to stay. Get out if you want."

The cabby began driving towards the address I had given. All the while Peggy and I were arguing back and forth. "He's my son," she said, "I gave birth to him and he has been in my care ever since."

"He's the son of both of us," I snapped back. "He's not a possession. Nobody owns him."

As we reached the intersection, I jumped out of the car with Rick, wrapping him more tightly in the fur to protect him from the cold. He was wide-eyed and his arms were clasped tightly around me. I had to squint against the driving snow to see which way to go. By now Peggy had also jumped out of the car and was kicking me and pummeling me with her fists. I broke away from her and walked quickly in the direction of Josette's building.

Peggy got back in the cab and took off, I assumed, to get the police. I knew they would look for us at Josette's, so I doubled back and ran a few more streets to the nearby apartment of a friend of Josette's whom Peggy had never met.

I had to knock several times before she awakened and came to the door. I told her we had no place to go and begged her to let me stay the night with Rick. She didn't want to let me in. Her husband, who was away at the time, was very jealous and she was afraid of his reaction should he arrive home suddenly and find me there. Only when she saw the desperation in my eyes and the way my son was clinging to me did she reluctantly invite us in.

When I think of what Rick endured that night watching his mother and father fight over him in a snowstorm at 1:30 in the morning, I still feel sick. I soothed him as best I could and he slept the rest of the night cuddled closely against me.

We ended up staying with Josette's friend all the next day and one more night. No one knew our whereabouts and we were safe as long as we stayed inside. I couldn't dare risk renting a car in my own name and the one friend I asked to drive us out of Edmonton, refused. "Do you think I'm nuts?" he responded to my request.

My father instructed me to sit tight; once again Leon Côté flew to Edmonton, rented a car, and drove us out of Alberta to Saskatoon. From Saskatoon, the three of us were to fly to Winnipeg and then on to Ottawa, where we would rent another car to Montreal. Now I was a fugitive. I was so scared – never knowing if I would be arrested at any moment. Rick wouldn't let me out of his sight. "Don't leave me, Papa," he repeated over and over. "Don't leave me."

Changing planes in Winnipeg, we encountered our first hint of trouble. We were sitting in the boarding lounge waiting for our flight when an RCMP officer walked over to speak to us. I'll never know if he was on the lookout for someone who fit my description or if it was purely coincidence that he stopped to chat. Rick was on my lap. We were playing some little game and he was smiling up at me. Whatever else the Mountie noted, it must have been obvious that Rick was quite content to be with me, and after a few pleasantries, he went on his way. I was numb with relief. We were the first in line when the call for boarding came over the loud speaker.

It was only when we reached Montreal and the familiar surroundings of my parents' home that I began to relax. Rick, too, brightened under all the attention he got from my parents and aunts and uncles. He never asked for his mother. One day when we were looking through a family album and we happened across a photograph of Peggy, he just turned the page over and continued to look at the other pictures.

We had been with my parents a few days – perhaps as long as a week—when I awoke one night in a cold sweat. I had dreamt that the police had raided my parents' home. By now I had learned to trust my feelings. The next morning I told my parents it wasn't safe there anymore, and Rick and I had to leave.

A friend of mine with contacts in the police force had my file checked out. That's how I learned there was a warrant for my arrest both in the Montreal area and in the Laurentians, north of the city. But for some reason, the south shore was clear. Through that friend's intervention, Rick and I moved temporarily to an apartment in Longueuil, a suburb directly across the St. Lawrence River. That same night, the police arrived at both my parents' and Toni and Richard's homes.

They went through both houses looking for any trace of Rick or myself. Closets, pantry, basement – they were very thorough in their search. I learned later that this was one of the few times when my mother spoke up on my behalf. "People are always complaining about fathers who show no interest in their children," she berated the police. "Now you have a father who really wants to look after his son. Why don't you just leave him alone?"

Rick and I spent the Christmas holidays in the Laurentians with Robert Roy. I had met Robert back in my construction days in Port

Cartier and we had become good friends. He was a shop steward at the time and later rose to prominence in one of Quebec's largest labor unions. In the years that followed, he, too, fathered a child, except in his case, he failed to maintain regular contact when he and the girl's mother split up. Years later, when he and his daughter did meet, she only wanted to know one thing: why he hadn't fought to be with her.

Every few days, I called Margaret Turfus for news of how the whole custody issue was progressing. About mid-December, she informed me that the Alberta Court of Queen's Bench had ruled that because of Rick's "real and substantial connection" to the province of Alberta, it was within its jurisdiction to hear the case. This effectively cancelled the interim custody order from B.C. However, nothing could proceed until Rick was back in Edmonton, so Margaret Turfus was doing everything she could to get the kidnapping charge that Peggy had laid against me suspended long enough for us to safely return.

In the meantime, Peggy wrote a long letter to my father saying she was willing to soften the charges against me if only I would come forth voluntarily with our son. "You must know that my main concern for the past six months has been to insure that my little boy couldn't be torn away from me if I was to displease your son...I knew that Ricaardoe cared for Branden and I have never intended to close him out entirely... All that has taken place does not indicate any dislike or revenge on Ricaardoe. What I've said is give Branden and me our freedom...you don't hang somebody up by grabbing their children..."

"What about our son's freedom to be with both his parents?" I said to my father, after reading the letter. "I wish she had thought about that before hiding him away in Revelstoke for months without letting me see him or speak to him or telling me where he was."

The days passed. Rick and I went for long walks, played in the park and saw my parents and the rest of my family as often as we dared. It was hardly a normal life, but I far preferred the strain of being a fugitive to being separated from him indefinitely.

One bitterly cold night, Rick and I had gone to visit some trusted friends in a neighboring apartment. A young couple with kids of their own, they knew the details of my story and would often invite

Rick and me over during those difficult days. The kids had already fallen asleep when their father and I decided to go out for a smoked meat sandwich. We had just finished our sandwiches and were at the cash paying when in walked a police officer.

"Cold night, eh?" I said, nodding to him and putting on as pleasant a smile as I could muster. Those days, my stomach went into knots every time I saw a uniform. The officer barely answered, looking me up and down coldly. "Did he know who I was? Was he after me?" I wondered, fighting my fear. We left quickly and then I saw his partner waiting for him in the squad car at the curb.

"Richard!" I heard my name called in French from the direction of the cruiser.

"Make a run for it!" my companion muttered under his breath. Luckily, I turned instead and walked over to the car. Inside sat one of my cousins who happened to be in the police force. He had recognized me coming out of the restaurant and was just being friendly.

Another time, Rick and I went for brunch with the same friends to a hotel on the Boucherville islands—a park just a few kilometers downstream from the city. As we pulled into the parking lot, we heard the sound of a helicopter landing. Looking up, I saw the police crest on the helicopter's side, at the same time that several provincial police cars pulled into the lot.

We quickly went inside and sat at a booth. To my dismay, several policemen installed themselves at the table right behind us. Rick was intrigued by all the commotion and the officers were soon smiling at him and making small talk with us. I kept waiting for something to happen, but eventually realized their being there must have been pure coincidence. All the same I couldn't wait to get out of there and we quickly ate our meal and left.

In late January, the call finally came from Margaret Turfus advising that the kidnapping charge against me was temporarily suspended and that an order was also in place preventing Peggy from leaving Edmonton with Rick. The court was placing Rick under the care of the Child Welfare Department until the matter of custody was settled.

That night, I explained to Junior that it was time we returned to Edmonton. I didn't say anything about the court case – just that we had to go back and see his mom and all our friends there. "That's OK, Papa," he said. "We'll still be together."

We had a tearful good-bye with my family at the airport. There wasn't one member of my family who wanted me to leave. They were all now convinced that I should stay in Montreal and eventually apply for custody. "I think you're crazy to go back," my dad said, just before we went through the gate, "but you know you can count on your aunt and me. We'll be there in Edmonton when you need us."

I still thought there was a chance that Peggy and I could come to some agreement to share in our son's upbringing. Amputating him from either parent went against everything I believed in. Surely my willingness to cooperate with his mother would count for something. I couldn't believe that anyone could be blind to the bond that grew stronger daily between my son and me.

Rick and I arrived in Edmonton just in time for his third birthday and we organized an impromptu party for him at Josette's with Wayne and Crystal Kading, their children and several other friends. At the end of the party, I was to bring Rick to the Tokens where, as a ward of the court, he was to live in the weeks leading up to the trial.

I had been putting off telling him about the court proceedings. Finally I had no choice. I broke the news as gently as I could. "Rick, in a little while I'm going to court so that no one can ever take you away from me. In the meantime, you're going to be staying with your grandparents until everything is settled. Papa will come to see you every other day and your mom will be there with you on the days I'm not there. We both love you very much."

The pain of that separation still haunts me some 20 years later. "No, Papa," he said. "I don't want to go. I want to stay with you. Why can't I stay with you?" He looked so vulnerable and his eyes were big with unspoken questions. Then he put his arms around me and started to cry. His tears soaked my shirt. "Don't leave me," he repeated, choking through his sobs. "Don't leave me." He was crying, I was crying, every adult in the room was crying, while the other kids gathered around us. "What's wrong with Rick?" they asked, concerned for their friend. "What's the matter? It's OK, Rick. Don't cry."

Slowly I picked him up and as we went downstairs to my car, our friends moved about wordlessly, gathering up the last bits of wrapping paper and birthday cake.

Ricaardoe Jr. and author:
Renovation of one of author's
properties, Edmonton, Alberta,
Spring 1980.

Author and Ricaardoe
Jr.: Edmonton, Alberta,
Easter 1980.

Grandfather (godfather) Di Done, Ricaardoe Jr. and Aunt Toni (godmother): Baptism of Ricaardoe Jr., Montreal, Quebec, May 1980.

Ricaardoe Jr. and author: Time when author reunites with son five months later in Revelstoke, November 1980.

Author and Ricaardoe Jr.: Country house of Robert Roy, Vice President founder of FTQ Construction, Ste Calixte, Quebec, December 31, 1980.

Author and Ricaardoe Jr.: Jr.'s third birthday, January 1981.

THE DEA JUDGMENT

Rick remained in the Token household barely a week. When we arrived at what was supposed to be neutral ground, I learned to my dismay that Peggy and Jack were also staying there. Each time I came to visit Rick, Jack would intentionally give me a little shove or find some other way to deliberately irritate me. It was as if he was trying to set me up – to rile me to the point that I would do something foolish in front of witnesses who could then testify to my "violent" nature.

I soon protested this arrangement and the court agreed that Rick be moved to the home of close friends, Wayne and Crystal Kading. The Kadings were a warm, generous, loving couple, whom both Peggy and I liked and trusted. They had two young children of their own, one of whom was close to Rick in age. Peggy and I were able to visit with him on alternate days – she on odd ones, me on even. Though hardly a happy arrangement, it was the best one possible under the circumstances.

In the two months that Rick spent with the Kadings, Crystal, more than anyone, noticed differences in the way he interacted with Peggy and myself. She told me she would support me in court, but then Wayne was strongly opposed to any involvement on her part. In the end, to my great disappointment, she followed his wishes. I couldn't understand how he could take this position when he was among those who witnessed how upset my son had become the day of his birthday party when he learned he would be separated from me. After that decision, there was a rift between us, even though I will always be grateful for the care he and Crystal gave Rick under such difficult circumstances.

Early in the preliminary proceedings, the court had appointed Alexander (Sandy) Hogan to act as the Amicus Curiae, a Latin term meaning "friend of the court." As Amicus, his role was to represent Rick's interests throughout the trial and, based on a thorough investigation of the family situation, to make a recommendation to the judge concerning custody.

Through Margaret Turfus' brother, John Odishaw – also a practicing Edmonton lawyer – we learned that Sandy Hogan invariably favored the mother in his custody recommendations. Odishaw suggested that I ask for someone else to conduct the investigation on the Amicus' behalf, and this is how social worker Gerry Way became involved. In the end, we fared no better.

In the weeks leading up to the trial, Gerry Way interviewed Peggy, myself and various friends and family members in Edmonton, Kamloops, Revelstoke, Calgary and Montreal. We received his final report around 4:00 p.m. of the day immediately preceding the start of Rick's custody hearing. It recommended that Peggy be named custodial parent.

Several disturbing incidents occurred during the investigation process. At the beginning of March, during a pre-trial meeting that included the judge, Margaret Turfus and Peggy's lawyer, Lawrie Smith, Gerry Way had already made it clear that he saw no reason why Rick shouldn't be removed from the Kading home and returned to his mother's care for the rest of the interim period. It seemed he had already made up his mind about who would be the better custodial parent even though he had barely begun his interviews with any of the people to whom I had suggested he speak.

On another occasion, he called to arrange an appointment to interview me. I was feverish with a bad flu that particular day and asked if we could put off our meeting for another day or two. He responded that this wouldn't do as he had to finalize his interim report. "I'll simply write that you don't want to meet with me," he added, sarcastically. Feeling trapped, I agreed to meet him in the lounge of the Four Seasons Hotel that night around 10:30 p.m. – the only time he said he had available. Aching in every part of my body, I dragged myself to the interview.

Moreover, once he did begin interviewing some of my family and friends, they came back to me with very troubling comments. Howard Starkman was one reference I had given to Gerry Way and he called me immediately following his meeting with the social worker. "I would have convinced any judge in your favor," Starkman told me, "but this guy is looking for something – anything – bad against you. He's trying to nail you."

Similarly, Stagen Warness reported that Gerry Way had cancelled an appointment with him in Calgary at the last minute because he was "running out of time." "That," I reflected, "and the fact that you happen to be a medical doctor whose opinion could carry considerable weight."

In fairness, Way did travel to Montreal to meet with my parents, two aunts and two long-time family friends. However, at the time he assured them that what they had told him was sufficient and there was absolutely no need for them to travel all the way to Edmonton to appear in court.

That piece of information weighed heavily on my mind on the morning of Thursday, March 26, 1981, when my father, my aunt Toni and I, entered the Law Courts building where Rick's custody hearing was about to get under way. Gerry Way was seated in the hall, going over his notes, as we passed by; his face turned a milky shade of white when he saw the three of us together.

At last, we were at the point of decision. This was my first experience of a court proceeding and I was extremely nervous. I knew very well that the odds weighed heavily against my being named Rick's custodial parent. My friends and associates had repeatedly cautioned me that custody went to the mother in the vast majority of cases. "For a father to get custody, you pretty well have to prove that the mother is totally unfit – that she's a confirmed alcoholic or drug user," they said.

Be that as it may, I had made up my mind to press on and would not be discouraged by trends or statistics. If Peggy had agreed to remain in Edmonton and share the parenting of our son with me, I could have lived with either of us having official custody. But I could never agree to her uprooting our son and taking him to live in another province and jurisdiction.

My lawyer had told me that if I had several strong witnesses testifying for me, there was still a chance we could turn the tide. So, though I was scared and nervous, I was not completely without hope, knowing that my father, my aunt and several friends were present to support me.

Although I was the one who had insisted on this Alberta hearing, my lawyer strongly advised me to let Peggy take the position of applicant. In any court proceeding, the applicant's testimony is heard first. She reasoned that, as respondent, I would have the benefit of hearing what Peggy had to say and be better prepared to respond. It was only later as I began to accumulate research on such matters that I discovered this wasn't the wisest choice.

In Canada in those days, it was far more common for women to be the applicants in custody proceedings than it was for men. Furthermore, when mothers were the applicants, they obtained custody in 95.7% of cases. However, when fathers were the ones to apply for custody, something very interesting happened: they obtained custody 42.6% of the time.[3]

I still wonder whether my being applicant would have had any bearing on the decision that was eventually reached. After years of being in and out of court, if I have learned anything, it is that any form of litigation is, above all, a gamble whose outcome depends not only on the strict merits of the case, but on the built-in biases of the court system and the judge who makes the ruling. Like any smart gambler, I wouldn't overlook any card that could give me an advantage.

But that is how I see things today. Back then, I was – in a word – intimidated. Faced with the stiff formality, austere surroundings and unfamiliar language and rules of the courtroom, I put my trust in my lawyers, often letting their advice overrule my own judgment.

The Honorable Mr. Justice Dea presided over the hearing, which stretched over four days. Peggy and I each had eight witnesses. Both Peggy's mother and sister Tania testified for her, as did Jack, a former babysitter, and other family friends and acquaintances. They maintained that Peggy had cared for Rick (or Branden as she now always called him) since birth and that as far as they were concerned, his home should be with her. When Peggy herself took the stand, she said that while I loved Rick and had his best interests at heart, I hadn't actively participated in his upbringing until after our separation. She also said that we hadn't lived together as man and wife since before his birth and that we had only stayed together "on occasion."[4]

Despite the fact that I had several years of photographs documenting our lives together and my almost constant involvement with Rick, Peggy was an excellent actor. She managed to say all this as calmly and collectedly as if she firmly believed it. I had planned to introduce these photos as evidence of our close relationship, but Peggy's lawyer somehow got wind of this and staged a pre-emptive strike. The testimony against me made it sound like my interest in my son was strictly superficial: that while I was always eager to get him to pose for the camera, once the photo session was over I would largely ignore him.

In cross-examination, Margaret Turfus grilled Peggy about how she perceived my future relationship with Rick, should she be awarded custody. Would she be prepared to cooperate in granting me access to him on a regular basis? I well remember Peggy's answer. "Ricaardoe has a very definite role to play in the child's future," she said. "I have no intention and never have had of obstructing him from seeing the child."[5]

She added, however, that she lived in constant fear that I would "snatch" the child away and would want some kind of safeguard that Rick be returned to her at the end of any access period. Margaret Turfus pointed out that Peggy, too, had "snatched" our son away for months without telling me where he was or letting me see him, justified by an interim custody order about whose existence no one had bothered to inform me.

During the afternoon of the second day of the hearing, my aunt Toni was called upon to testify. We were all feeling the strain, and I know for her, the experience of appearing in court was especially trying. She still had a great deal of affection for Peggy and had been deeply saddened that our relationship had come to such an unhappy pass. "I felt like I lost half of my life there in that court room," she told me after it was all over. "It's so hard to be a witness. You don't know if you've said the right thing."

Peggy had such a way about her – very few people could break through her composure. Not long ago I heard Rick tell a friend: "My father never stood a chance against my mom in court. She looks so innocent."

On the stand, Aunt Toni tried deliberately not to put Peggy down— in fact, she repeated several times that she loved her as if she were her own daughter. But she also insisted that I loved my son and was deeply involved in his care. She related how, when Rick was about 16 months of age and we had lived with her in Montreal, I had been the one to get him up in the morning, dress him, change his diaper, feed him, teach him new words. "Rick loves his father so much," she said.

When Margaret Turfus asked her opinion of Peggy's parenting skills, she responded simply: "She may be a good mother, but I think my nephew would be a much better mother to the baby."

Any skeptic might have said, "This woman loves her nephew deeply: of course, she'll say whatever she can to advance his cause." But as far as I was concerned, the fact that my aunt had traveled close to 4,000 kilometers to appear in person on my behalf, spoke volumes. As did her straightforward, warm and fundamentally decent personality.

In retrospect, it is ironic that my aunt – a kind and "mothering" individual if ever there was one, should so strongly defend a father's desire and ability to play more than a cursory role in his child's upbringing. Even my own sister, who was fully aware of the details of my case refused to have anything to do with my contesting Rick's custody. Her view was very simple: a child's place was with his mother. She was far from alone in this way of thinking.

Fathers were still often seen as mere accessories to their children's care and development – both in society's mind and in their own. A child's mother was his or her primary caregiver. In the event of marital breakdown, the balance of public opinion tipped almost unfailingly in favor of the mother, maintaining her right to nurture her child – particularly during his or her early years. This thinking persisted even to the detriment and sometimes-virtual exclusion of any meaningful father-child relationship.

The pendulum had swung far from the terrible extreme of the previous century where wives had no legal say in how their children were raised. In the rare event that a divorce occurred, guardianship of the children automatically went to the husband and mothers could be left virtually childless and penniless.[6]

Today, one hopes we are approaching a point of balance between two extremes, though I believe we still have a way to go before our culture recognizes – and fully supports – that children need a healthy relationship with both parents. The idea of either parent having "custody" is not only outdated; it goes against the best interests of children.

Peggy herself often referred to Rick's need for his mother's care during his "tender years." As Stagen Warness pointed out during his testimony for me, Peggy basically felt, the mere fact that she was the boy's mother was sufficient to warrant her being granted custody. It took a lot of courage for my aunt to tell the court that I was "a mother and a father" to him. In doing so, she was definitely going against the grain.

True, I wasn't typical of those fathers – then or now – who, due to the pressures of work, culture, lack of education or some other want, see their role principally as "providers" and leave the major share of child rearing to the mother. But there are also many fathers who find themselves in a similar position to mine, wanting to care for their children and play an active part in their upbringing, but who feel powerless against a social and legal system that still gives more credence to the mother's parenting role than it does to the father's.

In applying for Rick's custody, I had been prepared to retire from business – at least for a few years – to devote myself full-time to his care. I could have done it. By then I had accumulated enough wealth in real estate that, carefully invested, we could have lived off the interest. I wanted to let the judge know this and share with the court just how seriously I took my responsibility towards my son.

My lawyer and several others strongly advised against this. They said no judge would ever believe that a father would abandon a successful career in mid-stream to stay home and take care of his son. In the end I followed their advice and made arrangements to have a nanny for Rick, should I be granted custody. A kindly woman in her mid-fifties, Opal Collier had five grown children and nine grandchildren. She was following a nursery program through the Mormon Church and was prepared to accept Rick and I into her Edmonton home.

I thought highly of Opal Collier and I believe the judge perceived her as a warm and very competent caregiver. But she was not Rick's parent. If I could go back in time, I would ignore the legal advice I received and tell the judge simply and honestly that I wanted to take care of my own son.

Margaret Turfus had other concerns. She knew that we had to have a very credible argument as to why, in the face of Peggy's interim custody and restraining order, I had fled with Rick to Montreal in December. During my testimony, she asked me if I had contacted my lawyer before taking Rick to Montreal and was I aware at the time that there were charges pending against me. "Yes," I said, "but we didn't know what kind of charges they were and I didn't really understand them." I went on to say that I didn't consider it kidnapping when I was, in reality, taking the only action left to me to protect my son's basic right to free and ongoing communication with both his parents. "That's why I insisted so strongly on a full and open court hearing in Edmonton," I added.

And so the testimony continued, with each witness giving his or her version of key events. At one point, Peggy's lawyer questioned an expert-witness, Norma Ferguson, about a psychological assessment of Peggy she had submitted as evidence. Essentially Ferguson had found Peggy to be "a very stable person" with a well-integrated personality and "many fine developed qualities." She referred to her strong sense of loyalty and suggested that "she had tried to sustain the relationship (with me) longer than maybe was wise for her."

But it was Ferguson's opinions about Rick's well being that triggered my internal alarm. Although she had never even met him or evaluated him professionally, she expressed her concern that going back and forth between parents must be having a disruptive effect and that what he needed most was a stable home and a quiet, consistent environment. I feared that this very general statement could be used as justification for limiting my access to my son.

Norma Ferguson's conclusions were drawn strictly on the basis of her interviews with Peggy. In contrast, Ronald Harshman – the psychologist who testified on my account – had not only evaluated me, he had interviewed Josette Gauthier, the Kadings and Opal Collier, and he had observed how Rick interacted with me. He also spoke with Howard Starkman and others who had business dealings with me and had reviewed all the affidavits that were prepared for the hearing.

He concluded that I had consistently "demonstrated a very sincere concern for the welfare" of my son and saw nothing to suggest I would be anything but an exemplary custodial parent. He noted, however, that it wasn't his place to make a general recommendation about custody as he had not had the opportunity of meeting Peggy or evaluating the home environment that she offered Rick.

He indicated that I had "on all occasions indicated a strong concern for the child maintaining a healthy relationship with the mother." In fact, we had discussed this on several occasions when he had pressed me about how much access Peggy should have to Rick in the event that I was given custody. My answer had always been the same. "Free and easy access." I didn't want Rick separated from his mother anymore than I wanted him separated from me.

In Harshman's view, the issue of access was critical to any decision centered on Rick's best interests. "One of the basic things I look at," he said, "is which parent will be able to allow the child to have a healthy relationship with the other parent, or the corollary of that, will either parent prevent this." Should Peggy be given custody, he emphasized that "it would be most important to maintain as healthy and strong a relationship between father and son, with very generous and, obviously, because of what has been happening, clearly specified access."

This differed markedly from what Gerry Way recommended in his report – and reiterated in his testimony before the court. One of the very last witnesses to be called, he held that my access should be carefully restricted in order to allow Rick time to establish a "normal" family relationship with his mother and her new husband.

Earlier, Harshman had testified that he found Way's report biased against me. Based on the former's own stringent psychological testing as well as the evidence he had just heard in court, he didn't recognize me as "the person who is portrayed in the social worker's report." At the same time, he suggested that the report's treatment of Peggy "leaves many questions unanswered and, apparently, from the report, unasked."

When confronted by Margaret Turfus, Gerry Way stuck to his recommendation. Even though he believed, Peggy and I had, at separate times, both been guilty of "spiriting away" Rick from the other parent, he acknowledged openly that Peggy's actions caused him less concern than mine.

He was clearly of the opinion that a mother's relationship with a child was more important than the father's, and that she should have custody, particularly in light of the fact that she planned to stay home to look after Rick. When Margaret Turfus asked him if his opinion would change were Peggy to start working outside the home as she had done before moving to Revelstoke, he responded: "I would want to know the complete circumstances, how far from home, what were her hours of work and who the babysitter was."

This would become a sore point a few months later when Peggy did get a full-time job at an accounting firm and neither Way nor the Amicus did anything to verify if Rick was still receiving appropriate care.

To a casual observer reading the 500 pages of testimony that those four days of hearings produced, the statements and counter-statements of Peggy, myself and our various witnesses must seem a sad and sorry affair as we contradicted each other, and, through our lawyers, did our best to show why each of us was a more fit parent than the other. For us, however – and especially for Rick –the drama was very real. The decision of Mr. Justice Dea would shape the future relationship that our son would have with each of us. Its repercussions would endure a lifetime.

As the hearing progressed, I came to hold great respect for Justice Dea. Fiftyish, he seemed a decent, intelligent man, and very "simpatico" as one would say in Italian. But, more than anything, I was in awe of him. Seated high on the dais in his judge's black robe, he might as well have been God, holding all our fates in the palm of his hand.

Within the limits of a system designed to create winners and losers, I have never doubted that his decision was guided by what he sincerely believed to be Rick's best interests. At 2:00 p.m. on April 1st, we assembled in the courtroom to hear the judgment. The judge didn't mince his words. From the start he let it be known that he found the past behavior of both parents lacking. Yet, softening his tone, he allowed that despite the past, each of us loved Rick and had, during the last year, made an effort to provide a "reasonably satisfactory" home atmosphere for him. He went on to say:

> "Both parents are capable of caring for this child. The opinion of the Amicus is that the best interests of the child would be served if custody were granted to the mother. Having regard to all of the evidence before me, I think that

opinion is correct though I recognize that if there is a marked change in the mother's conduct or life-style from that of housewife, albeit with some part-time employment in her husband's trailer park, that that decision would have to be reviewed. A similar review will have to occur if the mother's marriage, the stability of which has been questioned here, should prove unstable to the detriment of the child.

"On the issue of access I am not prepared to accept the view of Mr. Way. The Harshman Report recognizes more, I think, than the Way Report, the factor of father's involvement with the child as part of what is in the best interests of the child; and while it is true that the track record of the father leaves much to be desired over these past hectic months, I was very impressed with his family background. His father and his aunt came here from Montreal to testify on his behalf, and I am left with a picture of a solid and supportive and responsible family which can and no doubt will influence the father in a positive way."[7]

All the lawyers I knew believed that, compared to the norm, the access rights to Rick that were granted to me were very generous. We would be spending the months of January and July together every year, as well as the Christmas holidays every even year and the Easter holidays every odd year. I could also be with him or speak to him by phone at any other times to which Peggy and I agreed. Under the terms of the custody order, Peggy was to bring Rick to Edmonton to her parents' home at the beginning of every access period, and I was to return him there at its end.

The judgment also stipulated that the Amicus Curiae should regularly monitor the situation to ensure that the conditions of the order were being followed. While he didn't specify any amount that I should pay in child support, he advised me "that a reasonable sum paid monthly" would demonstrate my goodwill in helping to bear the costs of raising Rick.

In contrast, one of Margaret Turfus' colleagues demonstrated a typical confrontational attitude: "Don't send her a penny," he advised me adamantly.

— "But wouldn't she then be able to argue that I had abandoned my son?" I asked.

— "You wait and see. After a while she'll get fed up with all the expense and bring your kid back."

Mr. Justice Dea obviously had a far better grasp of the enormity of the situation. If Rick was to flourish in the physical and emotional security every child needs, Peggy and I would have to set aside our differences and learn quickly to cooperate for the sake of our son. He left us with this message:

> "For the mother and father, the decision today may be either one more step in a prolonged legal battle or it may be the beginning of a new regime between them. If the latter, then it is time for the parties to call a halt to the differences between themselves and to begin with the admittedly rigid framework which the Court has constructed to do what is in the interests of the child.

> "That the child has not been injured to date by your actions is more a testimonial to the child than to either of you. Your suspicions of the actions and motives of each other will not disappear overnight but unless each consciously tries to encourage the child to love and respect the other, the child will feel the suspicion and animosity and will be affected by it. It is clearly in the best interests of the child that he grow to love and respect both of his parents."[8]

These were wise words and a sign of what was to come. Sadly, it was the dark vision that would prevail.

I walked out of the courtroom feeling like the sky had collapsed on my shoulders. Even though I had steeled myself for the likelihood that Peggy would receive custody, I had continued to hope against hope. Meanwhile, my lawyer and many of my friends thought I couldn't have asked for a better judgment.

My father and aunt Toni were returning to Montreal the next day. They did their best to console me, reminding me that the judge had stressed the importance of regular father-son contact and that Easter – my first access visit – was only a couple of weeks away.

Had Rick and I been able to enjoy the ready access that Justice Dea envisaged, our lives would have unfolded quite differently. But, to be honest, I expected nothing but trouble from Peggy and Jack.

After the judgment, Peggy left almost immediately with Rick for Revelstoke. I didn't get a chance to see him or to explain why I couldn't live with him anymore. The first cracks in the system were appearing. Eventually they would look more like crevasses. Although months of preparation had been devoted to arriving at a decision fundamental to Rick's well being, what – if any – thought was given to how that decision would be explained to the child? Who reassured him that he still had two parents who loved him with all their hearts? Those are the gut-wrenching questions left dangling before many a non-custodial parent.

Regardless of my disappointment, I had had my say in court and resolved to make the best of a difficult situation. Furthermore, I had not resorted to unethical behavior in a misguided attempt to gain the upper hand. Not that the temptation hadn't surfaced.

A short while before the case went to court, I ran into an acquaintance at a gathering of friends. A psychologist by profession, she was aware of the upcoming hearing and had often seen me in the company of my son. "It doesn't matter how much you love each other," she told me point blank, "you don't have a hope in hell of getting custody. If you really want your son, there's only one thing to do, but it'll cost you $5,000. She went on to explain that she knew people who, for that kind of money, would arrange a set-up by planting drugs in Jack's truck. "Just one little tip-off to the cops and he won't get near your son," she said.

I wasn't interested. But the incident was an eye-opener to just how easily the system could be manipulated with the right contacts, the wrong intentions and a pocket full of cash.

* * * * *

As Easter approached, my spirits brightened. My access, as stipulated in the Dea order, was to begin at noon on April 11, the day before Palm Sunday, and Rick and I were to have 10 days together.

I arrived at the Tokens a little before noon. Sandy Hogan, the Amicus, was supposed to be there to oversee that everything went as planned. When I rang the bell, Tania Token answered and seemed surprised to see me.

— "Are Peggy and Rick here?" I asked. "I've come to pick up Rick."

— "I'm the only one home," she said. "I have no idea where Peggy and Rick are. Nobody told me about any arrangements."

— "Oh. Well, I'll drop by the clinic. Maybe they're there with your parents."

I left phone numbers with Tania where I could be reached and drove the short distance to Vina Clinic. "Stay calm," I told myself. "There may be some perfectly reasonable explanation." The Tokens couldn't help me any more than Tania. They said they hadn't heard from Peggy or the Amicus.

There was little that could be done over the weekend. The Amicus' office was closed and I couldn't reach Margaret Turfus. The afternoon passed with no sign of Rick and no word from Peggy, Sandy Hogan or any of the Tokens.

I was at Josette's around 6:30 p.m. when the phone finally rang. The big booming voice at the other end of the line belonged to Gerry Way.

— "So, Ricaardoe, how are you?" he began.

— "I'm fine," I replied guardedly. My instincts said not to let myself be provoked into saying something I might later regret.

— "Are you sure?" he continued. "You must be pretty mad. If I were you, I'd be very mad."

— "Not mad, just disappointed. But where is my son? Weren't you or Sandy Hogan supposed to be at the Tokens today?"

"Your son's fine," he said, "but before he can be released into your care, you will have to sign a solemn undertaking agreeing to use the Alberta courts for anything to do with Rick's custody." In other words, they didn't want me to get any ideas about taking off to Quebec and making an application to reverse custody there.

"What do you mean sign an undertaking?" I responded, my voice rising. "Don't we have a judgment saying I am to have access to my son today? That judgment said nothing about a solemn undertaking. What's going on here? Are you saying you can go above a court order?"

— "What I'm saying is that if you don't sign the undertaking, you're not going to see your son," Way replied calmly.

— "Fine. If you want me to sign an undertaking, I'll sign. Remember, I was the one who insisted on using the Alberta courts. But if I sign, Peggy's going to sign, too."

Three days later, Peggy and I met at the courthouse to sign the document. Only after we both swore to respect the undertaking and it was duly incorporated into the custody order, was I finally reunited with Rick. I had already planned to take him to Jasper for the Easter holiday, and had invited Margaret Turfus, Josette Gauthier and her boys to come along. To make up for the time already lost, my access was extended by three days. All the same, we had to do some last minute juggling of reservations. Furthermore, the surprise condition of the undertaking, which I felt the Amicus and Peggy had conspired together to make me sign, just added on to my legal bills.

These bad feelings were soon eclipsed by my happiness at being with Rick in Jasper. One night we all went out for a special dinner. The dining room had a breathtaking view of the surrounding mountains with the sun setting over an emerald-colored lake. I loved to dance and when the orchestra began to play, I picked up Rick in my arms and together we danced first with Josette, and then with Margaret. I danced that entire evening out of pure joy and my son never left my arms.

When it was time to return to Edmonton, he didn't want to leave. "Can't I stay with you, Papa? Why can't I stay?" How do you explain to a three-year-old the legal intricacies of a custody order? All I could do was hug him and try to reassure him. "No one will ever stop us from seeing each other," I told him as we prepared to part. "Sometimes it may take longer than we like and it will be hard, but you can be sure that I'll always come back for you."

Shortly after Rick's return to Revelstoke, I sent Peggy a cheque for $100 to help cover his expenses. I had also sent him back with a suitcase full of new clothes, a practice I would continue over the years. The cheque went uncashed.

—"Did you get the cheque I sent you?" I asked her by phone.

— "No," she said. "What cheque? I haven't received any cheque."

During the following weeks, I sent two more cheques, both times via Margaret Turfus and Jimmy Di Pinto – another lawyer and friend who worked for the same firm as Margaret. I took this precaution so they would be witnesses that I was attempting to shoulder my share of our parental responsibility. Neither of these cheques was ever cashed or returned to me. Several months later, I discovered that Peggy had turned the cheques over to a lawyer who filed a complaint on her behalf concerning inadequate child support. The complaint was withdrawn when she and Jack decided they preferred instead to proceed with an application for adoption.

Between Easter and my next formal access period in July, I twice asked Peggy if Rick and I could spend a weekend together. Both times she refused, complaining that he was whiny and irritable after our last visit and that he needed a period of uninterrupted calm to adjust to his new home. When I phoned to try to talk to him, she refused to put him on the line. "The Court has already given you more than enough access," she told me. Then she asked me to refrain from calling her. "If you want to contact me in future, please do so in writing. I don't have time for all these phone calls."

More problems arose at the start of the July access, although this time, at least, Peggy, Rick and Gerry Way were present at the Tokens at the appointed hour. I barely had time to say hello to Rick when Peggy handed me a note from his doctor saying he was suffering from an ear infection and would be unable to travel by air for several days. We were supposed to be leaving the next day for Montreal to visit my family and I had made our reservations several weeks beforehand.

After a couple of hours alone together, Rick seemed fine. He wasn't complaining of any soreness or discomfort in his ear or anywhere else. Fearing another stalling tactic on Peggy's part, I called Gerry Way and said I wanted to take my son to another doctor for a second opinion. As any verdict from my own physician could be suspect, I asked if he could recommend someone. When he said he couldn't help me out, I phoned Margaret Turfus who soon came up with a name. That doctor examined Rick the next morning. "This child appears to be in perfect health," he told me. "If he had an ear infection, some trace of it should remain for at least 10 days. His ears show absolutely no sign of infection."

There was another upsetting element to the Revelstoke doctor's note. It referred to my son as Branden Token. Once again, my antennae were on full alert. Was Peggy giving Rick the Token surname strictly out of preference or convenience or was something else going on here? Could she have had his name changed legally? I made a mental note to ask Margaret Turfus to look into this. But it could wait for a while longer. I didn't want anything to spoil my precious time with my son. That afternoon we boarded our flight to Montreal as originally planned.

There the days passed all too quickly. We visited often with family and friends and made frequent trips to my parents' cottage in the Laurentians. There were quiet days, too, when we just enjoyed the simple activities that we used to be able to take for granted: a trip to the ice cream store, a see-saw ride in the park, a walk in the woods, a game of hide-and-seek. Only now I seized on every detail of every moment, storing it as a treasured memory to ease the pain that, surer than wind or rain on a sandstone cliff, would carve an ever-deeper hole in my heart during the long periods of separation between visits.

There was also some business to attend to as I still held property in the city, and I can't recall whether it was unexpected and urgent business or some other reason that caused me to bring Rick back to Edmonton a few days late. I asked Margaret Turfus to let Peggy know about the delay and our new traveling plans. Not surprisingly, with the mushrooming mistrust between us, Peggy thought and expected the worst.

As the day approached for our return to Edmonton, Rick's behavior changed dramatically. From the happy, smiling kid he had been throughout most of our visit, he suddenly alternated between sullen withdrawal and outright irritation and anger. On the flight back, his eyes darted fire, directing all his frustration at our coming

Ricaardoe Jr. and author: Author exercising his visitation right after original court case at Jasper Park, Jasper, Alberta, 1981.

Ricaardoe Jr. and author: The Laurentians, Quebec, Summer 1981.

Author and son Ricaardoe Jr.: "I love you this much... and all the way around!", says Jr. to his father, Ste Lucie des Laurentides, Quebec, July 1981.

Author Ricaardoe Di Done and son Ricaardoe Jr. : First summer vacation spent together after original four day trial, at Ste Lucie des Laurentides, Quebec, July 1981.

KIDNAPPING AND JAIL

Within six months of the ruling on Rick's custody, Peggy and I reached an impasse in our ability to cooperate over anything that had to do with our son. Peggy persisted in preventing me from seeing or speaking to Rick at any time other than the access periods spelled out in the judgment and even then, I had run into difficulties on both occasions. Unfortunately, greater conflict was to come.

Margaret Turfus had also confirmed my suspicions about Rick's name. Peggy had officially changed it not once, but twice: first from Ricaardoe Branden Di Done to Ricaardoe Branden Token, and then, just days later, there was a further change to Branden Ricaardoe Token. She was obviously trying to cut him off from his roots and I feared what would come next. What astounded us even more was, the name change took place, back in February – before the hearing with Justice Dea, and before she knew whether or not she would receive custody!

Later, under oath, Peggy maintained that she had revealed the name change to her lawyer in the days leading up to the custody hearing. Apparently her lawyer suggested she avoid mentioning the name change so as not to "confuse the court." According to Peggy, both Sandy Hogan and Gerry Way were also advised.[9]

Imagine how I felt! Had the fact of the name change come out in court, the judge might have seriously doubted Peggy's willingness to let me maintain an open, caring relationship with Rick, compromising her chances of getting custody.

I was quickly losing faith in a system that could be so easily manipulated. And the doubts I already harbored about the effectiveness and objectivity of the Amicus only intensified.

When I had called Sandy Hogan to let him know that Peggy was refusing any additional access – even telephone calls, he said he would see what he could do. Nothing changed. Now Peggy was working outside the home for a firm of chartered accountants, barely five months after she had assured Justice Dea that she intended to stay home and care for Rick full-time. Still the Amicus saw no reason to review the custody arrangements.

There were also the petty irritations. When I picked up Rick in July for our trip to Montreal, his suitcase contained only dirty clothes. Peggy made some excuse about not having a washer or dryer, but this would become a pattern at every subsequent access. Then there was Jack, who must have viewed me as a constant threat to his relationship with Peggy. As long as he, Peggy and Rick were living together, he could count on Peggy to stay with him. But should Rick's custody ever be reversed, would Peggy soon follow her son, as she had done in the past? Whatever their motivation, it was increasingly obvious that both Peggy and Jack wanted me out of Rick's – and their – lives.

Things came to a head early in October. That was the day my sister called in tears with the news that my father had been rushed to Fleury Hospital in Montreal with life threatening double pneumonia. Only 53, he had already tangled with cirrhosis of the liver.

Who knows how great a toll the events leading up to the custody hearing, the appearance in court in Edmonton and now the problems I was experiencing getting regular access to my son, had taken on my dad. Like the children themselves, grandparents are too often the forgotten victims of divorce, separation and family breakdown. Over the years I have met many grandparents whose happiness was shattered by a bitter custody dispute that, from one day to the next, severed all contact between them and their grandchildren.

After speaking with my sister, I immediately called the hospital where my father had been admitted and asked to speak to him. After several moments, I was put through – but the voice at the other end was almost inaudible. I kept repeating, "Please, I would like to speak with Mr. Theodore Di Done." Only after several attempts, could I finally decipher a faint, "It's me." I was amazed at the extent of his deterioration.

He sounded suddenly old, feeble and more than a little sorry for himself as he gasped, "I've lost my son. You'll have yours soon."

— "What are you talking about?" I replied, sensing an opening. "You haven't lost your son. How can you talk that way? You want to abandon me now when I need you so much? Besides, I haven't lost my son. He's with me right now. As a matter of fact, we're leaving for Montreal in a few days. We wanted to surprise you. When we get there we can look for that farm you always wanted to buy together."

My bluff seemed to perk him up ever so slightly. I hung up, after telling him he had to get better because we would be there soon. I didn't bother calling Peggy as I was sure what her reaction would be. Instead I asked Margaret Turfus if she could arrange special visiting rights that would enable me to take Rick to visit his grandfather – perhaps for the last time.

On October 9, 1981, because of the gravity of my father's illness, the Alberta Court of Queen's Bench granted me access to Rick for a 10 day-period, starting the following day. It was understood that Rick and I would travel to Montreal so he could be with his grandfather.

The next morning I arrived at Edmonton's municipal airport for my flight to Kamloops, where I was to pick up Rick. From there we were to fly on to Montreal. But instead of my ticket, the counter agent handed me a telex from Peggy saying "Meeting adjourned; flight cancelled." When I talked to her, she told me she had cancelled because she didn't believe my dad was that sick!

— "Sick?" I said, "don't you understand he could be dying. I have a court order saying I can bring my son to Montreal. Who do you think you are to cancel our reservations?"

She claimed that she had called Fleury Hospital the previous evening and the nurse on duty had told her my father was much improved. As far as she was concerned, I had completely exaggerated the extent of my father's illness just to get Rick away from her. But she couldn't give me the name of the nurse she had talked to, nor could she explain how she had managed to obtain information about a patient's condition so easily over the phone.

I was frantic – and stuck without reservations. In those years of economic boom, flights in and out of Alberta were invariably booked days in advance; with my father gravely ill, I was in no mood to sit around hoping for a cancellation. Margaret Turfus advised me to drive to Revelstoke immediately. She also suggested I take someone along as a witness.

My friend Jacob Vanderschaaf agreed to accompany me, but he couldn't leave until the next day. At the time, Jake was assistant to the leader of the Alberta Liberal party and we had met at various social functions. Jake had his own share of domestic pain. He and his wife had recently separated and she had obtained custody of their three children: a daughter and two sons.

Those kids meant everything to him; when their mother picked up and moved the family first to Ottawa and then to Timmins in northern Ontario, and then later back to Edmonton, he walked away from a promising career in government and business and took whatever odd jobs were available just so that he could crisscross the country and be near them. At one point, his sole means of communicating with his children was through a set of walkie-talkies he had given them as a gift. Yet, as his children grew, they wanted the freedom to be with their father whenever they chose. Today he remains very close to all his children – but the personal cost to him was enormous.

By the time Jake and I reached Revelstoke, it was already early evening. Anticipating trouble, we had sought the aid of the local RCMP detachment and showed them the special court order. Two officers followed us to Peggy and Jack's home. They and Jake parked in the shadows, while I rang the doorbell.

Our precautions were well taken. "Get the f—k off my property," Jack shouted as soon as he opened the door. Even Jake who is more than six feet in height described him as extremely belligerent. The Mounties quickly intervened. Nevertheless, it took at least two hours of arguing, non-stop negotiation and finally threats of arrest before the two officers succeeded in getting Peggy and Jack to agree to let me take my son the next morning at 10 o'clock.

All that night I paced the floor of our hotel room. As far as I knew, my dad lay dying and it had taken me three precious days just to get near Rick. And that was with a court order! How did I know the whole mess wouldn't start up again in the morning? And what was all this doing to Rick? It didn't help that one of the officers had told me outright that if it were his son, he would never bring him back to that house again. "That guy's totally mad," he said.

I was completely exhausted from worry and lack of sleep when Peggy and Jack arrived in the morning with Rick. Once again, they were late. At least, we all managed to be civil to each other in front of the child. However, the long drive to Edmonton still stretched before us and, after that, the flight to Montreal.

We weren't ten minutes down the road before Rick blurted out: "Mama hit me."

— "Why did she do that?" I asked.
— "Because I throw things at her."
— "Why do you throw things?"
— "Because I hate her."
    I was still absorbing that when he asked me, "Do you like Jack?"
— "Do you?" I responded.
— "No," came his answer. And then, "Do you know what I'm gonna do?"
— "What?" I asked him.
— "I'm gonna throw Mama and Jack off the cliff so they can't ever take me away again."

From the intensity with which he said it, I knew this wasn't just peevishness or a childish bid to use one parent to manipulate the other. The pain and confusion in his eyes were all too real.

I could have put up with a lot had I been sure that my son was happy with his mother and Jack. But knowing that he was miserable was too much. I had already asked around about my chances of obtaining a reversal of custody in Alberta, based on Peggy's unwillingness to comply readily with the access provisions of the custody order. But every lawyer I talked to told me the same thing : there was no way I would succeed.

They suggested that if I was really serious about reversing custody, I make an application in my home province of Quebec where a different legal code from the rest of the country might work in my favor. They also warned me that timing was essential; if I waited too long, no judge would even consider reversing custody. This latest confrontation with Peggy and Jack was the last straw. By the time, Rick and I arrived in Montreal, I had made up my mind to try for a reversal of custody in Quebec. The only question remaining was when.

We went straight from the airport to the hospital. There I was relieved to learn that my father had actually rallied a little, although he was far from being out of danger. My aunt Toni was there and I left Rick with her while I went in to see my dad. His face was swollen painfully and his breathing labored, but he managed a feeble smile when he saw me.

— "I told you we were coming," I said cheerfully, masking my dismay at his appearance. "Rick and I. We're both here. And since we came all this way to see you, I hope you're going to do something for us and get yourself well again very soon."

— "I'm getting old, Ricaardoe, and I'm not feeling good at all. This time, I think maybe it's the end." His voice was shaky, every word an effort.

After a long pause, he added, "You've really brought Rick with you?" and his eyes – until then dull and unresponsive – momentarily flickered with interest. Then he sighed and fell back on his pillows.

— "A grandson shouldn't see his grandpa looking so bad. I'll scare him."

—"You won't scare him, Dad, he'll just come in for a couple of minutes to say hello. He's traveled all the way from British Columbia just to be with his grandpa."

I went and got Rick. We only stayed a few minutes – but it was long enough for a big hug and a shy "I love you, Grandpa. Get better, Grandpa."

— "We'll be back tomorrow for another visit," I told my dad. "You remember what I said about getting better." As we turned to go, I saw my father's eyes wet with tears.

That short visit marked a turning point for him. From then on, he stopped talking about dying and began a very slow, but steady recovery. His doctor told him he was a lucky man indeed when, though still very frail, he was eventually discharged from the hospital and allowed to return home.

But in the days immediately following my arrival, nothing was certain. I spent my days running back and forth to the hospital, worrying about my father, and also trying to reassure my son. He insisted he didn't want to go back to Revelstoke; he wanted to stay with me. That's when I called my friend Tony Deltone to ask his advice.

Tony, who was by then, well into his seventies, was a lawyer who had known my father for many years. Despite our age difference, we had also become close friends and confidantes. Over lunch, the conversation quickly came round to my son and he listened carefully as I related all the problems I had been having with my access visits.

It was a story that hit close to home. Several years earlier, Tony and his wife had separated and she had moved to Italy with their then teenage son. Two or three years elapsed before he was able to see his son again. At this point in the story, his son was back in Canada, but unfortunately there was to be no happy ending. A few years later when his son reached his early twenties, he committed suicide. I was the first person Tony called with the news. Devastated, he forever blamed the tragedy on the trauma of their family breakdown.

Tony's own problems must have weighed heavily on his mind as he let me go on for a long while. Then all at once, he leaned over, looked me straight in the eye and said, "Ricaardoe, how long are you going to play the fool? Aren't you tired of this yet? What do you think all this is doing to your son – do you want to ruin him?" He insisted I should make an application to reverse custody in Montreal – and the sooner the better.

"I am going to apply for custody here," I responded. "But I was planning to wait till January when my son will be here for a month. My lawyer in Edmonton advised me that if I want to try to reverse custody, it has to be done while my son is legally with me, and he's due back in Revelstoke on the twentieth, just a few days away."

Then I mentioned that Peggy and I had both sworn an undertaking to restrict any action related to our son's custody to the Alberta courts. Tony brushed this aside as a minor concern.

— "So what if there's an undertaking. Has the mother respected it? C'mon Ricaardoe, she's laughing at you. You just finished telling me she didn't respect the court order you got when your own father lay dying. Do you think she's going to pay attention to an undertaking? As long as your son is here in Quebec, the Quebec courts can hear this case!"

When I still hesitated, he invited me to come to his office where together we could call Margaret Turfus and ask her opinion. Margaret stuck by her original advice: if my motion couldn't be heard in court during the ten-day period in which I had legal access to my son, I should forget about it until January when he would be with me for a full month. In the meantime, she said it was imperative that I return Rick to Peggy on time; otherwise I would risk being in contempt of the Alberta judgment.

Deltone argued with her, saying that that might be the law in Alberta, but this was Quebec and the law was different. He was equally adamant that as long as Peggy was served notice of my custody application before my visiting rights expired, there would be no problem. By serving notice, he claimed I was automatically relieved of my obligation to return Rick.

I was caught between two lawyers arguing the fine points of a law I knew nothing about. Who was I to believe? Finally, Deltone slammed down the phone in anger, but not before Margaret Turfus had let me know she would have to resign as my lawyer if I failed to follow her counsel.

Either way, I had to make up my mind as time was quickly running out. When I still expressed my doubts about going ahead to my friend, he banged his fist down on his desk, and shouted at me with all his Latin fervor, "Who's the lawyer in this province anyway – me or your Margaret Turfus? Go ahead, think about it some more. But while you're thinking, your son is suffering."

I returned to his office the next day, this time accompanied by my aunt Toni. Once again, Tony Deltone assured us there was nothing to worry about. No one's going to take your son away when you're fighting this hard for his benefit. "It's not like you're running off and hiding," he added. "You're bringing matters openly before the court. It's obvious to anyone how concerned you are about your son's welfare. Why are you wasting time hesitating?"

What neither of us realized was that a very recent change in Quebec law concerning jurisdiction over custody applications would go completely against me.

Just a few days remained before Rick was due back in B.C. I agreed to proceed immediately with the application for custody, understanding that I must keep my son with me in Montreal until our case was heard in court. It would be another month before I realized just how disastrous this decision was.

Because of our friendship and the fact that, with age, he had greatly curtailed his practice, Deltone told me he would not personally represent me. Instead, he arranged for a colleague to handle my case. "He's a young lawyer; he'll take good care of you," he said. Within a day, he had me scheduled for a meeting with Giulio Gritto.

I couldn't have spent more than five minutes with Gritto during that first meeting in his office late in the afternoon of October 16. Surprised that he didn't want to know more about the details of the case, I assumed that he must have been well briefed by Tony Deltone. When I started to offer more information, he said there was plenty of time to get into that once we knew whether Peggy planned to contest. For the moment, he was most concerned with getting the hastily prepared custody motion filed. To save time, he asked me to sign two slightly different versions of an affidavit, as he was still unsure which one he would use. Before I knew it, he was ushering me out the door. "Go home and sleep well, Ricaardoe," he said. "No one will take your son away from you."

On October 19, Gritto sent Peggy a telephone-telegram informing her of my pending court action and that a hearing was scheduled for November 5 in Superior Court in Montreal. The formal notice left by registered mail that same day. By the time it reached Revelstoke, Peggy had already left for Kamloops, where she was expecting Rick and I to arrive by plane on the twentieth.

When Peggy realized we weren't coming, she wasted no time in reporting my breach of access to the RCMP in Revelstoke. Then, once she was aware of my custody motion, she traveled to Edmonton, where on November 2, she filed complaint of contempt of court against me and a warrant was issued for my arrest. She flew to Montreal the next day, hired a lawyer, and on November 4 obtained a writ of *habeas corpus* from the Quebec Superior Court. Essentially, the *habeas corpus* stipulated that I must bring my son to court the next morning to enable a judge to determine whether my reasons for detaining him were justified.

But on the Thursday morning when I entered the Palais de justice, I was still completely unaware that any of this had happened. I thought I was going into a custody hearing. Tony Deltone had arrived before me and was standing in the corridor outside the room where the hearing was to take place, determined to attend court even though he was not representing me directly.

Gritto didn't show up deliberately – calculating that our case would be postponed. His reasoning – which he didn't share with me until later – was that Peggy might be discouraged by the mounting expenses of a prolonged stay in Montreal and give up and return to B.C. He obviously didn't know Peggy if he believed she could be deterred so easily.

Peggy's lawyer, Bertha Choke, was far better prepared. As soon as she saw me standing with Tony Deltone in the corridor, she attempted to serve the *habeas corpus* on Deltone. He refused to take it as he wasn't representing me. She then turned to me. "What should I do?" I asked Deltone. He glanced at the document and said, "Take it, it's nothing."

A few minutes later, we were all called into a courtroom before Mr. Justice Maurice Lagacé. With the *habeas corpus* in hand, he asked me where my son was. By now I was very nervous and becoming more and more confused about this latest turn of events. Gritto was nowhere to be found and I had no idea how serious the motion of *habeas corpus* was. I couldn't conceive that anyone would think I was holding my own son a prisoner. I told the judge that Rick was at home with my father, and that since I had just received the documents a few minutes before, there was no way I could have known to bring him to court with me. He ordered an adjournment until mid-afternoon when I was to return to court with Rick.

I didn't go home. Instead, I went to a small coffee shop with my Aunt Toni, who had come with me to court. Deltone knew where we would be and had instructed me to wait there until I heard from Gritto.

"Suppose I do bring Rick to court?" I said to my aunt. "What if the judge just hands him over to Peggy? There's nothing to stop her from walking out of the courtroom and taking the first plane back to B.C. Except this time she may disappear with him for good. We'll be back where we started – with Rick trapped in the middle."

My aunt was equally mystified, but she also worried openly that if I didn't listen to the judge, I might end up in jail. "How can I bring him back," I argued. "The risk of losing him is too great."

What I really wanted to do was go public. If I could draw media attention to the plight of fathers whose access rights were not being respected, there might at least be some pressure on the court to hear me out. I had convinced myself this was the route to take when Gritto finally telephoned.

He totally disagreed. Like many other lawyers I would come to know, he didn't want any media involved. "It's too big a gamble," he said. "If you call in the media, you never know which way it could go." Instead he suggested that when we returned to court, I simply say that I didn't know where my son was. He added that he knew Judge Lagacé – that he was a sympathetic man – and might just decide to put aside the *habeas corpus* issue temporarily and proceed with the custody hearing. This, he pointed out, was exactly what we wanted.

Over the next few days, I would become all too familiar with Gritto's misguided tactics – although even now I believe he was sincere in his desire to help me. But he was no expert in family law. Had he specialized in family law, he would certainly have anticipated the measures Peggy would take to contest my petition. At the very least, he would have been better prepared with social and psychological evaluations from expert witnesses justifying my case. Above all, he lacked any specialized training that might have helped Peggy and I put a lid on our growing conflict rather than inflame it further in the arena of the courtroom.

Mostly I regret not listening to my own instincts and calling the media. In the end, that might have done the most good. But I was vulnerable, inexperienced, and in a way, over my head. I was a real estate developer, a businessman. What did I know about the law? I followed my lawyer's advice.

That afternoon, when Judge Lagacé asked why I had not brought my son to court, I replied that I had been unable to reach his grandfather and that the two of them must have gone off for the day to the family's country house. Although Peggy's lawyer was already pressing for a contempt of court charge against me, the judge seemed satisfied with my explanation. He ordered me, without fail, to bring Rick the next morning. Then he adjourned the session.

Outside the court on Notre Dame Street, I walked with Gritto towards his office.

— "What do you think?" I asked him. "Should I bring my son tomorrow or not?"

— As your lawyer, I can't advise you not to bring your son," he responded. "But as a father," he added, "I know what I would do."

I returned home, convinced that if I brought Rick to court the next morning, I might never see him again. Nothing could persuade me that this was in the best interests of the son I loved and who loved me. After hours of agonizing indecision, I arranged for him to stay with some very close friends for the duration of the court proceedings. Not even my parents or my aunt Toni knew where he was.

Both Gritto and Deltone had encouraged me in this direction. They warned me I might be jailed for a few days if I were found in contempt, but added: "So what. We'll appeal. It can't go on forever. Eventually the court will listen to you." They believed that most judges would be sympathetic to a father who was so concerned about the safety of his child that he would defy a court order and endure imprisonment, rather than deliver his child into what he perceived as real danger.

The hearing resumed around eleven o'clock the next morning with Mr. Justice John Hannan on the bench. He was replacing Judge Lagacé, who had informed us the day before that a conflict in his schedule might preclude his continuing on our case. This wasn't a good omen. Judge Hannan was known for being rigid and extremely conservative in his views.

Things went badly for me right from the start. Although Judge Lagacé had been prepared to hear both the *habeas corpus* and custody motions simultaneously, Judge Hannan resolved to proceed only with the *habeas corpus*. Once that was settled, he would then decide whether it was within his jurisdiction to hear the custody motion.

During the lunch break, Gritto noted with considerable interest that the motion for *habeas corpus* referred to Branden Token, whereas my custody petition specified my son's name as Ricaardoe Branden

Di Done. This confusion in names could provide a legal loophole for not complying with the *habeas corpus*, he implied.

Around 2:30 in the afternoon, the hearing resumed with testimony from Peggy that set the scene leading up to the motion of *habeas corpus*. After she concluded, Judge Hannan turned to me and asked if I had brought my son to court as ordered. "No, your honor," I replied, "I did not bring him out of concern for his physical and mental well-being." I tried to explain the difficulties I was having with my access visits, but the judge wasn't interested. Nor did he take Gritto's concern about the discrepancy in names seriously. At 3:45 that Friday afternoon, he found me guilty of contempt of court and ordered me imprisoned until Monday morning at 9:30 when the hearing was to resume with my son present.

Gritto immediately informed the judge that he would be filing an appeal. While he rushed off to set the appeal in motion, Judge Hannan ordered the guards to keep me in the courtroom until 4:30 p.m. However, by the time Gritto returned to bring me before another judge who could have freed me pending my appeal, it was too late. I was already on my way to the Parthenais Detention Center.

The guards, it seemed, had their own agenda. Anxious to finish up their shift, they started to hustle me away a few minutes before the 4:30 deadline. Nor were they above a cruel joke at my expense, even while my aunt was still present. As they were handcuffing my wrists together, one guard asked the other, knowingly: "Should we take him to Bordeaux or Saint-Vincent-de-Paul?"

Both were prisons for serious offenders with extended sentences, and there was no question of my going to either. Parthenais – where I was headed – was strictly a holding center. But with the speed with which events were unfolding, neither my aunt nor I could be sure of anything. She was crying as the guards led me through the courtroom exit reserved for prisoners. "This has to be a mistake," I called back to her, putting on my bravest front. "I'm sure I'll be freed within a matter of hours."

****

Parthenais is a large, multi-story, concrete box of a building that was built in 1966. It's within sight of the Jacques Cartier bridge in

Montreal's east end. I had passed it many times, but had never expected to find myself within its walls.

Immediately upon my arrival, I was taken to a small room where all my personal belongings – wallet, rings, watch, tie – were taken away and I was told to strip naked. Satisfied that I wasn't concealing anything that could be used as a weapon on myself or others, the guards allowed me to dress once more in the suit I had worn to court. Handcuffed, I was led to another room where my picture and fingerprints were taken.

I couldn't believe what was happening, that I had been reduced in an hour from loving father fighting in the court for his son, to being treated like a criminal. It was no longer possible to deny the gravity of my situation: it was reflected everywhere in the dismal surroundings, the troubling anonymity of the other prisoners, and the grim faces of the two guards who never let me out of their sight.

Within a matter of minutes, they had guided me into an elevator; when the doors slid open, we walked down a hall until we came to a set of two heavily bolted doors, leading to a long corridor containing some 15 or 20 cells, running along the length of one side of the corridor. The guards ushered me into an empty cell, locked the door and left.

I fought back panic as I stared at my surroundings. The cell, approximately 6 by 10 feet, contained only a narrow cot, a small sink and a toilet. There was no such thing as privacy. You did your business in the open. Bars ran the length of the cell adjacent to the corridor, across which you could see out windows with more bars. The cell's other three walls were solid concrete. From inside the cells, inmates could see anyone walking down the corridor, but we couldn't see each other.

That first night was awful. Trapped like a chicken in a cage, I lay unsleeping on the hard cot, staring into the darkness. Every so often I would hear the screams of those who could no longer control their fear or desperation. Then there were the sounds of the doors. First the buzz, then the click of a lock release, heavy bolts sliding open, and finally the loud clang as metal slammed against metal.

After what seemed hours, I finally dozed off, playing those sounds over and over in my mind. The next thing I knew I was shielding my eyes from the harsh glare of florescent lighting that suddenly filled the cellblock. Then a cart-full of breakfast trays rattled down the corridor. It wasn't yet five in the morning. Bleary-eyed from the near sleepless night and the stress of the previous day, I choked down some dry toast and took a few sips of weak, watery coffee. I had had no news from either Gritto or Deltone and had no idea what awaited me.

It didn't take long to learn the routine of life in jail. Meals were brought to our cells, but three times a day we were allowed out to mix with other inmates, play cards and get some exercise. Cigarettes and soft drinks were the currency to acceptance. Luckily, I had enough money for both and was generous in passing them around. Everyone wanted to know why you were there, and I fought back a wave of nausea as one inmate boasted about how he had beaten up some woman. Another one took me aside and told me he was getting out Monday. He offered "to take care of my boy's mother" if I just let him know where she was. I had the feeling he might be a detective trying to set me up.

Either way I steered clear of him after that.

Finally, late Saturday afternoon, Gritto and Deltone came to see me. Gritto explained that he had tried on Friday and Saturday with two different judges to have me freed, but had been unsuccessful in both attempts. The big question was whether or not I should obey the judge and bring my son to court on Monday. Deltone was adamant that I should continue on the same course.

"If you bring your son on Monday, there's a very good chance the judge will hand him back to his mother and she'll be gone like a flash with him back to British Columbia. Once your son physically leaves this jurisdiction, you're finished – you'll no longer have the right to make a custody application in Quebec.

—"And if I don't bring him back, won't the judge find me in contempt again?" I protested.

— "So what if you spend a few more days in jail?" Deltone thundered at me in disgust. "Are you a man or not? We're talking about your son's life here. If you're not man enough to spend a few days in jail for your son, I'll have nothing more to do with you."

Gritto agreed that I should stick it out and refuse to bring my son to court. Based on their advice, I resolved to remain in prison indefinitely if that's what it would take to prevent my son's return to Revelstoke where I knew he was unhappy.

Long before sunrise on Monday morning, a guard arrived at my cell and told me to get up and get dressed. Prisoners due in court were awakened even earlier than usual, fed and then transferred to a large holding cell where we waited like cattle for transport to the courthouse. The cell was full of nervous, smoking, sweating men. It felt like an eternity before we were finally herded into the transport van. I overheard one of the guards stating that they needed to place shackles on one of the prisoners. I was chosen to be shackled with him and was told that that is what would happen to me if I didn't smarten up. By 9:30 a.m. I was back in Judge Hannan's courtroom, along with Peggy and our lawyers. Hannan confirmed that we were proceeding with testimony related to the *habeas corpus,* rather than the custody hearing. He didn't ask me about Rick.

As the morning passed, Gritto questioned first Peggy, and then me, about the events leading up to our present predicament. It was close to noon when Judge Hannan finally asked if I had brought my son to court as ordered. Gritto tried to argue that it was impossible for me to bring my son since I had been imprisoned since Friday afternoon.

The judge ordered me detained over the lunch hour. His patience was running out and he insisted in no uncertain terms that Rick be present at 2:15 when we were to resume and conclude the hearing.

In the afternoon, both lawyers summarized their arguments. The transcripts reveal a lot of attention to points of law: was the Alberta judgment valid in Quebec? How significant was the discrepancy in Rick's name between the writ of *habeas corpus* and the petition for custody? Did such and such a case represent a precedent? Did the Quebec courts have any say over who had custody of Rick? It was a legal fest for those in the profession. The real core of the matter – what was in the best interests of a three-and-a-half year old child whose parents were accusing each other of bad faith and deception – was somehow lost in the shuffle.

At the end of the day, I steadfastly refused to say where Rick was. "You're asking me to betray him," I told the judge, "and that is something I cannot do." Though outwardly calm, I was quaking inside when an exasperated Judge Hannan again found me in contempt. This time he sentenced me to a week in jail. As I was taken, handcuffed, from the courtroom, Deltone slapped me broadly on the shoulders, and, with a big smile, declared: "That's a boy!"

The following day, while I was locked away in Parthenais, Judge Hannan ruled that Rick had been illegally detained and ordered him returned to the care of his mother. He also concluded that Rick wasn't a Quebec resident despite my lawyer's argument that he had lived with me almost as long as he had with his mother. As a result, he dismissed my petition for custody, on the basis that he had no jurisdiction to hear the case. He also ordered me to reimburse Peggy for the costs she had incurred because of my action.

All this I learned through Gritto and Deltone who visited me several times during that additional week I spent in Parthenais. Gritto was still attempting to appeal my sentence, but so far without success. At one point, Peggy herself paid me a visit, pleading with me to tell her where Rick was. "Why should I help you?" I asked her. "So you can cut me out of his life completely? The child already has a father who loves him, but you admitted in front of the judge last week that you and Jack are considering adoption. And you have the nerve to ask me to help you? I'll tell you where our son is if you agree immediately to a joint custody arrangement. Otherwise, I'd rather remain in prison indefinitely than help you take him back to Revelstoke. "

"That's blackmail," Peggy responded angrily, as she turned to leave.

My words were brave, even as I knew my situation was turning graver by the day. Shortly after Peggy's visit, two detectives showed up at Parthenais, bent on extracting from me the whereabouts of my son. They used a combination of good cop/bad cop tactics. One treated me kindly and tried to cajole an answer out of me. The other threatened to charge me with kidnapping. If found guilty, he warned menacingly, I could face as much as 10 years in prison. I still refused to tell them where Rick was. "You have to understand I'm doing this for my son's sake," I told them. "If I had been serious about kidnapping him, do you think I would have applied for custody through the courts? Please, I just need a little more time to try to settle this thing reasonably." The "good cop" said they'd be back in a few days.

Then it was my father's turn to visit. He hadn't been out of the hospital more than a week or so, but had stubbornly insisted on coming to see me. Pale, drawn and extremely weak, he collapsed into the visitor's chair, the distress he felt at seeing his son behind bars evident in every line of his face. Between that and his illness, he looked terrible.

"Ricaardoe," he said, once he had caught his breath, "Pay attention to your father. Things have gone too far. What do you hope to accomplish by all this? It's time you stop listening to your lawyers and face reality. You have to obey the judge and bring your son to court."

He might as well have asked me to abandon Rick forever. "How can I just give up now?" I responded. "Let me ask you this. If this had happened to you when I was Rick's age, what would you have done? Would you have walked away to save yourself and left me abandoned?"

— "Everyone knows you love your son. You're not abandoning him. But this isn't doing him or you any good. I never thought I'd see the day I had to visit my only son in jail."

That brief exchange with my dad left me discouraged and disappointed. My father must have spoken with Gritto as well, because when the latter next came to see me, he, too, began to backtrack. "Your father's taking this very hard," he told me. "This could kill him. Maybe you should think about giving up on this case for now. You have many years to see your son. But your father may only be here a short while longer."

I couldn't believe my ears. This was the man who just a few days earlier had insisted that I stand firm for the sake of my son. In my mind, I could see my father and my son both hanging from a thread and only one could be saved. It was up to me to choose.

A social worker at Parthenais who had overheard my earlier conversations with Gritto and Deltone took me aside and suggested I get myself a new lawyer – quickly. He put me in touch with Micheline Parizeau.

Parizeau was a highly successful and tough-minded divorce lawyer who had a knack for quickly sizing up her opponents and ferreting out their vulnerable spots. Colorful, and flamboyant, she was also relentlessly competent. She was the only one of my many lawyers who could truly rattle Peggy's composure. And her billings reflected her success rate.

I called her from Parthenais late Thursday afternoon and breathed a deep sigh of relief when she agreed to take on my case. Because of Gritto's involvement from the beginning, I didn't want him totally out of the picture and asked if they could work as a team. Now I was paying two lawyers.

I had been ordered to bring my son before Judge Hannan on Monday, November 16, 1981. It was Saturday when Parizeau met me at Parthenais. She made it very clear that she could do nothing for me as long as I remained in contempt of court by hiding my son away. At this late date the best we could hope for was to have him placed under the protection of the Youth Tribunal, where she would try to arrange an emergency independent hearing. I could see she was also concerned for my father's health, so I told her where Rick was and by Monday, November 16, he was under the Tribunal's protection. An inquiry was to take place before one of its judges the following day.

Even though Judge Hannan had already ruled that I should return Rick to Peggy, Parizeau hoped to persuade him to delay carrying out his ruling in order to let the Youth Tribunal conduct its investigation. She also planned to argue that since I had now served three separate jail sentences for contempt, no further action should be taken against me until we had a decision from the Tribunal.

Things did not go as planned. Judge Hannan called the session to order at 9:30 a.m. At first, only Gritto was present to represent me, as Parizeau was still busy making arrangements with the Youth Tribunal. I told the judge that my son was with her now and she should be arriving soon.

In the meantime, the judge rejected Gritto's request that Rick not be turned over to his mother before we knew the outcome of the appeal. If we wanted to pursue the appeal process, we were free to do so; but he was not budging on his order.

There was a long recess until mid-afternoon as we waited for Parizeau to arrive with Rick. During that time, I was returned to a cell within the courthouse. At one point, the same detectives who had questioned me at Parthenais arrived and had me taken under guard to another court room before yet another judge who informed me I was being charged with kidnapping. While this was happening, I had no opportunity to see or speak to either of my lawyers.

It was well into the afternoon when Parizeau arrived at last and we knew my son was safely in the building. Judge Hannan requested yet again that Rick be brought before him. For almost an hour, Parizeau tried every argument she could muster to delay the judge from turning Rick over to his mother. But not even a pending Youth Tribunal intervention would sway him. He stated emphatically: "It was the decision of the court that, *for better or for worse*, the child be returned to his mother". He finally ended the stalemate by threatening Parizeau herself with contempt of court if she didn't immediately get Rick and bring him into that court room.

Ever since that day, Judge Hannan's words continue to ring in my ears as a thundering symbol of the inadequacy of our judicial system in dealing with the sensitive human dramas that can rip families apart. "For better or for worse," he had said about his decision to return Rick to Peggy, if that would absolve anyone of the responsibility for a decision that would profoundly affect Rick's life and the lives of everyone close to him.

This was a judge who ruled by the book. My quarrel is not that he upheld the existing Alberta custody judgment – that was his right and duty. But I believe he revealed a serious flaw in the system by refusing to allow the Youth Tribunal the extra time required, then and there, to intervene, study the file, and determine if my son's mental or physical health was being jeopardized in any way. Had this happened, Judge Hannan's ruling might have been quite different, and Peggy and I might have avoided the years of court battles that would consume Rick's childhood and a large portion of our own lives.

My experience that gray November day triggered my determination to find a better way to settle family disputes, especially where children are concerned. Eventually this would crystallize in an ongoing campaign for widespread, accessible mediation within the framework of specialized family courts. Here, too, was born my deep-sprung conviction that the parent-centered notion of "child custody" must give way to the child-centered practice of "parental responsibility."

But for the moment, it was 5:20 on a Monday afternoon and I was sitting handcuffed in Judge Hannan's courtroom. Micheline Parizeau had just gone to find my son who had spent the last hour with my aunt Toni in a nearby corridor. While we waited for them to arrive, Gritto asked the judge, if for the child's sake, the handcuffs couldn't be removed from my wrists.

The judge refused, noting that unfortunately, it was my own fault that I now found myself in this sorry situation.

Then the door opened and in walked Rick, holding my aunt's hand. A three-year-old doesn't stand on ceremony. He immediately bounded towards me with an exuberant "Papa, Papa," passing right by his mother. Automatically, he opened his arms wide in our standard "I love you this much all the way around" greeting, but stopped when I didn't respond as usual.

— "Papa," he said, in a voice that carried clearly throughout the now silent room, "why aren't you putting your arms out wide?"

— "I can't," I whispered back, as a huge knot rose in my throat. Then I showed him my shackled wrists.

Rick continued to chatter on, as the lawyers argued over one final piece of business. I was no longer listening, my attention fully on my son. With only a handful of people in that large court room, it was obvious to anyone with ears where Rick was, but Judge Hannan still made a point of asking formally: " Is the child in the court?" At last satisfied that Rick was present, he brought the proceedings to a close, telling Peggy she was free to leave with our son.

Peggy approached and tried to coax Rick to go with her. Rick refused. Peggy tried to persuade him saying: "Mommy has a big toy truck for you downstairs." But he only tightened his hold on me. "I want to stay with you, Papa. I don't want to go," he said.

After several awkward moments, I finally said, "You go ahead with Mommy. Papa will come after a little while. Go ahead," and I gave him a gentle push.

— "You promise you're coming?" he asked me, still tugging at my sleeve.

— " I promise," I said, quickly brushing aside a tear.

Just before the two of them walked out of the courtroom, Peggy turned to me and said loudly enough that Micheline Parizeau and others around me could hear, "Don't worry, Ricaardoe, I won't ever stop you from seeing your son."

I badly wanted and needed to believe her. Never would I have thought that the "little while" I had promised my son would stretch into more than two and a half years. Once Peggy and Rick had vanished out the door, I broke down completely. Even the two guards who remained with me were moved. As they led me away, one of them, with tears in his eyes, muttered under his breath, "Some women can be real bitches".

I was held in jail one more night and released the next day after a bail hearing related to the latest kidnapping charge against me. A trial date was set for February 1982. I was placed under a 9:00 p.m. curfew and my freedom was conditional on my refraining from any contact with either Peggy or Rick.

My attempt to reverse custody was, to put it mildly, a fiasco. Once again, my son was four thousand kilometers away; there was no way I could see him, let alone talk to him. And if found guilty of kidnapping, I faced the possibility of an extended prison sentence. I also owed some $25,000 in legal fees and my bills were continuing to mount.

Once she returned home, Peggy asked the Alberta Court of Queen's Bench to amend the existing custody judgment to deny me any access whatsoever to Rick until further notice. The *ex-parte* order was granted by Mr. Justice Dea on December 4. About this time, she and Jack also began adoption proceedings through a lawyer in Kamloops, B.C. Of this latter action, I was never served any notice.

It didn't seem things could get much worse, when one day in February, just before my trial was to begin, a snowplough accidentally ran into my mother's parked car. When I went early in the morning to a nearby police station to report the accident, a routine computer check revealed that the RCMP in Alberta had an outstanding warrant for my arrest on yet another kidnapping charge. The Montreal police informed me they were holding me until the RCMP arrived from Edmonton to transport me there for trial.

Thankfully, I was able to reach Micheline Parizeau on my first attempt. She, together with Margaret Turfus in Edmonton, succeeded after several hours and many phone calls, in having the arrest warrant put on hold until we had a judgment in Quebec on the same charge. I was released late in the afternoon, but the hole I found myself in just kept getting deeper.

FIGHTING AN ADOPTION; FOUNDING **OPCR**

It is my nature to maintain a positive outlook and to look for ways of overcoming obstacles, not be pulled down by them. Some might say I'm just plain stubborn. However you describe it, that philosophy kept me going in the early weeks of 1982 when my every thought and action were colored by the knowledge that I had forfeited all access to Rick and had yet to stand trial for kidnapping.

After the catastrophe of my failed custody petition, I broke off any further association with Giulio Gritto and asked Micheline Parizeau to defend me on the kidnapping charge. She remained optimistic that I would be found innocent when all the circumstances were taken into account. Tony Deltone also assured me he would testify on my behalf.

I assumed it would be a fairly straightforward matter to reinstate my visiting rights once the kidnapping issue was resolved; I didn't even want to think about the consequences of a guilty verdict.

The trial began in early February and continued over several days, with adjournments of a week or more in between sessions. I was officially charged with kidnapping my son between October 21 – the first day after my legal access expired – and November 6, when I was first imprisoned. The evening before we went to court, Parizeau and I were going over the details of my defense, when I called Tony Deltone to confirm the time I should pick him up in the morning. That's when he told me he wouldn't be testifying after all. "You don't need me, Ricaardoe," he said. "Who's going to testify against you? I'm certain you'll be acquitted."

That was one major strike against me. The second one came when we arrived in court the next day to learn that Gritto would be testifying – for the Crown.

In my defense, Parizeau did her best to show that the quality of legal representation and advice I had received from Gritto and Deltone was sadly lacking (despite the invoice for $12,000 that had since arrived). She maintained that even though I was wrong in defying the court orders to return Rick, I had acted in good faith, concerned only for his well-being. She also argued that a person seriously intent on kidnapping in the criminal sense of the word wouldn't voluntarily come before the court with a request for custody.

Gritto, however, denied encouraging me to proceed with the custody application in October even though my legal access period had almost expired. He also denied telling me that the Alberta judgment couldn't be enforced in Quebec. He claimed he had never suggested ignoring the *habeas corpus* because it called my son by a different name than the one stated in my custody petition. Most damning of all, he said he had always advised me to comply with the orders of Judges Lagacé and Hannan to bring my son before the court. Defying them, he said, was strictly my idea and my doing.

In the end, it was Gritto's word against mine – and his prevailed. On Friday, February 26, Judge Bernard Grenier, who had listened patiently and carefully during the whole of the proceedings, found me guilty. He could understand that a father might risk everything for his child, but he did not believe I was "an innocent victim of errors or negligence on the part of my lawyer."[10] "I am convinced," he said, "that the accused took advantage of his son's presence in Montreal to try to overturn the ruling of Judge Dea and obtain a judgment in his own favor through the Quebec Superior Court."[11] He rejected my defense of good faith, convinced that I was fully aware of what I was doing.

I stood motionless as Judge Grenier delivered his verdict. His words barely floated on the surface of my brain as I struggled to grasp their meaning. Then the sickening reality sank in. All I could visualize was a jail door slamming behind me and my son's face growing fainter and fainter until it finally dissolved like a presence in a dream that, try as we might, we can no longer remember.

Sentencing was scheduled for March 3. We had five days to react. Parizeau intended to push for an absolute discharge based on the very unusual nature of this case, and the fact that, until now, my legal record was unblemished.

She asked me for the names of credible witnesses who could vouch for my personal and professional reputation, and who could attest to the closeness of my relationship with Rick. I suggested two friends and colleagues: Robert Roy and Marcel Trudeau.

Rick and I had spent considerable time with Robert Roy and he had seen first hand how much we thrived on each other's company. I couldn't have asked for a more glowing reference. He testified that I was an honest person, respectful of others, and that my son was more important to me than anything. More importantly, he was able to say that, back in November, he had overheard Gritto outside the courtroom encouraging me not to bring my son to court.

Marcel Trudeau was a senior chartered accountant with a prominent Montreal firm, a close family friend with whom I had also done business. His parents had died when he was still a child and his adoptive mother was my father's cousin. He had known me practically since birth.

He, too, went out of his way to emphasize my love for my son and my personal integrity and good judgment, which had allowed me to flourish in business. He also pointed out the serious consequences that a criminal record would have on my ability to earn a living. Because I managed investment projects on behalf of associates that often involved hundreds of thousands of dollars, it was essential that I be bonded by an insurance company. They weren't likely to bond anyone with a criminal record, he noted.

Then I spoke in my own defense. Up until the day of sentencing, Micheline Parizeau had debated the wisdom of this move. She feared that the judge might react badly if he thought I was trying to introduce new evidence in a case he had already ruled upon. But I felt I had to speak. "This is my future," I said. "I'm the one who's facing prison and the loss of my son."

The words just poured out. I confirmed that a criminal record would jeopardize my chances of ever working again in my present field. But more importantly, I emphasized that Peggy could try to use it against me to bar me from my son. I explained the difficulties I had already experienced at every access visit and how Peggy had refused to grant me additional access when my father was gravely ill. I related how, even after I obtained a court order for access, she had cancelled my flight, and that it was only because of the intervention of the RCMP that I had been able to see my son. I showed the judge the card of one of the RCMP officers who had offered to testify for me, should I ever need his help.

I related how, in the car leaving Revelstoke the previous October, my three-year-old son had told me he hated his mother with an intensity that shook me. I swore that I had been assured by both Deltone and Gritto that I could legally keep Rick with me while we waited for a custody hearing in Quebec, and that throughout the whole process, I had taken for granted that my lawyers were giving me sound advice. Finally I mentioned how Deltone, the day before my trial, had suddenly refused to testify for me, and how I only discovered when the trial was in process that Gritto would actually testify against me.

Judge Grenier let me continue for several minutes, before he finally interrupted. "I understand why you are doing this," he said, adding that I was the one with the judgment hanging over my head. "I'm not reproaching you. But *right or wrong*, my judgment has already been given. The question before us now is what sentence I am going to give you."[12]

I had no idea what effect my words had had; I could only hope that I had succeeded in explaining my actions simply and honestly. As it turned out, even the Crown lawyer wasn't interested in sending me to jail. She said I clearly wasn't a criminal, but had become embroiled in a very human situation. She recommended a three-year probation.

Judge Grenier chose instead to grant me an absolute discharge. As a father himself, he sympathized with the attachment I felt for my son, and said he was convinced that my son truly loved me. He took into account my earlier 10-day imprisonment and the damage a criminal record would cause my professional reputation. He didn't believe that by discharging me, he would be encouraging others to try what I had done. People accused of this kind of kidnapping were usually fathers or mothers – without any criminal intent – who acted impulsively, out of concern for their children; they weren't likely to be dissuaded by someone else's sentence, he noted.

Instinctively he knew that the best safeguard the court could have against my committing a repeat offence was the painful knowledge that this would swiftly and surely destroy any chance I had for a lasting relationship with my son.

I left Montreal's Palais de justice considerably less naive about the legal system and the role of lawyers than when I had first entered that same building back in October. It had been a hard lesson. And while I had cleared another major legal hurdle, I had no idea just how many more still lay ahead.

For one, there was still the kidnapping charge in Alberta. Margaret Turfus agreed to represent me once more, and that summer, based on my absolute discharge in Quebec, she succeeded in having the charge dropped.

With both kidnapping charges behind me, I tried unsuccessfully to contact Peggy, hoping she had meant what she said the previous November about never stopping me from seeing my son. She had a new, unlisted phone number. I also sent several letters to Rick by mail, but they were always returned marked "unknown at this address."

That year, I spent a lot of time in Edmonton, attending to business matters that had been sorely neglected throughout the months in court. Sometimes I would visit the Tokens to see if they had any news of Rick and Peggy. Despite everything that had happened, they still accepted me as a member of the family. They must have mentioned to Peggy that I was very anxious to see Rick.

In December 1982, she wrote me directly, saying "You are a most extraordinary man and I give you your due in many areas…I hold you no malice whatever and my last wish would be to do you harm. Branden is extremely healthy and growing very tall," she went on. "He has a great imagination and sings a lot…You can be sure he's eating well and is always safe." But the one thing I desperately wanted to hear was missing: there was no mention or even hint of when I might see him.

I re-read that letter many times, unsure how to interpret it. She had gone to great lengths to reassure me that Rick was doing well. But did she really think I would be satisfied with occasional brief reports about his newest interests and activities? Did she think so little of a father's role or influence in his child's life?

I understood that I would have to return to court if Rick and I were ever to be reunited. That meant a formal petition to the Alberta Court of Queen's Bench to reinstate my visiting rights. But this time I wanted Micheline Parizeau to represent me; if anyone could penetrate Peggy's innocent veneer, it was she.

To be able to practice law in Alberta, Parizeau first had to be admitted to that province's Bar. This entailed additional costs, which I agreed to absorb. She also believed I would stand a much better chance of having my visiting rights reinstated in Alberta if I could demonstrate that I had been the victim of poor legal counsel in Quebec. She strongly recommended that I sue Gritto and Deltone for damage. Assuming all went well, it would cost me an additional $30,000 in legal fees to have my visiting rights reinstated.

It was a never-ending process, with weeks, months even years, between each step. While we waited, Rick was growing; he was approaching his fifth birthday. More than a year had passed since we had seen each other and it was a rare night when I didn't cry for him, myself and the lost moments we could never regain.

Lawsuits rippled into more lawsuits - and more lawyers. Because of her personal involvement in the events leading to my suit against Deltone and Gritto, Parizeau said, it would be a conflict of interest for her to represent me against them. Instead, she introduced me to Reevin Pearl, another Montreal lawyer.

He had a good reputation, was straightforward, and I liked him immediately. After listening to my story, he asked me if I would mind if he spoke to Gritto directly. "Please, go ahead," I responded. "Find out whatever you need to know." Within a short time he called me back. Before deciding whether to take the case, he wanted to meet with both Gritto and myself. The outcome of this meeting was quick and clear. Reevin Pearl stated, "He's lying. Let's get him!"

Bringing legal action against another lawyer was an expensive proposition: it was going to cost $5000, just to get to the courtroom stage. I didn't at all relish the idea of suing my old friend, but went ahead, persuaded it could make the difference between seeing my son or not. In short order, Gritto counter-sued both Reevin Pearl and me for defamation of character. If we pursued this, we would need yet another lawyer to defend both of us. This legal impasse dragged on for several years, until eventually we settled out of court.

On top of my mounting legal bills, I was running into financial problems in other areas. The Alberta economy had fallen into recession, interest rates were high, and the financing costs on the investment properties I owned in partnership with Stagen Warness and others, continued to rise.

Stagen was carrying the load financially, and he and many of my other business associates were quickly running out of patience with my preoccupation with my court cases. We were moving in opposite directions. They thought I was spending too much money on hopeless legal battles and should concentrate on business. "You can build your relationship with your son when he's older and can make up his own mind," they would tell me.

No matter what they said, my son came before all else in my life and I was prepared to take whatever legal means necessary to see and be with him. My own recent experience had also awakened me to the sad realities of family breakdown and I was searching for ways to sensitize others to its tragic after-effects.

At that point, some 40% of marriages in Canada were ending in divorce and approximately half of them involved children. I wanted to reach people through film or television – to create a dramatic series that would enable people to see divorce and custody through the eyes of a child. "You're a dreamer," Stagen told me, when I tried to convince him that such a project could help people and be profitable, too.

Between the prolonged separation from my son and my mounting debts, it wouldn't have taken much to have spiraled into a deep depression or alcohol-induced despair. As it was, I was barely sleeping more than three hours a night. What saved me was my need for other people. I forced myself to work out, dress up each day in a neatly pressed suit and tie, keep a smile on my face and downplay my financial worries.

The Bistro Praha became my second home. It was a simple, European-style restaurant with a huge heart emanating from its gregarious, prosperous and popular owner. A big man of Czech origin, Franticek Cikanek loved champagne almost as much as he loved to laugh. Every evening, I would find refuge there amidst friends, lively conversation and the classical music I loved. It was a place frequented by journalists, theatre people and other professionals, as well as a core group of expatriate Czechs. The genuine camaraderie I found there over the years helped preserve my sanity.

Wherever I went, it wasn't long before people found out about my son. One evening, another group of friends got together and presented me with a four-foot-tall stuffed Yogi Bear. "For your son," they told me. "You mustn't give up hope – you will see him again."

Several had encountered their own problems with child custody, and through them, I met more and more people who were being prevented from seeing their kids. We began to develop a network of concerned parents who had become but occasional visitors in their children's lives because of custody arrangements that were either overly restrictive or weren't being respected.

Learning of each other's experiences opened our eyes to the need for reforms in the legal system that oversaw the custody of children after marital break-up. For that we needed to found a national organization dedicated to making reform happen.

I had to learn everything about setting up such an organization. A friend advised me we would need a minimum of three founding members to qualify for a federal charter as a non-profit charitable group. Jake Vanderschaaf agreed to come on board as number two and our third member was another Montrealer, Mohammed Ali Alebouye, whom I had met through Micheline Parizeau.

He had a thriving business selling Oriental carpets, and his wife had recently left him for someone else. She had gained custody of their two-year-old daughter and only child, leaving his life in tatters. He loved his daughter dearly and was heartbroken from the forced separation. From the beginning, his ex-wife refused to respect his visiting rights and he had to go to court five times over a period of three years, to have his legally sanctioned visiting rights enforced. His wife continued to ignore court order after court order. Only on the fifth attempt did the court impose a token and ineffective penalty - his wife was fined $500.

A few years after we met, he eventually managed to gain access to his daughter and out of sheer frustration fled with her to Europe and the Orient, where they remained for a long time. "Do you know what it's like to live like that?" he asked me recently. "It's miserable

– you're hiding all the time. But you love your child so much, you see no alternative." Today his daughter is in her early twenties. At her father's instigation, she has recently become reacquainted with her mother.

At any given time during her formative years, Alebouye's daughter had to endure separation from either one or the other of her parents, an unhappy fact that was the result of a legal system that simply didn't work in a child's best interests. Furthermore, the very ineffectiveness of that system was driving parents like Alebouye to such rash and desperate measures.

In May 1983, the Organization for the Protection of Children's Rights (OPCR) came into being with the aim of creating a more child-friendly legal system that would meet the real needs of children by routinely insisting on joint custody and shared parenting arrangements. Free and obligatory mediation services for separating or divorcing parents was then, and continues to be, one of OPCR's primary goals. From the very beginning, OPCR has also pushed for the creation of specialized family courts to handle all family conflicts.

While I was back in Montreal setting up the new organization, Parizeau was cleared to practice law in Alberta. That May, I was finally able to apply to the Court of Queen's Bench to have my visiting rights reinstated. Peggy immediately contested my application and an initial hearing was scheduled for June 9, 1983. On June 8, our respective lawyers had agreed to a meeting where Peggy and I would be questioned on our affidavits.

To save hotel costs, I had booked two tickets for Parizeau and myself on an early flight to Edmonton on the morning of June 8. This would get us in on time for the afternoon meeting. However, last minute business delayed Parizeau and by the time she rushed up to the gate, our seats had been given to someone on standby. The only seats left were in first class. I had little choice but to purchase the more expensive tickets, and the flight ended up costing me much more than I had budgeted. It may seem a small detail, but it's indicative of how quickly the costs associated with any legal action can rise.

And cost – rather than a child's need for love and parental guidance – too often forces our hand. I personally know many non-custodial parents who have abandoned their struggle to obtain access to their children for the sole reason that they can no longer support the financial and emotional burden of pursuing their case through the courts. Apart from the substantial legal fees, there are the extra costs of taking time off from work for court appearances, the fees required by psychologists and other expert witnesses for the preparation of reports and the time spent testifying in court. And if the hearing takes place in another city, you have to factor in all the travel and living costs for yourself, your lawyer and any other witnesses who are testifying for you.

After so many court appearances and legal fees, my own cash reserves were exhausted and I was living strictly on credit and the goodwill of friends and relatives. Between Peggy and myself, we were keeping a lot of lawyers employed.

That afternoon meeting in Edmonton was full of surprises. We met Peggy and her lawyer, Paul Curran, at his Edmonton office, where Parizeau proceeded to question Peggy in detail. In her affidavit, Peggy claimed that restoration of my visiting rights would jeopardize the stability of the caring family unit, she and Jack were striving to create for Rick. She entreated the court "to take the position that access should be suspended for an indefinite length of time, until Branden is past his tender years and capable of making many of his own decisions."[13]

Parizeau was in top form. Before long, she succeeded in wrestling a confession from Peggy – for the very first time – that she always knew she could reach me by phone or letter through my aunt Toni in Montreal. By extension, had she really wanted, Peggy could have served me with many documents and court orders that, in the past, had never reached me because "no one knew how to contact me."

Parizeau also managed to get Peggy to admit to having received at least one cheque from me towards Rick's support back in 1981. Up till now, she had always denied receiving any money from me.

But the most startling revelation was the fact that Peggy and Jack had legally adopted Rick in June of the previous year through the Supreme Court of B.C.! Again this occurred without my knowledge or consent – and without the knowledge or consent of the Alberta courts. With this, yet another name change was exposed. As of mid-1982, my son had been legally known as Branden Ricaardoe Roaff.

Both Parizeau and I were thunderstruck. If the B.C. adoption order took precedence over the Alberta custody order, I no longer had any legal relationship to Rick. The slate was wiped clean – it was as if I didn't exist.

Peggy claimed she didn't know how the Alberta court would view the adoption.

— "Is it not your intention, Mrs. Roaff, to make sure that your son forgets completely the existence of his natural father and that he becomes a total stranger to his father? Parizeau pursued.

— "I don't at this particular time in Branden's life see the purpose of the position that Mr. Di Done can fill..." Peggy responded.

— "You feel that you are married to another man who can very well replace the father; is that correct, Mrs. Roaff?"

— "That is true."

— "Do you feel that the family of Mr. Di Done has anything to offer to that child, who has in his heritage, part of the Di Done family?"

— " I would suggest that it would not be injurious to Branden that Mr. Di Done's family play a part in future years," answered Peggy.

— "And how would that be done if access is cancelled?"

— "By somewhere considerably down the line."

Parizeau reminded Peggy that she had previously testified in court that she recognized how much I loved my son and that Rick was very attached to me. Then, referring to Peggy's recent letter to me, she asked her if she thought that "that most extraordinary man" has nothing to offer his own child?"

While Peggy persisted in claiming that her purpose in seeking the adoption was not to cancel all my legal rights, she also said that it should be up to her and Jack to determine when and if I saw my son. The problem was that she thought an appropriate time for my family and me to become involved once more in my son's life, was perhaps around age 12!

The following day, with the exception of Peggy, who was represented by her lawyer, we gathered again – this time in the chambers of Justice Dea. Sandy Hogan, the Amicus, was also present at this meeting.

Peggy's lawyer began by suggesting there wasn't any proof that I even was Rick's father.

"What!" Judge Dea, responded. "Are you trying to say that your client has been perjuring herself all this time?"

If that line of argument didn't play well with the judge, the adoption was Peggy's trump card. Justice Dea first learned of it from Micheline Parizeau. Peggy's lawyer then used that opening to question the Alberta judge's jurisdiction to hear the case, given that his client had already sought and been granted the adoption in B.C.

For a split second, the only sound in Justice Dea's chambers was the whir of the air conditioning on this hot July day. Then, Dea's eyes widened and his face darkened in anger as he looked straight at Peggy's lawyer. "Your client did what?" he said, as his normally calm voice rose with his fury. Never in all my court appearances have I seen a judge so enraged. Not even Judge Hannan.

Parizeau counter argued that the hearing should continue, because the adoption was invalid. Dea himself seemed inclined to proceed. Ironically, it was Sandy Hogan, the Amicus, who persuaded the judge that as long as the adoption stood, he had, in fact, no further jurisdiction in the case. At this, Dea questioned Hogan about his involvement.

— "Where were you all this time? Your office is supposed to be supervising this case." Hogan replied that the adoption had also come as news to him.

Dea strongly suggested that Peggy immediately take the necessary steps to have the adoption set aside. We were to reconvene at the end of July to continue with the hearing.

Dea's words had no effect. When we met again before Justice Dea on July 28, nothing had changed. Furthermore, Peggy's lawyer continued to argue that the case should be dismissed because the Alberta court no longer had the authority to reinstate my visiting rights.

This time, Dea reluctantly agreed – having failed in his attempt to get Peggy to voluntarily undo an adoption that, under normal circumstances, should never have occurred. In his ruling that day, Dea reiterated his view that it remained in Rick's best interests that we be reunited.

He also noted that Peggy must have been "less than frank" with officials in B.C. when she applied for adoption. "Her very custody of the child was subject to supervision by the Amicus Curiae of this court," he said. "She led the father to believe that he would see the child again. She apparently did not disclose the quality of her custody or the existence of the Alberta Court Order pursuant to which she had custody." Dea further remarked on Peggy's "bad faith" in proceeding without notice to me or to the Amicus Curiae charged with supervision of her custody to secure the British Columbia adoption.

Dea acknowledged that his hands were tied. It wasn't his place to question the validity of the British Columbia adoption, which, in effect, terminates all visiting rights by any third party, even the father. "I come to that decision with regret," he stated, adding that he would otherwise "without hesitation" have reinstated my access rights.[14] All he could do was leave an opening for me to reapply for reinstatement of my access should we succeed in having the adoption set aside in British Columbia.

I left the Law Courts building in a state of shock. The parent-child relationship was something so basic, so fundamental, so essential to life itself. Yet, even though I had been engaged in three continuous years of litigation in both Alberta and Quebec to prevent exactly this from happening, loopholes in the legal system had allowed a third jurisdiction to completely sever my relationship with my son. To undo this required another costly legal action – in yet another province. What kind of a system, I wondered, can so cavalierly play with the lives of our children and their families?

I didn't know anyone in British Columbia – never mind a lawyer sufficiently selfless or foolhardy to take on a thorny case on behalf of a 31-year-old with an increasingly poor credit rating.

Like it or not, if I wanted to see my son again, I had to hire a lawyer in B.C. I could no longer afford to retain Micheline Parizeau for long-distance legal work, and was grateful when she found Cheryl Hass's name in a directory of lawyers. A young lawyer based in Kamloops, Cheryl would have a huge impact on my case; she was also one of the most caring, selfless individuals I would encounter.

When I first called and recounted my situation to her, she was far from optimistic. She explained that to her knowledge, adoptions in Canada were rarely, if ever, overturned. Moreover, the rights and obligations I had had as Rick's natural father could no longer be taken for granted.

From the outset, Cheryl would have preferred to see me agree to the adoption on the condition that my access rights be restored. She was very concerned that if I opposed the adoption straight-out and we lost the case, what little window remained to bring my son and me together could close forever.

I had been through too much to accept the adoption on any condition and I could never believe that this is what Rick would have wanted. What parent could? "He's my son," I said. "We love each other; we belong together."

Even if, for the sake of argument, I had agreed to the adoption in return for visiting rights, what guarantee was there that my access would ever be respected? By the very fact that they went ahead with the adoption when they knew full well I would have opposed it, Peggy and Jack had left no doubt that they wanted my relationship with Rick to cease. How could I trust them now? As far as the courts were concerned, Jack was Rick's father and I had no legal say whatsoever.

Seeing my determination, Cheryl reluctantly pressed on. By mid-August we were to appear for a hearing before the Supreme Court of British Columbia in Kamloops. I had returned to Montreal following Judge Dea's ruling and now had to make the trip West once more. It was a waste of time. Peggy's Kamloops lawyer, Barry Carter, requested a postponement.

On the second attempt, the presiding judge thought it better, for the sake of continuity, that the case be heard by Judge Arkell. He was the judge who had granted the adoption order, as well as the original 1980 interim custody order. Each delay entailed extra costs in terms of time, legal fees and travel expenses.

It took two more attempts before we finally appeared before Judge Arkell in early September. As we entered the courtroom, Cheryl was so nervous about the final outcome that her hands never stopped shaking. And on September 9, 1983, we succeeded in having the adoption cancelled. After months of anticipation and worry, the whole matter was resolved in a matter of a few hours.

At that time, British Columbia law stated that if a biological parent's name appeared on the birth certificate of a child born outside of marriage, that parent had to be notified before the child could be adopted. Although my name was clearly indicated on Rick's original birth certificate, I had never been advised of the adoption. On that basis, Judge Arkell overturned the adoption so that a full hearing could take place at which I would have the right to testify. Justice Dea's strongly worded judgment, written just over a month before, no doubt helped to influence the B.C. court in my favor.

We had done what most had thought impossible: the adoption was set aside. But there was little time to celebrate. I still had to reapply in Alberta to have my visiting rights reinstated. That required the written version of Judge Arkell's decision, which would take another few weeks to arrive. While I waited in Edmonton, I decided to put that time to good use.

By now OPCR had numerous members in Quebec and Alberta, and some journalist friends had helped me to introduce the organization to the media earlier that summer. The positive coverage we received from those initial interviews encouraged us. It also convinced us that the media was a fast and effective way to publicize the downside of a judicial system that makes the children of separating parent's voiceless pawns in a war of escalating litigation. Our media campaign had a simple message: the existing adversarial legal system tends to aggravate, not resolve, family conflicts. And the biggest victims are the children.

Soon OPCR members were giving interviews, condemning a legal system that pits father against mother in a bid to prove who is "more deserving" to be trusted with the children's upbringing. Instead of soothing strained relations between parents, the system itself was heightening them, at exactly the time when cool heads and cooperation were most needed to ensure the kids' well being. We were armed with example after example of custody arrangements that had gone sour and a legal system that offered little recourse for correction.

We supported the idea of reciprocal reinforcement of provincial and international custody orders as well as a national computer record that would discourage parents from kidnapping their own children or neglecting support payments. We went so far as to suggest that custody arrangements be removed from the hands of the legal system and given over to mandatory mediation in the same way that labor disputes are handled.

The system was out of touch with the real and urgent needs of families, and seemed more swayed by years of antiquated jurisprudence than the best interests of children.

Articles began appearing in several newspapers and magazines across Canada with headlines like "Children caught in custody wars," "To the victor, the children" and "Why children lack rights in custody cases." We were building a momentum for change.

One story that appeared in the Montreal Gazette in 1983 was especially heart-rending. It was about an eight-year-old girl who stayed initially with her father when her parents decided to divorce.

> *"In the nine months it took for the case to get to court, her parents' relationship deteriorated , their bitterness escalated and her father sank into a deep depression. The little girl became convinced that unless she stayed with her father, her father would die. She told the judge all she wanted was to stay with her father. The judge awarded custody to her mother . . . For months, living in her mother's home, she had nightmares . . . She still believed her father would die without her."*[15]

* * * * * *

I was back in Montreal in late October when Margaret Turfus called with the long-awaited news that the Alberta Court of Queen's Bench had reinstated my visiting rights. I had lingered in Edmonton almost a month waiting for the B. C. judgment to arrive, but was eventually obliged to return to Montreal to deal with pressing business. I had been concerned about not being able to attend the reinstatement hearing personally, but Margaret had assured me that my presence wasn't necessary. She said reinstatement was almost a certainty based on the Dea ruling in July.

In fact, it was Justice Dea who again heard the case and restored my visiting rights with two new conditions. First, all visits were to start and end in Revelstoke (and not Edmonton as was stipulated in the original judgment, but which had rarely been enforced). Second, I was to post a $20,000 bond with the court prior to every visit. The bond would be refundable upon Rick's safe return.

My joy quickly turned to panic when Margaret Turfus mentioned the $20,000 bond. "I don't have anywhere near that amount," I told her. There was silence on her end. "What do you mean?" she asked, quite aware that in the not-very-distant past this amount wouldn't have posed any problem. I explained the current state of my finances and asked if we couldn't appeal. She refused. "They asked for a $50,000 bond and I got it down to $20,000. I don't believe we could do any better."

In the weeks preceding the decision, I hadn't given any thought to the possibility that a bond might be required, nor had we discussed my finances to any great degree. In addition to representing me in my legal entanglements with Peggy, Margaret Turfus was also a partner in some of my real estate investments. To protect my reputation in the business community, I had deliberately downplayed the strain my legal bills were causing me. Including the most recent costs involved in setting aside the adoption and restoring my visiting rights, I was now some $100,000 in debt.

For the next few months, I tried every possible avenue to raise the bond money. No bank or insurance company would agree to give me a loan. True, my Montreal property alone was evaluated at close to a million dollars, but it was heavily mortgaged, and my credit rating had taken a real dive. My family had been feeding me and helping me whenever they could, but even if they wanted to give me a loan, they had nothing close to the amount of money required.

Finally I wrote to Peggy, her lawyer and the Amicus, offering to sign over everything I owned as collateral in order to take advantage of my visiting rights. The answer came back a resounding no: nothing short of a cash bond was acceptable.

Once more, I contacted Sandy Hogan, asking him to reconsider the decision.

"The idea of never seeing my son again is intolerable," I wrote. "I am sure you are well aware of the psychological effects suffered by any child who is deprived over a long period of time of the love and caring of one parent. I do not want this to happen to my son…and am prepared to agree to anything logical in order to be able to see, love and care for him again." I got a five-page letter in answer, but the refusal remained.

The need to see my son was so urgent, it sometimes took my breath away. The thought of him consumed me day and night, and the memory of one particularly vivid dream still affects me. In it, Rick had his arms around me and was hugging me with all his might, as he cried repeatedly, "Please don't let me go, Papa."

The frustration was ripping me apart. I had inched my way back from the terrifying precipice of jail, kidnapping, and my son's adoption, only to be hurled forward again to that sickening height by the mundane constraint of money.

Money problems plagued me on a daily basis. I had no cash. Everything was tied up in properties. Even if we wanted to sell, in those recessionary years of skyrocketing interest rates, no buyers were interested in meeting our price.

It got so bad that back in Edmonton in late November, I had nowhere to sleep but my car. Until then I had camped out in an old vacant house that Stagen and I still owned, where my bed was a sleeping bag on the floor. The snow and cold had set in early that year, and during that particular period, the nighttime thermostat held stubbornly at minus 20 degrees Celsius. When the utilities were cut off because the bills had gone unpaid, I moved into my now aging Lincoln that was parked in the back lane. You could hardly call it sleeping. Every few minutes I would start the motor just long enough to generate a bit of heat to get me through the night. Even so, I had to keep the window open for fear of asphyxiation.

In the morning I'd go to a nearby gym, where I had a lifetime membership. There I'd thaw out with a hot shower and change into clean clothes. I thought no one was the wiser. However, after several cold and uncomfortable nights, I opened my eyes one morning to find Vile'm Weber, a Czech friend from the Bistro Praha, knocking on the frosted window of my car.

— "I thought so," he said quietly. He had suspected I was in bad financial shape and had come by to see if he could help. He wasn't well off himself: an aspiring movie producer, he also worked as a chef-cook and lived in a small bachelor apartment. Nevertheless, he insisted I move in with him for the rest of my stay in Edmonton.

Meanwhile, just in case I somehow managed to scratch together the bond money, Peggy and Jack were taking their own means to keep Rick and me apart. In late December 1983, they re-opened adoption proceedings and petitioned the B.C. court to suspend my visiting rights until the adoption matter was settled. They also asked that all jurisdiction related to Rick's custody and access be transferred from Alberta to B.C. (In his October ruling ordering reinstatement of my access, Justice Dea had recognized that B.C. was now clearly Rick's home province and had opened the door for a transfer of jurisdiction.)

Peggy and Jack initiated this process just days before my access would have started if I had raised the bond. With Cheryl Hass's assistance, I counter-filed a motion, calling for jurisdiction to remain in Alberta. I also asked that the adoption request be dismissed or, failing this, that a full hearing take place where I would have liberty to testify.

Magically, the adoption petition was withdrawn shortly after it became evident that I couldn't fulfill the access conditions. According to Peggy, they could no longer afford the financial burden a legal adoption would entail; as far as I could tell, they had simply taken advantage of one more loophole in a system that could be manipulated to deprive the non-custodial parent of access.

Two other events occurred around this time that strengthened my resolve to continue fighting for my son, no matter what hurdles came my way. A couple of weeks before Christmas, I was having lunch in a Montreal steakhouse with Mohammed Ali Alebouye. We were talking about our plans for OPCR when in walked the most attractive woman I had seen in a long time.

She and a woman friend were seated at a nearby table. I could barely take my eyes off her and sent her an admiring note via the waitress. On the way out, I stopped at her table for a moment, introduced myself and apologized for my forwardness. "If you'd ever like to have a coffee together, here's my card," I said and took my leave.

When I got back to my office, there was a message to call a Madame Vanderchamp from a downtown firm of architects. I don't know any architects, I thought, puzzled, as I dialed the number. It was the woman from the restaurant. Her name was Jackie and the still unfamiliar voice was saying, "This may sound crazy and I've never done this before, but if you want to have a coffee together, I could meet you for 10 or 15 minutes, no more."

Two days before Christmas we agreed to meet at a nearby restaurant at 11:00 a.m. More than 14 hours later, we finally stepped out into the street again, dizzy with champagne and the joy of finding each other. At one point earlier in the evening, my romantic nature had gotten away with itself when I spied a beautiful arrangement of flowers. Picking up the arrangement, I made a show of presenting it to Jackie and then proceeded to drop the whole thing, flowers and vase. When the manager came over to see what was causing such a commotion, we realized we were both Italian. Not only did he let me get away without paying for the flowers and shattered vase, the whole evening was on the house!

Jackie and I would continue to see each other for the next year and a half. She had a daughter, Natasha, who was just a couple of years older than Rick, and could empathize with my predicament. Her help in getting OPCR off the ground was priceless.

About this time, I was also interviewed on Canada AM, a national TV news show that aired every weekday morning. Following that exposure, one of the cast of Canada AM put me in touch with Marilyn Weston, host of *As It Is*, a popular Sunday night public affairs show on CFCF-TV in Montreal.

When I first met with her, she was highly skeptical of my story. Her initial reaction went straight to the point: "What did you do to Peggy to drive her to act this way?"

— " All I ask is that you listen to what I have to say," I answered. "Investigate all you want. Talk to Peggy, too. By all means. Then if you think I'm at fault, say so. But what really counts is my son and I would appreciate your support."

She did her homework. After meeting with me, she and the show's researchers poured over photographs and read through all the court transcripts, affidavits and judgments. She also interviewed Peggy. In that interview, Peggy said that she and Jack were working hard to create a home for Rick. "I simply feel very strongly that for our child's benefit, all access should be denied." She went on to say that Rick no longer remembered me.

The research took almost three months to complete and the result was a half-hour documentary that aired in March 1984. It was highly sympathetic to my plight. I was immensely relieved and encouraged. At last people were starting to listen – and understand.

Over the next year, *As It Is* did several follow-up segments on my story. One of the show's researchers even wrote to the Insurance Board of Canada on my behalf saying " 'As it is' would like to be able to update our program with the happy news that (one of the board's member-companies) has put up the bond money and Ricaardoe Di Done will be able to see his son again.

The plea didn't work, but such an active demonstration of support gave me a tremendous boost. The staff of *As It Is* helped me in many other ways. So many of my friends and acquaintances had already questioned the sanity of my pursuing legal action after legal action in what they considered a hopeless struggle. Marilyn Weston took the opposite tact. "You must never give up, Ricaardoe," she said. "It would be devastating for your son. You must never abandon him."

REUNION AT LAST

It was in the spring of 1984 that I called Marilyn Weston with the news. I was so excited she had to tell me to calm down so she could understand what I was saying. "I'm going," I shouted, my joy unrestrained. "I'm going to see my son. After two-and-a-half years! We're going to be together again!"

A chance encounter with a sympathetic credit manager a few weeks earlier had at last resolved my financial crisis. He approved a re-mortgaging of the Lajeunesse Street apartment complex that Stagen Warness and I still co-owned, enabling us to pay off outstanding debts that had been accumulating on our business holdings in Alberta and Montreal. Stagen then agreed to let me borrow $20,000 from the company short-term to cover the bond money.

I had actually hoped to see Rick at Easter, but Peggy had refused, since my access provisions only entitled me to Easter visits during odd calendar years. So I waited impatiently for July.

My plan was to pick up Rick in Revelstoke on July 1st, spend a few days getting reacquainted in the West, and then bring him to Montreal for the remainder of the month. My family was already planning his welcome-home party. My aunt Toni was bursting with happiness, as if a dear one who had died was suddenly restored to life. "He's like a grandson to me," she confided. "When I lost him, I lost something very precious."

Peggy now had two lawyers in B.C. – one in Vernon and one in Kamloops – and Cheryl Hass advised both of them of my intentions. By the time I was leaving for Revelstoke, we had a good idea that things might not go smoothly. Peggy was not at all happy that I was about to re-enter our son's life, and her lawyers let us know that she was seeking to block my access. On my arrival in Revelstoke, I was to meet Cheryl Hass, who by then, would hopefully have been able to sort out matters with Peggy and her lawyers.

Vile'm Weber kept me company on the long drive from Edmonton. As I got to know him better, I learned that he, too, had a son he rarely saw, from a marriage that had ended in divorce several years before. But he had chosen not to contest the custody arrangements.

His own mother had been married five times and he had little faith in the legal system. Some time later when his son was in his late teens, I was with Vile'm when they met after a long separation. He was taken aback by how little he knew about the young man his son was becoming. "Vile'm," I reminded him gently, "you weren't there while he was growing up. What did you expect?"

Vile'm and I drove to Revelstoke in my old blue Lincoln. I was going on sheer adrenaline – just hours away from seeing my son. I ranted non-stop about the absurdities of the present custody system and how countless children, parents, grandparents – whole families – were suffering needlessly as a result. "We've got to make changes," I said to Vile'm. "And we will."

He let me talk. It was hard to know whether he thought me a valiant crusader or an idealistic fool. Maybe I was both. He did remark on my confidence. At one point he asked me:

— "Ricaardoe, what will you do if Rick doesn't remember you? He was little more than a baby when he last saw you. What if he refuses to go with you?" He wasn't the first person to pose those questions.

— "He'll know me," I answered. "We love each other so much and the bond between us is so strong."

— "And if he doesn't?" he responded.

— "Well, we'll just have to start back slowly, one day at a time."

When we arrived in Revelstoke, Cheryl was waiting at the RCMP station. One look at her face told me we had a problem. In her hands was a copy of a petition Peggy had filed three days earlier with the Vernon registry of the B.C. Supreme Court. Vernon was a town approximately 150 kilometers southwest of Revelstoke. Once again, Peggy was formally requesting the B.C. courts to assume jurisdiction for all matters relating to Rick's custody. She was also asking the court to refuse me any access until a full hearing was held on the question of Rick's adoption.

Cheryl had already contested the petition on my behalf and we were to attend a hearing in Vernon on July 4. Until then we would just have to sit tight. So much for the flights and hotel reservations I had pre-arranged for Rick and myself.

On the fourth, Peggy was present with her Vernon lawyer, K.W. Tollestrup, when we met before Judge Arkell. Within minutes, the judge dismissed Peggy's petition. Because of our undertaking to use the Alberta courts, he maintained it would be an abuse of process for the Supreme Court of B.C. to now step in. He also didn't like the idea that Peggy had submitted a last-minute application trying to prevent my access.

To make up for the time lost, my access was extended to August 5. It was agreed that I would pick up Rick the next morning at 6:30 a.m. at the Frontier Restaurant in Revelstoke. I was also given leave to telephone him at home that evening to say hello and prepare him for my sudden re-appearance.

For well over an hour after supper, I sat by my motel phone, dialing their number over and over. Six, seven, eight times, it would ring, but there was no answer. About 8:30 p.m., I finally got through, but Peggy informed me it was too late: since Rick had to be up so early the next morning, she had already put him to bed.

The first rays of morning sun were streaming through the windows of the Frontier Restaurant where I waited shortly before six-thirty. My stomach was in knots; in front of me the steam rose from a still untouched cup of coffee. The restaurant was a sprawling log structure, stained dark on the outside with red trim around the windows. Inside, the wood-paneled walls displayed old saws, ploughs and other farm implements. Over the next few years, I would get to know its every nook and cranny very well.

I had been too anxious to sleep and had risen just before daybreak. Not long after, Vile'm had roused himself and we had packed up the car, checked out and driven to the restaurant. Still sleepy, Vile'm said he wanted to doze in the car until Rick and Peggy arrived; he also wanted to give Rick and me a few minutes alone.

Some twenty minutes later, I was out in the parking lot, my eyes trained on the road. My heart sank when Peggy drove up alone.

She said Rick was still at home, and that before she would turn him over to my care, she wanted me to sign some papers she had brought with her. I refused.

— "Peggy, what more do you want. I paid the bond money. Yesterday, the judge agreed that I should see our son. It's been two-

and-a-half years. Please have some compassion and don't try to keep us apart any longer."

She turned, got into her car, and drove away. I called Cheryl Hass who, after a delay of several more minutes, succeeded in reaching K.W. Tollestrup. He informed her he had just spoken to Peggy and explained to her it was senseless to ask me to sign anything further. The arrangements had been agreed to the previous day. He apologized on her behalf and said that she should be arriving back at the restaurant with Rick any minute.

I was back outside when the car drove up. Out climbed Rick, almost a foot taller than I remembered. He was wearing black pants and a matching T-shirt and his blond hair was trimmed short and fell in bangs across his forehead. There was a flicker of hesitation as his keen blue eyes rose to meet mine and then a shy smile lit up his face.

— "Hi, Rick," I said, crouching on a level with his eyes and taking both his hands in mine. "It's Papa. I've missed you so much. Do you remember me?"

— "Yes," he responded in a quiet voice. "You used to live with Mommy and me." For the next few minutes, his hand remained in mine, his small fingers stroking my palm with the lightest of touches. I asked Peggy if she would stay to have breakfast with us, but she declined. We transferred his suitcase from her car to mine. Then, after a few awkward moments, she leaned over, gave our son a big hug and reminded him that he could call her anytime he wanted.

As soon as her tail lights had disappeared, Rick turned to me, and before I even realized what he was doing, he had encircled my waist with his arms and was uttering our old familiar refrain, "I love you this much all the way around." Then he hugged me for all his worth.

I brushed tears of joy aside as I hugged him back as hard as I could. "You really do remember me – after all this time," I said. "You're quite the boy, Mr. Ricaardoe Di Done Jr.!"

After a little while, he said, "Mommy told me I had to go with you or she would go to jail."

— "Don't you worry," I responded. "Mommy isn't going to jail. But how would you like to go see Grandpa and Grandma and Auntie Toni and all your cousins and friends in Montreal?"

His head nodded yes.

— "Well, that's what we're going to do in just a couple of days. But as for right now, let's go have fun!"

I introduced him to Vile'm, and after a substantial breakfast, the three of us were heading down the highway out of Revelstoke. It was a beautiful sunny day and I left it up to Rick to decide how we should spend it. He said he'd like to go to a beach. We rolled down the windows, pointed the car towards Kelowna and the Okanagan Lake, and set off, with the breeze blowing through our hair and big smiles on our faces.

On the way, we passed a small theme park called the Enchanted Forest. Rick said he had always wanted to go there and asked if we could stop. "Why not?" I responded. "You're the leader!"

Once inside, it was obvious he knew his way around and had visited there before, but wanted to share his enthusiasm for the spot with Vile'm and myself. We continued on to Kelowna and spent the rest of the day playing ball on the sand and splashing in the calm, warm water of the lake. Rick was all over me – jumping off my shoulders into the water, then pulling me by the hand to show me some treasure on the shore. Wherever I was, so was he. Vile'm remarked how easily Rick had adjusted to my presence and how natural and effortless our reunion had been.

That evening, we stopped at an Italian restaurant for dinner. After Rick had consumed a full plate of spaghetti, I was amazed to see him eyeing my rigatoni longingly. "You should have told me you were going to have rigatoni," he lectured me. "I would have ordered that, too." "You want some?" I asked him and he nodded yes. A plate of rigatoni disappeared almost as quickly as the spaghetti had. Even with the passage of time, there was no denying his Di Done roots. He had certainly not lost his fondness for good Italian cooking!

Just before we landed at Montreal, I explained to Rick that in addition to our relatives and friends, there would probably also be a nice lady with a TV camera, waiting to see us. Marilyn Weston had asked if she could film our arrival for an *As It Is* update. "Do you mind if she takes pictures of us?" I asked him. "No," he said, "not if you're going to be there."

I needn't have worried about his being nervous or camera-shy. When Marilyn Weston approached and asked him, "What was the first thing you said when you saw your dad?", he smiled right into the camera and said without any hesitation: "I love you this much all the way around!" A few years later, he had forgotten all about that tape at a time when he was growing increasingly angry and confused about who really was his father. Then I would count myself fortunate indeed to have a copy to show him.

My parents, Toni and Richard, my aunt Ida, her husband and their children had all come to the airport to greet us. Jackie and her daughter were also there, as was Jake Vanderschaaf, who had made the trip from Ottawa especially for the occasion. After much hugging and kissing, we all gathered at my parents' home where a huge "Welcome home, Rick" banner was strung across the hallway. Set out for him were all the cards and letters I had sent to him over the past two and a half years that he had never received.

That day the hollowness that his long absence had created in our family was suddenly and wonderfully filled with the laughter and non-stop energy of a healthy and active six-year-old. Over the next four weeks, Rick and I were glued to each other; it was a fantastic month.

So many people find it hard to believe that after such a long separation, we could have rekindled our relationship so quickly and so easily. For me, there was only one simple explanation: it never burnt out. Over the years, even strangers have approached me to say they have rarely seen a father and son who were so close. Personally, I can't imagine anything more natural. As a child I would follow my father anywhere. He was my best friend. It didn't seem in the least strange or extraordinary to me that my son and I should feel the same way.

At night, before bed, Rick would curl up beside me and we'd talk about what we'd done that day or what we had planned for the next one. Once he said that in Revelstoke he often cried himself to sleep at night. "When Mom comes in to see what's the matter, I tell her I don't want her to go to court anymore." Then he added that the real reason was that he wanted to come and live with me, but was afraid she would be hurt and get upset.

There was something very wrong about a child so young shouldering such a burden. In a winner-takes-all version of custody, courts impose decisions, and children are expected to live accordingly, regardless of their own personal feelings.

During the month he spent with me, I made sure Rick called his mother regularly and did my best to avoid any negative references to what had happened between us. I deliberately steered away from the subject unless Rick asked me a direct question. I wanted this to be a happy time; God knows, we all had had enough sadness.

The extent to which children of separated parents are torn in different directions was driven home by three separate evaluations of Rick's emotional and psychological state that were carried out that year.

To support her latest legal action, Peggy had submitted a report by a Kamloops psychologist named Jim Fornelli. It had been prepared several months before Rick and I were reunited and it stated that, physically, emotionally and intellectually, Rick was developing well in the security of his present family. Not only did it say, "There was no indication that Branden has suffered by not seeing his natural father," it added: "It is more appropriate to suggest that he has benefited from not visiting with his natural father." It conceded that "Branden continues to be anxious and unsettled about his natural father," but indicated that this was due to some lack in our relationship and had nothing to do with our long separation. The report recommended that access be denied out of concern for Rick's best interests.

This ran completely counter to all the research I had recently been exposed to through my involvement in OPCR. That's why, towards the end of our visit, I took Rick to be evaluated by two experts of my own choosing who had been highly recommended to me. One was family psychotherapist, Patricia Hunter and the other Dr. André Masse, the then head of child psychiatry at Montreal's renowned Sainte-Justine children's hospital. Dr. Masse had studied the father-child relationship for many years, both in intact families and in ones where one or both parents were absent due to separation, divorce, death or the demands of migrant work.

After Peggy's last-minute attempt to block my access to Rick, I had no illusions that she wouldn't continue to pursue every avenue – including adoption – to prevent any further access. I knew she would come armed with more psychologists' reports favoring her point of view. I wanted to see what other impartial experts would say about Rick's relationship with me.

Patricia Hunter noted "a strong bond between father and son" and said that our relationship "appeared natural, caring and happy." She observed that occasionally Rick would climb onto my lap and hold me tight. She also reported Rick saying that "he is told to call Jack 'daddy,' but that he does not want to do so since his real 'daddy' is the one he wants to be with."

"In my years as a family psychotherapist," she concluded, "I have seldom seen a parent/child relationship which seemed so strong, happy and desired on the surface, but in reality faced a very insecure future due to outside influences. It is my firm belief that Mr. Di Done has only the very best in mind for his child and is very willing to share him with the mother as long as he has reasonable access to his son."

Dr. André Masse also recommended that, to reinforce the identification of son to father, Rick and I be able to see each other frequently and regularly. He was convinced that Rick and I shared a good relationship, and that it was a relationship we both desired. As an example, Masse indicated that not only was Rick happy to say he had the same name as me, but he said it "with an Italian intonation – and smiling."

What was essential, he emphasized, was for both parents to cooperate in helping the child during the transfers from one home to the other. "It is common that the child, at the time of these meetings, be more anxious, restless or sad," he wrote. "These emotions are those of a normal individual faced with an emotionally charged situation. The child must evidently be helped in keeping the symbols of his ties (name, surname, mementos, photos, activities) and the availability of the 'other parent' must be encouraged at a maximum in a stable manner both foreseeable and free of any animosity."

It was hard to believe that the child described by Hunter and Masse and the one portrayed by Fornelli was, in fact, one and the same. If the acknowledged experts differed so greatly in their opinions, how was a six-year-old child to respond? Small wonder that, as time progressed, Rick would become increasingly confused about who he was and where he belonged.

The day we returned to Revelstoke was especially poignant. We had spent the last few days of our visit together at my parent's cottage in Sainte-Lucie. Jackie and her daughter had joined us there. Rick had taken a real liking to Natasha and proudly introduced her to everyone as his "sister." The weather was perfect and we lazed about by the lake, went for long walks, camped out and enjoyed many a family barbecue. Every evening at twilight, my dad would bring out his old accordion, and the music and our laughter would last well into those long summer nights.

But as the date of our return flight drew nearer, Rick's mood changed abruptly. Every morning as soon as he awoke, he asked anxiously, "How many days left till I have to leave?" Then he would start: "I don't want to go back. I want to stay here with you."

When I explained I had to bring him back to his mother or the judge might not let me see him again, he would start to cry and tell me he hated me.

The actual day of departure was the worst. Once again, the family gathered at the airport, trying to hold back their tears. On the plane, the stabbing looks I got from my son hurt more than any physical knife. Here I was, his supposedly all-powerful father, useless to help him when he most wanted it.

The knowledge that we would see each other again at Christmas was little consolation. Five months is an eternity for a child. Only during the drive back to Revelstoke did he relent and hug me at every opportunity. When we pulled into the parking lot of the Frontier Restaurant exactly one month from the day of our reunion, Peggy and Jack were waiting.

In the trunk of my car were a new bicycle, a photo album crammed with family pictures taken during Rick's stay, a pair of walkie-talkies and a few other toys I had gotten for him. I had also bought him a soft Gremlin doll, based on the little reddish-brown character in the movie "Gremlins", that was then at the height of its popularity. He took the doll everywhere and had cuddled it the entire trip home.

As I started to unload Rick's suitcase and take out the bike and other gifts, Jack quickly intervened. "We don't need all that stuff," he said, adding under his breath, "and we don't need another father."

Rick turned to me with a sad and confused look: "What shall we do?"

Not wanting to make things any more difficult or cause a scene in front of my son, I loaded the bike and other items back into the car.

—   "It's all right, Ricaardoe. Don't worry about it. I'll put them away for you until we see each other again."

The only gift Peggy and Jack let him keep was the little Gremlin doll. I promised to call him as often as I could get through, and with one last hug, he was on his way. I stood riveted to the spot for several minutes after the car carrying him, Peggy and Jack drove out of sight. Months later, he told me that the Gremlin doll disappeared from his room a few days after his return home.

* * * * *

Now that Rick and I had finally been reunited, I decided to take additional legal steps to ensure ongoing contact with my son. In theory, there was nothing to prevent Rick and me from filling the gaps between visits with frequent phone calls and letters. However, experience had taught me that Peggy and Jack wouldn't hesitate to block or intercept such communication. That's why I asked the Alberta court to clearly state that I could telephone Rick or write to him on a regular basis. I also applied for the return of the $20,000 cash bond that had been deposited with the court in June, and I requested that for future access visits, the bond be reduced to $5,000.

The red tape surrounding these cash bonds would cause endless headaches in the years to come. Aside from the difficulty of raising the money and arranging its deposit (which entailed a court order and legal fees), a second court order confirming Rick had been returned to his mother (and more legal fees) were necessary to get the money back. At each access period, this process had to be repeated, and several months could pass before the money would be released.

At approximately the same time that I was requesting this change in my access provisions in Alberta, Peggy and Jack re-applied to adopt Rick in British Columbia. Accompanying their adoption petition was a follow-up psychological evaluation that Jim Fornelli had conducted shortly after Rick's return from Montreal. His report noted that Rick's behavior had deteriorated since his visit with me and referred to "the disruptive influence of extended visits with his natural father." Fornelli concluded that these visits would only confuse and disrupt Rick's development, and if they were to continue, they should be limited and minimal. Once again, he supported Rick's adoption by Jack.

Peggy also filed an affidavit in Alberta, contesting any reduction in my access bond.

At the end of September, Mr. Justice Bracco of Alberta's Court of Queen's Bench amended the access conditions – lowering the bond requirement to $7,500 and granting me formal permission to write to Rick regularly and to telephone him on specific days at set times. I was to be notified of any change in Rick's address or phone number.

Taking into consideration Rick's new school schedule (he had just started grade 1), the judge also eliminated the annual month-long January access. In its place, I was entitled to visit my son anytime I was in the Revelstoke area, as long as these visits didn't exceed once every two weeks and I provided Peggy with 48-hours notice.

Even with the Bracco order supporting me, I was unable to contact Rick. The phone number Peggy had given me in July was no longer in service, and registered letters to my son were returned "moved, address unknown." At the end of October, I filed a contempt-of-court charge against Peggy.

Before taking this step, I wrote to her, asking for her new phone number. "It is in the best interest of our child to have communication with both parents," I pleaded. "Ricaardoe Branden asked repeatedly that I telephone him regularly. It is his right as well as mine. Peggy, I do not wish to complicate matters more than they have already been. God knows enough time has passed wherein we should be able to come to some reasonable understanding regarding our son."

I received no response to this letter.

Only after the contempt charge had been filed did Peggy counter that she preferred not to give me her phone number as this would cause problems between her and Jack. At the end of November, the Alberta court – this time through Mr. Justice F.R. MacNaughton – adjusted the access conditions once again. Now Peggy and Rick were to call me collect in Montreal every Wednesday and Sunday evening, instead of my calling Revelstoke.

This arrangement, which persisted on a more-or-less regular basis for the next couple of years, had its share of frustrations. Often it meant frequent juggling of schedules so as not to miss one of those precious calls. Sometimes my parents, aunt Toni or other relatives would sit with me by the phone at the appointed time, waiting for a chance to speak to Rick and hear his voice. The anticipation before each call was tremendous, and the letdown even greater on those not infrequent occasions when the phone didn't ring, or the call came late after other family members had returned home, or it came altogether unexpected on another day.

When Rick and I did connect, I made sure I had a store of jokes to keep up his spirits and lessen the awkwardness of our long-distance communication. It was far from the kind of father-son relationship I had always envisioned. Nevertheless, I was still very grateful for those brief calls that enabled me to share in a larger part of my son's life than had been previously possible.

Through all this, the threat of adoption continued to loom. Despite our uneasy truce over the phone calls, Peggy and Jack were still bent on eliminating me from my son's world. They argued it was in Rick's best interest to have one clear family affiliation in the home where they lived together. Even though they knew Rick and I loved each other, they tried to portray my insistence on being a father to my son as some stubborn, vengeful meddling designed to destroy their happiness together. Whatever their motivation, their actions were clear – they saw no role for me as Rick's father.

It seemed we were never to reach a middle ground. I did – and still do – believe that it was vital for Rick to maintain a close relationship with his mother. But I was equally adamant that my son would know without question that I was his father and would always be there for him.

Towards the end of November 1984 – as the date for my Christmas access approached – I learned that in addition to the adoption application, Peggy now had two other petitions before two different registries of the B.C. Supreme Court. She was leaving no stone unturned in her attempt to prevent any further access between me and Rick.

The first – in the Vernon registry – once again asked the B.C. court to assume jurisdiction for all matters related to Rick's custody, and at the same time, deny me access. The second – in the Kamloops registry – sought to prevent my access to Rick until such time as the application to adopt him could be heard.

Peggy's timing was sublime. Both Rick and I had been counting the days until we would see each other again. Our visit was to begin on December 20 and continue through to January 6. It would be the first Christmas Rick would spend in Montreal with my family since he was three – and the first time since then that I had really looked forward to the holidays.

Now Peggy was again trying to block my access, as she had done in the summer. Both motions were heard December 4 before Mr. Justice Hamilton of the Supreme Court of B.C. Cheryl Hass represented me; I couldn't afford to make yet another trip to B.C. – just two weeks before I would have to travel there anyway to pick up Rick for Christmas.

Thankfully, the motions were denied. The ruling was consistent with past ones: because Peggy and I had signed undertakings to use the Alberta courts, Justice Hamilton refused to assume jurisdiction. Rick would still be coming home to us for Christmas!

And what a Christmas it was. Late in the afternoon of Christmas Eve, Rick, Jackie, Natasha and I drove up to my parents' chalet in Sainte-Lucie. Even though my finances were strained to the limit, we arrived with such a carload of presents for everyone that there was barely room for all of us to sit. After the holidays, I would face my ever-present debts, as the credit card bills stacked up in the mail.

But for a few days I wanted to savor the memory of this special Christmas with my son.

The lights from the chalet sent a welcoming glow through the snow-covered pines that surrounded the house, as we made our way up the path. Large, moist snowflakes drifted gently downwards, tickling our eyelashes and turning our coats and scarves instantly white. A snowman that someone had built at the end of the drive stood in official greeting. The whole scene had an old-fashioned, Christmas-card-perfect feel to it – and it remains one of the few truly happy memories that stand out during that long and difficult period of my life.

With my parents, aunts, uncles, and cousins, we were a big group. For the next twenty-four hours, we opened presents and feasted like royalty. Once everyone had finally had their fill, out came the accordion and we started to sing. Rick and Natasha bounced around the chalet, trying out new toys and basking in the love and excitement of a big family gathering.

After Christmas, we spent a few more days in Montreal with Jackie and Natasha before Rick had to return to B.C. and to school, with a party to celebrate both our birthdays the day before we left.

That brief magical interlude quickly gave way to the reality of a long anxiety-filled winter. The adoption petition continued to inch its way through the courts. While my real-estate investments occupied a portion of my time, more and more of my energy was focused on OPCR and my struggle to be with my son.

By now the organization was "headquartered" out of a 3°-room basement apartment on Robert Street, part of a 336-unit complex that Stagen, I and several partners had purchased back in 1980. OPCR consisted of close to 20 people – all volunteers, working in cramped conditions, with one phone and an old manual typewriter. Some, like Jackie, had full-time day jobs – and yet would still spend many an evening and weekend helping to compile the endless lists of politicians, community groups, trade organizations, journalists and anyone else we thought could add support to our cause. We spent hours preparing letters and briefs aimed at changing a system that aggravated the problems of divorce and child custody because it failed to equip separating parents with the positive tools and mechanisms they needed to build a secure and emotionally stable future for their children.

One of OPCR's early volunteers was a divorced father – a teacher, with a daughter about the same age as Rick. The little girl lived with her mother who had been given sole custody. The father had just four days access to his daughter each month. Even though he and his ex-wife lived quite close to each other, she wouldn't agree to him seeing their daughter more frequently – even to baby-sit! Undoubtedly there was more to the story than that, but I recall an intelligent, involved father who loved his daughter dearly being arbitrarily prevented from being anything more than an occasional presence in her life.

This was the level of heartache and injustice that drove me on. For the better part of that year, I put in 16, sometimes 18 hours a day, seven days a week. Surrounded by a constant litter of paper, it was a wonder any of us accomplished anything, but we churned out an enormous quantity of letters to elected representatives at both federal and provincial levels, and succeeded in drawing up a platform of essential reforms that remain the basis of every OPCR intervention to this day.

In those early years of OPCR, the notion of joint custody was just beginning to surface in the public awareness. The Conservative government under then Prime Minister Brian Mulroney was spearheading changes to Canada's divorce law and, in June of 1985, the House of Commons Standing Committee on Justice and Legal Affairs held public hearings into the proposed changes. The new legislation aimed at humanizing the divorce process by largely eliminating the notion of fault and making it possible to obtain a divorce after a one-year separation solely on the ground of marital breakdown. Under the existing legislation, a three-year separation was required for a "no-fault" divorce to be granted. However, the process could be significantly speeded up if the grounds used were adultery or mental cruelty. So, ironically, the law itself may have been encouraging couples to commit perjury and falsely claim adultery or mental cruelty, simply to hasten the divorce.

The proposed legislation sought to correct this situation. It also contained several other important advances, including recognition for the first time of the interests of the child. Nevertheless, to

OPCR's mind, it fell far short of the mark when it came to promoting the idea of joint custody and shared parenting, or the use of mediation as a constructive tool to reach divorce settlements and future parenting plans. Other criticisms revolved around its ability to enforce support payments – Justice Minister John Crosbie noted himself that from one-half to three-quarters of all support orders in Canada at that time were wholly or partly in arrears. Nor did the legislation help in ensuring that access provisions for non-custodial parents would be respected.

On behalf of OPCR, I appeared before the Standing Committee, which consisted of members of Parliament from the three main political parties of the day. Our brief maintained that any reforms to the law should favor joint custody – or the continued involvement of both parents in the upbringing of their children. "If and when a relationship between two parents comes apart, they will still be married to their children until the children are fully grown," we said. "No one owns his children; both parents have the responsibility to give their children the love and care they require. And children have the right to full communication with both parents."

Joint custody, we emphasized, did not mean that children must move back and forth between each parent's home every other week; it was far more concerned with creating a climate where mothers and fathers would cooperate in providing their children with a balanced, loving and healthy upbringing. "The law should not favor any sex," we said, "because the best parent is the balance of the two."

OPCR also stressed the need for greater education about the enormous responsibilities that go hand-in-hand with parenthood. A system truly geared to the well-being of children would not only make such courses available to separating parents, it would also incorporate this type of education into the basic curriculum of elementary and secondary schools.

At this hearing, and other similar hearings where I presented briefs, I met Sheila Finestone. A long-time Liberal member of Parliament – and now a Canadian senator – Sheila Finestone has labored for social reform for close to two decades. She was the first MP who truly listened to my story and made a real effort to understand and take action to correct the heartbreaking experience that I and so many other parents, grandparents and whole families were living on a daily basis.

These initial efforts to bring about reform allowed me to channel the frustration and bitterness I felt about my own situation, into something positive. But no matter how hard I worked, I could not escape the knowledge that my relationship with Rick, which was so painstakingly nourishing, could be totally uprooted should the courts eventually agree to his adoption by Peggy and Jack.

That Easter, Rick and I had spent several days together in B.C. and Alberta. One morning we were having breakfast with friends at a popular Edmonton restaurant when we turned to see Wayne Gretzky at the next table. Rick still has a treasured photo of himself with the then Edmonton Oilers hockey legend.

The last day of my access we went boating on Okanagan Lake. The water was choppy and we thrilled to the speed of the high-powered boat jumping the waves. "Faster, Papa, faster," Rick shouted gleefully over the noise of the engine, as the wind and the spray temporarily obliterated the gnawing hurt over our impending separation that we were both trying so hard to mask.

Immediately after Easter, the first step in the long-awaited adoption hearing unfolded on April 10 in a courtroom in Salmon Arm, approximately mid-way between Revelstoke and Kamloops. With the passage of time, the issue had become ever more complicated. Peggy had changed legal counsel and her new lawyer, Robin Jackson, was contesting my application to appear and testify before a full adoption hearing, such as Judge Arkell had envisioned when, a year and a half earlier, he had set aside Rick's original adoption order.

Jackson's argument centered on a Court ruling concerning another adoption case. That ruling had concluded that the natural father of a child born outside of marriage had no standing in adoption proceedings.

This newest episode took place before Local Judge of the Supreme Court of British Columbia, K.D. Houghton. I attended in person with Cheryl Hass. On May 1st, 1985, Judge Houghton's breakthrough ruling safeguarded my right to participate fully in any subsequent adoption proceedings. The judge disagreed with

Jackson's argument that I be excluded, declaring that it was an elementary principle of justice – and in my son's best interest – that I be heard, especially since an adoption would automatically override my current access rights. His judgment noted that access provisions are as much for the benefit of the child as for the non-custodial parent.

He concluded: "When the record shows that the father of an illegitimate child has acknowledged the child and taken an interest in the child, either from his name on the birth certificate, an access order or otherwise, that parent must be given notice of the adoption proceeding and heard on the application if he comes forward. He has a common-law right to be heard and the court in seeking to act for the welfare of the child should hear his submission ."

Two weeks later, Peggy and Jack appealed the Houghton decision.

Meanwhile, in a counter-move against the adoption, I had filed an application with the Alberta Court of Queen's Bench for joint custody of Rick. To see this action through, I had the services of a new lawyer in Edmonton. At the end of my rope financially, I had applied for legal aid. While I waited for my application to be processed, Helyna Freeland had accepted me as a client, as a favor to a mutual friend.

The good professional relationship I had enjoyed with Margaret Turfus since the original 1981 custody hearing had floundered over money. I owed her a substantial amount and my account had been outstanding for months. My Christmas spending spree hadn't helped, but that was a drop in the bucket compared to my ongoing legal fees and court costs.

My predicament wasn't uncommon. What was uncommon was my determination to pursue the matter through the courts for as long as it took to guarantee my relationship with my son. Very few people would persevere for 16 years as I did. In many cases where a non-custodial parent's access rights are not being respected, the sad truth is that he or she eventually gives up and drifts away, crushed by the overwhelming financial and emotional burden of endless court actions. And the real tragedy is that children don't always know this and they can spend years agonizing over why their parent doesn't want to see them. Eventually their relationship with that parent disintegrates and is swept away by pain and misunderstanding.

Frankly, I was too sickened by a system that allowed this to happen to ever cease my efforts. Weighed against my son's happiness, money was just one more obstacle to overcome.

Perhaps people were moved by the force of my resolve – or maybe I was just plain lucky – but it was often when things were at their most desperate that someone – sometimes a complete stranger – would arrive with a solution. My luck also had a way of running out – as it did when Margaret Turfus finally gave up on me.

I had borrowed the $7,500 bond for my Easter access from friends who were anxious for its return once the visit was over. However, without my knowledge, the money was withdrawn from the court and used to pay a part of my outstanding account with Margaret Turfus. I never got it back and, understandably, no friend wanted to lend me money again for a long while after. More than a year would pass before I would again have sufficient bond money to see my son.

So this is how Helyna Freeland became involved with my application for joint custody. During an examination on affidavit, she questioned Peggy directly about why she and Jack were seeking to adopt Rick.

"Our intention is to make him legitimate," Peggy responded. "We feel this is very important to his sense of pride and to his standing in society, and . . . would increase the strength of the emotional ties of our family unit in Revelstoke."[16] When asked point blank whether the real purpose of the adoption was not to deny me access, Peggy's lawyer advised her not to reply.

Peggy conceded that "a certain warmth" existed between Rick and myself, but she added that this was offset by the unsettling and confusing effect my presence had on Rick. "Very minimal and very controlled" access could be beneficial to our son, she said, but she would not guarantee my access to him should the adoption go through. Nor would she support the idea of joint custody. That, she said, would suggest "a greater involvement on the part of Mr. Di Done, and he already creates a great deal of friction in our lives."

As I had emphasized in OPCR's briefing to the House of Commons Standing Committee, joint custody didn't mean that a child must travel endlessly back and forth between two residences. In any case, the sheer geography between Peggy and I precluded this possibility for Rick. What I was really suggesting was the notion of shared parenting – a still novel concept at the time.

Because it enables both parents to take an active role in their child's upbringing and to make decisions jointly on important matters like health and education, shared parenting demands a great measure of cooperation, teamwork and goodwill on the part of the former spouses. From Peggy's standpoint, we were long past the point of any such cooperation, but I was still willing to try. As sure as I was of my own heartbeat, I knew our son could only benefit from a strong, loving relationship with both his parents. And I can't help dwelling on how much he suffered – and still suffers – from being denied this most basic of childhood needs.

However, in the court structure of the mid-eighties when the large majority of custody decisions were made in favor of the mother, my bid for joint custody was far-fetched at best. It came as no real surprise when the case was dismissed.

That summer of 1985 was a stark contrast to the previous one. The euphoria I had experienced over my reunion with Rick had all but vanished with the bond money. Its loss prevented me from seeing Rick that July. My legal costs continued to rise, as I waited to hear whether I would be accepted for legal aid. My work with OPCR kept me constantly busy, but provided no income. And, to top things off, my relationship with Jackie abruptly ended.

It wasn't that we ceased to care for each other; for we did until the end. But she could no longer stand the stress of the endless legal battles that were the focus of my life. She had volunteered hours and hours to the cause of OPCR and had given me tremendous support personally. She and Natasha had become attached to Rick, as he had to them, and his departures were upsetting for everyone. And it was Jackie who was left to pick up the pieces each time I returned dejected from Revelstoke to face another long separation.

We were both in our mid-thirties and time was moving on. Finally, it was the reality of a life on never-ending hold, waiting always for the next court decision that Jackie could no longer endure either for herself or her daughter.

I threw myself even deeper into the work of OPCR. Despite the fact that some opposition members of the House of Commons Standing Committee were favorable to the concept of joint custody, it seemed increasingly unlikely that their voices would be sufficient to push it through in the majority Conservative government's new divorce legislation.

In mid-September, OPCR joined other parent groups in a demonstration on Parliament Hill in Ottawa. Though by demonstration standards we were a small group of about 50 people, we succeeded in attracting media attention from several major Canadian dailies. Carrying placards, well-fingered snapshots of sons and daughters, and in my case, a large framed photograph of a smiling Rick cradled in my arms, we pressed the government for legislation that would require the courts to presume joint custody as a matter of course.

We also petitioned Justice Minister John Crosbie to require divorcing spouses to seek mediation and conciliation rather than "fighting like animals." We hardly expected to change the world with one small demonstration, but at the very least, we were attracting attention and making contact with those who could make change happen.

All the while, Rick and I kept up our twice-weekly phone calls. As much as possible, I tried to avoid the subject of why I hadn't been to see him for so many months. What was I to say? That I had no money to give the Court – and that without that money, his mom wouldn't let me see him? No, I would just assure him that eventually we would be together and then quickly ask about his friends and schoolwork or whether he had any new jokes to tell me.

That summer and fall, I began dropping by the Piano Bar at Montreal's Ritz Carlton Hotel during the evenings. Stagen and I had recently sold our Lajeunesse property, and the Robert property was sold shortly after. The proceeds of these sales had allowed me to pay off some debts and gain some temporary respite on my credit cards. My newly reinstated credit, my gift for meeting people and making friends easily, and the one or two well-tailored suits that I still had in my possession, all stood me in good stead.

The Ritz was one of the places to go to mix with the city's powerful and influential people. But what really attracted me was the music. There I could relax for a couple of hours and lose myself in the romantic Mediterranean classics of the '40s, that my father and grandfather would play on their accordions and that I still loved to hear.

Within a short while, I became a regular and got to know several of the other patrons and staff. Sometimes an acquaintance would buy a round – and I didn't have to pay at all; occasionally a real-estate deal would emerge out of a chance conversation. Eventually, a few people learned about my legal battles for my son, but the Ritz was one place I rarely talked about my problems or the work I was doing with OPCR. I went there to escape.

As time went on, I was drawn to one of the barmaids – a strikingly tall blond in her early twenties whose name was Brigitte Jalbert. On one particular evening, a difficult customer was giving her a hard time and I intervened to smooth over the problem. Brigitte and I started to talk.

After the required "Are you married?" to which we both answered no, we got on to the subject of families, and then children. I asked her if she liked kids and did she want to have any eventually. "Oh yes," she said, "I want five of them." "I want five kids, too," I answered – and we both laughed – taken aback by the other's answer. It isn't often that you meet someone in a bar – or anywhere for that matter – who tells you they want five kids.

Then she asked me how old I was. "How old do you think I am?" I responded. "About 29," she answered. "Then 29 it is!" I countered with a grin. I was leery of telling her my real age or giving her too many details about my life. I didn't want to frighten her away before we even had a chance to get to know each other.

Before I left the Ritz that evening, she accepted my invitation to have brunch together the following Sunday. "Are you adventurous?" I asked. "Because I have somewhere special in mind. But we'll have to be on our way by seven-thirty in the morning." "Are you serious?" her voice showed her surprise, but she agreed to come just the same.

We set off the next day into a perfect October morning. The sun was shining, there was a delicious crispness to the air, and the sky — already a beautiful deep blue – was a glorious backdrop to the multicolored splendor that was autumn at its peak in Quebec.

We headed onto the Laurentian highway. Barely an hour later, we were drinking in the ·golds, reds and deep greens of the mountains reflected in the clear waters of the lake that lay just beyond the dining room windows of the venerable Auberge La Sapinière in Val David. Brigitte told me she had been intrigued by my invitation. "No one ever asked me for an early morning drive on a first date before," she said. "This is so beautiful."

After breakfast, we drove higher into the mountains and took a boat cruise on Lac des Sables in Sainte-Agathe. Then after lunch, we visited some land I had bought several years before, not far from my parents' chalet. The setting, overlooking a small lake, was very romantic – and her eyes, the loveliest shade of blue. It seemed we had known each other forever, and before long, I told her about Rick and some of the difficulties I had seeing him. But I stopped short of revealing my financial problems.

Eventually the sun and fresh air made us drowsy – and although we hadn't yet exchanged so much as a kiss, we nodded off for a few minutes in each other's arms.

Then we drove to my aunt Toni's country house nearby, where my parents and several other family members were gathered. Brigitte still teases me that I'm the only man she knows who would introduce a woman to his whole family on the first date!

Thanks to my last remaining credit card, we finished the day back in Montreal with dinner, wine, champagne – the works – at a small Italian restaurant downtown. When we finally returned to our respective apartments, I couldn't bear to go to sleep without speaking to her one more time. I called her and we talked until I don't know when. In the morning, I awakened, still cradling the receiver on my arm.

From then on, we saw each other every day. Then, one afternoon, I overheard her telling someone how rich I was. "You'd better sit down," I said, as soon as we met. "I need to talk to you. She looked at me, questioningly.

— "We have to get something straight right now," I began. "I know you think I'm loaded with money – and I didn't want to disappoint you. But the truth is, with all my legal cases, I owe close to $100,000."

— "Is that what you wanted to tell me?" she responded, and to my surprise, a trace of relief flickered across her face. "I thought you were going to break up with me. If you must know, I owe some $20,000 myself. So altogether that makes $120,000!"

— "What a pair we make," I said – and we both burst out laughing. From then on, there was no separating us.

As Brigitte learned more about me and the work I was doing to promote the rights of children, so, too, did I discover that her life had been far from easy. She grew up in Abitibi in northwestern Quebec. When Brigitte was born, her father was a lumberjack, who spent much of the year away from home in the bush. After an accident, he worked as a camp cook, until he and his wife opened a restaurant in the town where the family lived. Then, when Brigitte was only seven years old, her father committed suicide.

With no insurance, her mother was left to fend for herself and nine children. Through hours and hours of hard work, she managed to keep the restaurant going and the family together. But the children had to grow up very quickly. At 12, Brigitte was already waitressing in her mother's restaurant. At 15, she was a barmaid.

The emotional scars that mark every member of Brigitte's family run far deeper than the financial hurt. Sometimes Brigitte will tell me, "No matter how hard it has been for you and Rick, you both know that you love him and that you have fought hard for him and for what you believe in. That is so important. In my family, we loved our father – but it always felt like he abandoned us. I often wonder why, for our sakes, he couldn't try harder to work out whatever problems he had."

From the beginning, Brigitte was a strong supporter of OPCR; from her own experience she understood why the cause I was fighting for, was so important. It was her salary that helped keep us going when we decided to live together in the Robert Street apartment that had become not only the OPCR office, but also my living quarters. When I first moved there, I was still part owner and had lived rent-free, but now that the complex had been sold, we were paying rent. For seven years – up until she became pregnant with our second child – Brigitte worked during the day for OPCR, while in the evenings she kept her job at the Ritz.

At first, her family wasn't sure of me. Brigitte had told them about Rick and my legal struggles and they were very sympathetic that a father would go to such lengths for his son. But they had pre-conceived ideas about the trustworthiness of Italian males and my lack of money and a regular job, didn't help to inspire their confidence. Then, to make matters worse, Brigitte's mother saw an article about me in a Montreal newspaper that mentioned I was a 35-year-old divorced father.

She called her daughter immediately. "You see," she said. "He lied to you about his age and he never told you he was divorced. What else has he kept from you?"

"It's true I thought he was younger," Brigitte answered. "But he was never married. That's part of the reason he's having so many problems seeing his son."

Today Brigitte's family and I get along very well, but it took time to gain their trust. Brigitte, however, believed in me from the start. Even under the strain of all the court cases and a relationship with Rick that would become more difficult as he grew older, she made up her mind to stick with me.

Marriage in her mind was, for better or for worse. She reasoned that we would live "the worse" at the beginning, and hope for "the better" later on.

Ricaardoe Jr. and author: Within first hour of reunion after not having seen each other for almost three consecutive years, at the Enchanted Forest, British Columbia, July 1984.

Ricaardoe Jr. and author: Afternoon of first reunion after not having seen each other for almost three consecutive years, at Kelowna, British Columbia, July 1984.

Ricaardoe Jr. and author: At the end of the afternoon of the first reunion, British Columbia, July 1984.

Ricaardoe Jr. and author: Jasper Park Lodge; the morning following the day of the first reunion, British Columbia, July 1984.

Grandfather Di Done and Ricaardoe Jr.: Ste Lucie des Laurentides, Summer 1984.

Author and Ricaardoe Jr.: Safari Park in Quebec, July 22, 1984.

Author and Ricaardoe Jr.: Ste Lucie des
Laurentides, Quebec, July 1984.

Aunt Toni and Ricaardoe Jr. : Ste Lucie des Laurentides, Quebec, July 1984.

Author and Ricaardoe Jr. : Jr. clinging to his Gremlin doll while returning to Revelstoke, British Columbia, August 1984.

Ricaardoe Jr. and author: Nun's Island, Quebec, December 1984.

Grandfather Di Done and Ricaardoe Jr.: Ste Lucie des Laurentides, Quebec, December 1984.

A HUNGER STRIKE AND THE THREAT OF ADOPTION

Even in my newly found happiness with Brigitte, I was haunted daily by the very real possibility that Peggy and Jack might eventually succeed in adopting Rick and blocking my access to him. We were still awaiting the B.C. Appeal Court's hearing on whether I would have the right to testify at an adoption hearing.

All my energies – and much of OPCR's – were now concentrated on this case and its ramifications for all non-custodial parents. Throughout the months that followed, Brigitte worked alongside me each day, cranking out letter after letter on OPCR's old manual typewriter. Then every evening, she would set off for the Ritz where her income from her barmaid job helped keep a roof over our heads and food on the table.

With each new step in my court case, the waiting seemed endless. I talked with Marilyn Weston and other friends of the organization about how we could awaken people to the problems of thousands of non-custodial parents and their kids across the country who were being kept apart by custody laws that arbitrarily favored one parent over the other, to the long-term detriment of the whole family.

Marilyn pointed out that to rouse public opinion, we first needed to get the media's attention. That's when I decided to embark on a hunger strike.

At first my goal was a 10-day fast. For several years, I had been experimenting with natural approaches to medicine. The years I had spent with the Tokens had piqued my interest. It was not uncommon for me to fast for a day or two at regular intervals to cleanse my system. I had always felt better after it. Nevertheless, my five-foot-eleven-inch frame weighed only 145 pounds (despite my healthy appetite), and my family and friends worried that an extended fast would be courting danger. But I was fit as a result of regular workouts and karate sessions, and I was reasonably confident that my body could handle the stress of a hunger strike. Furthermore, the looming Appeal Court hearing would be a strong incentive to keep me going.

My colleagues at OPCR in Montreal and Ottawa supported me, though they feared for my well-being. But we had all been energized by our first attempts at direct political action through the Parliamentary Committee hearings and the demonstration on Parliament Hill, and needed to keep up the momentum.

The Conservative government's proposed new Divorce Act was still making its way through parliamentary reviews. Sheila Finestone was part of that process and I had been in touch with her several times since our initial meeting. But while amendments supporting joint custody and mandatory mediation had been proposed to the bill, she wasn't optimistic they would survive a vote in the House of Commons.

I had my own ideas about why the proposed reforms were meeting with opposition. In large part, it stemmed from the realities of the political system. Everyone likes to talk about the importance of protecting the "best interests of children," but when it comes to taking action and changing the laws, party interests over-ride every other consideration.

This has been the cause of many a worthwhile idea or reform being defeated — the "wrong" party proposed it. It may be good politics, but it is also flawed, shortsighted social policy. And in the case of divorce legislation where the future happiness of so many children, parents, grandparents and others was at stake, I found such partisanship appalling.

Moreover, there was another factor in the equation. For years, the divorce process had been the exclusive domain of lawyers and judges, and I believe that many in the profession saw the increased use of mediation as a potential threat. If significant numbers of divorcing parents suddenly turned towards mediators in the hopes of reaching less expensive and more collaborative post-divorce settlements and parenting arrangements, the legal profession would lose some of its traditional authority over the process.

It would have to share it with psychologists, social workers and others well versed in the intricacies of human relationships and the art of mediation and consensus building. Even more importantly, couples themselves – for too long sidelined by an adversarial legal system – would regain control over the decisions that would ultimately determine how they would reshape their parental roles and responsibilities after divorce.

As many of my lawyer friends themselves have told me, this was a turn-of-events that would not necessarily sit well with the powerful Bar Associations, many of whose members earned a significant portion of their revenues from divorce litigation.

There were other groups, too, who were wary of the types of reform that OPCR was championing. Among them were certain feminist organizations that viewed these reforms as a backlash to gains women were only recently achieving in divorce settlements. They perceived us as a radical proponent of fathers' rights at the expense of those of mothers. My answer to them was always the same: "It's not fathers' rights or mothers' rights that we should be talking about, but children's rights – children's rights to enjoy the love and care of both their parents. It's not a question of which parent is the better one. From the child's perspective, the best parent is both of them!"

All these conflicting viewpoints fuelled OPCR's sense of urgency to keep the need for reform before the public eye. I originally intended to begin my hunger strike in January, when the House of Commons resumed sitting after the Christmas holidays. My colleagues convinced me it would be better to start just before the holidays to bring home the point that not all families could share the joys of this season of goodwill and togetherness.

One of OPCR's members was Sami Mohanna, a medical doctor who lived in Ottawa where he worked in the Federal Ministry of Health. He had joined OPCR after his own experience with family breakdown. His ex-wife was a physician who had left him for another man; and she had custody of their two boys whom he greatly missed. At the time I met him, he was struggling to make ends meet – paying over one-third of his salary in support payments to his ex-wife who, together with her new boyfriend, was earning at least twice what he was making himself.

He volunteered to supervise me throughout the hunger strike and invited me to stay for a few days with him in Ottawa. This would keep me under his watchful eye and allow me to make the rounds of the Ottawa media – and hopefully attract the attention of the politicians and lawmakers.

I began my hunger strike on December 18, 1985, determined to take nothing but frequent drinks of water to keep me going. It was a bitterly cold day in the Capital, famous for its long, cold winters.

Two colleagues from other organizations I had met as a result of the September demonstration were supposed to escort me around the city to my meetings with different journalists. But the previous day they had had a falling out – and I was left on my own. In any case, one of them had wanted me to place all my emphasis on how the rights of fathers were being neglected. I disagreed. I was there to focus on the rights of children and their need to enjoy the love of both parents and extended families.

The first couple of days passed quickly. A number of journalists agreed to meet with me, and I tramped from bus stop to bus stop, making my way to my various appointments. The reporters listened sympathetically to my cause and the result was some very positive coverage. Physically I felt fine, except that after a full day of climbing on and off unfamiliar buses in -30⁰ Celsius temperatures, how I would have loved a plate of hot pasta and a glass of wine instead of the cold water I had to look forward to!

A couple of days before Christmas, Dr. Mohanna drove me back to Montreal so I would be home with Brigitte and our families during the holidays. Getting into his car, I stumbled as a wave of dizziness swept over me. But the faintness passed after a few seconds.

We spent Christmas day at my aunt Ida's and brought in the New Year with Brigitte's family. I maintained my fast throughout, despite the best efforts of my aunts and other family members who couldn't conceive of any festive occasion without heaping plates of food and plenty of good wine.

"Ricaardoe," they protested, "take something. It's Christmas. Who's going to know?" But when after repeated enticements, I still held out, they eventually gave up. "Have it your way," they said, "but don't be so foolish that you kill yourself." Although they understood my desire to fight for my son, they were also extremely anxious about my health.

Rick never knew about my fast until several years later. The last thing I wanted was an eight-year-old worrying himself sick that his father was starving himself on his behalf.

On day 10, still in good spirits, I resolved to continue my hunger strike at least until January 20 – the day of the Appeal Court hearing. But I was ready to go even longer if that's what it took to attract the attention of the members of Parliament.

Sami Mohanna was still monitoring me closely. When another fourteen days passed and my condition began to deteriorate, he ordered me to add vitamins and liquid protein to my water diet. "If you insist", I reassured my friend with a wry smile. "I didn't start this just to let myself die. I want Rick and me to benefit from whatever changes we succeed in bringing about."

Since the beginning of my hunger strike, I had stayed in frequent contact with Sheila Finestone and her staff. Now I told her of my plan to demonstrate on Parliament Hill on January 13 – the day Parliament reconvened after the Christmas break.

She offered to introduce me to several of her colleagues who were actively interested in the proposed divorce reforms. She also said she would draw public attention to my fast and the potential injustice of a natural father being faced with the loss of his son through an adoption that neither wanted.

Finally, she offered to read in the House of Commons the petition OPCR was circulating across the country. It called for divorce legislation that would legitimize the notion of shared parenting, and guarantee the children of divorce, the right to free and open communication with both their parents. The petition also called on the government to transfer custody from one spouse to the other, if the custodial parent – without valid reason – was deliberately interfering with the other parent's access.

Meanwhile, I continued to give regular interviews to the media. One of these brought me an unexpected phone call from Vincent Della Noce, who was then the federal Progressive Conservative member of Parliament for the Quebec riding of Duvernay-Laval. His wife had heard me on the radio and urged him to see if he could be of help to a fellow Canadian of Italian origin.

When I had explained the problems I had experienced maintaining my visiting rights and the huge expenses I had incurred in legal fees, he assured me I could count on his support when I arrived in Ottawa on January 13. He even said he would do his best to arrange meetings with then Health and Welfare minister, Jake Epp, and with Justice minister, John Crosbie.

Monday, January 13, dawned blustery and cold. In the company of several friends and supporters, I set off on the two-hour drive to Ottawa. This was the twenty-sixth day of my fast; I was down to 125 pounds and my body was craving anything edible. But I was also elated at the prospect of meeting legislators and sensitizing them to the real suffering that the existing legal system was forcing many children of divorced parents to endure.

A bitter wind blew off the Ottawa River when we arrived at the Parliament Buildings. As we braved the cold, I held onto the large framed photograph of my son that I had brought to our other demonstration. Within a few minutes, Sheila Finestone and several of her Liberal colleagues arrived to show their support. Then Vincent Della Noce greeted us and introduced us to other MPs, including two from British Columbia. One represented the riding in which my son lived, and the other was from Vancouver where the Appeal Court hearing would take place in just a few days.

Della Noce then introduced me to Jake Epp. As the Health and Welfare minister shook my hand, he acknowledged that he was all too familiar with the host of social, psychological and financial problems facing families in the throes of a divorce. He noted that the changes being made to the Divorce Act were intended specifically to help enforce custody and maintenance orders. He didn't need to be convinced that mediation and education were far better routes to post-divorce peace and child well being than litigation and court battles.

Later on, I ran into a journalist whom I had met on several previous occasions. I mentioned to her that I had just spoken with Jake Epp, but there seemed to be no way I was going to get in to see the Justice Minister. She said not to give up hope and suggested a plan for getting his attention.

Together we called John Crosbie's office from her cellular phone. When an assistant picked up the call, I introduced myself, saying:

— "Good afternoon. This is Ricaardoe Di Done of the Organization for the Protection of Children's Rights. Earlier today I was told the minister could not spare any time to meet with me. I am now with a member of the press who would like to know if Mr. Crosbie is too busy to be preoccupied by the best interests of children. . ."

There was dead silence for a couple of seconds, and then the aid asked me if I would hold on for a few moments. About two minutes later, John Crosbie himself came on the line and agreed to meet with me.

Shortly after, I found myself face to face with the Justice Minister across a large, impressive desk in his office overlooking Parliament Hill. He listened attentively as I told him our story.

"The worst part is that so many of these obstacles arise from the legal system itself," I said. "Imagine, Mr. Crosbie, that you're a divorced father who loves his kids and has been told by the Court that you can only see them four days a month. And then when the day of your visit finally arrives, their mother finds some reason to cancel it."

"And it just doesn't happen once. It happens repeatedly. So you go back to court and a judge orders your ex-wife to respect your visiting rights. But the story repeats itself and you still don't see your kids. Meanwhile, you're torn apart wondering how they're reacting and what they're being told.

"So you return to court once more and maybe this time the judge gives your ex-wife a fine. But it's not a big enough deterrent to stop her from continuing to interfere with your access. So what are you supposed to do? No one is getting to the root of the problem and you're running out of money to keep going back to court. Does the system automatically assume that fathers care less about their children than mothers? Is it any wonder that some fathers finally just give up, withdraw from their responsibilities and neglect their support payments? Or they kidnap their own children."

"And who suffers the most in all this?" My words just poured out. "The children. They are the ones who have to watch their parents fighting over them. And what about the grandparents? They, too, are innocent bystanders. Does it make any sense that they can be blocked from seeing their grandchildren because of a court decision that favors the custodial parent – and by extension, one side of the family – over the other?"

"Mr. Crosbie, we need a law that ensures that both parents can be deeply involved in their kids' upbringing. So many of the problems encountered today could be avoided if divorcing couples were required to try to reach a mediated settlement, before they could embark on any court action. In a neutral, non-threatening setting, a trained mediator could help them set aside their anger towards each other in order to focus on their children's needs. We could avoid many of the lengthy and expensive legal battles that currently clog our courts. Children would no longer serve as bargaining chips between bitter ex-spouses. And the money both parents save in legal fees could be better spent in raising the kids."

I sank back in my chair, exhausted by my long monologue. The Justice Minister slowly rose, came around his desk and placed his arm on my shoulder. He sympathized with my predicament and acknowledged that cases like mine were indeed problematic. But he also believed they were extreme and represented only a tiny portion of the population, and the government could not make laws based upon their experience. No legal system was perfect, he said, but the changes the government was already planning should make it effective in the majority of cases.

"If the numbers appear small," I responded, "it's because most people in my situation have lost the will to continue. They're just too poor and exhausted to keep on struggling. Yes, I am rare, because no matter what happens, I will not abandon my son."

I left that meeting with the distinct impression that nothing would convince the Justice Minister to incorporate any more changes –no matter how worthy – into the legislation he was shepherding through Parliament. At the snail's pace that reform was moving, I might well be a great-grandfather before any meaningful change occurred.

In a follow-up letter some time later, Crosbie acknowledged that while the expanded use of mediation was desirable, the government lacked the resources to provide mediation services with trained mediators in every community.

My answer to that was the same then as now. The cost of mediation is minimal compared to the huge social costs of family breakdown. Poverty, illness, high drop-out rates from school, juvenile delinquency and even suicide were just some of the consequences that researchers were uncovering at that time. If mediation could alleviate even a portion of those social costs, how many new mediators could be trained? And that didn't even begin to put a figure on the price of human suffering or tally the enormous financial savings that would be achieved if couples could settle their differences out of court.

"Patience," people would tell me. "You can't change the whole system overnight." But I was running out of patience with a system that, in my view, was only aggravating the already formidable problems that come with divorce.

My spirits rose a couple of days later when I learned that Sheila Finestone, true to her word, had addressed the House of Commons about the reasons for my hunger strike. Referring to Peggy and Jack's petition to adopt Rick and change his name yet again – this time to Roaff – she pointed the inconsistency in the laws of two provinces of the same country. Quoted in the official record of the House of Commons debates, she said: "Here we have a non-custodial parent faced with the potential extinguishing of his rightful claim as the father of his child in B.C. ...while in Alberta, his paternity rights were acknowledged and visiting rights accorded".

Where divorce and family law is concerned, she urged that, "There must be some way, through federal and provincial ministers of Justice, to come to an understanding. There should be a mutual undertaking to respect judgments of any provincial jurisdiction which has rendered a decision impacting upon the life of a child." She recommended the creation of a national central registry system that would have the power to intercede in cases where decisions were not being respected. "For it is the child that suffers," she concluded. "That's the sad reality."[17]

A week later, when the new divorce legislation was presented for third reading, Sheila Finestone again spoke on my behalf in Parliament, this time reading our petition that now contained thousands of names. Half a dozen other members of Parliament joined her in reading similar petitions they had received supporting our cause.

In the end, the amendments to the Divorce Act stopped far short of what OPCR had hoped. The Act did not recommend joint custody as the norm; nor did it give any serious weight to mediation. It only obliged lawyers to advise their clients of the availability of mediation services should they wish to use them in negotiating custody or support orders.

Days after the legislation was passed in the House of Commons, Peggy and Jack's case was heard by the B.C. Appeal Court. Now there was nothing further to do but wait for the decision that would come in late March.

That week my family and friends openly voiced their alarm about my weakened condition. "You've done what you set out to do," they told me. "What else can you gain by continuing your hunger strike? It's time to think of your own health while you still can."

What they said was true. Each time I looked in the mirror, I was shocked at the gaunt image that stared back. My once firm muscles had all but dissolved as my famished body consumed itself; I was literally skin and bones. By the thirty-eighth and last day of my hunger strike, I was down to just 115 pounds.

Late in the afternoon of Friday, January 24, 1986, I decided to call off my fast. I had met with OPCR colleagues earlier in the day, but they had long since left. Brigitte was at the Ritz. I was alone in our apartment, staring out the window at the passers-by, bundled up against the cold, who were hurrying down the street. I imagined them arriving at their homes and sitting down to a hot supper with their families after a long week.

A knock at the door interrupted my thoughts. It was my upstairs neighbor who had taken to checking in on me at least once a day. But this time he held a steaming plate of osso bucco.

– "Ricaardoe," he said. "Enough is enough. It's time you eat. I made us some supper and I'm not leaving till you take something."

– "My friend, I think you're right. That's it. Tonight we feast!"

Grinning broadly, he excused himself and returned a few moments later carrying a gallon of homemade red wine.

I knew I should have taken only a little clear broth or some other light nourishment to get my stomach readjusted to eating. But after 38 days, the osso bucco was too tempting and, though it took me several hours, I consumed a respectable portion. The next day, Sami

Mohanna lectured me for my foolishness, but fortunately the meal didn't cause any apparent harm. Nor, it seemed, did the red wine. That night I slept soundly for the first time in months.

The next morning I was gratified to learn that another divorced father, Denis Landry, who lived in nearby Drummondville, had heard about me on the radio, and was taking up the cause by embarking on his own hunger strike.

******

In very real terms, the hunger strike was a turning point for OPCR and gave us credibility with both the politicians and the media. The months we had spent researching our facts, documenting our positions and doggedly pursuing the decision-makers who could bring about reform, were witness to the seriousness of our efforts.

Sheila Finestone later confided to me that I was the first person who alerted her to the problems that non-custodial parents came up against. "It's hard to find such tenacity," she once told me. "When you first came to my office, I thought you must be trying to cover something up. But when I heard your story, and saw your persistence and your pain, I knew you were genuine. You were also the first person to push for grandparents' rights."

My hunger strike was also a personal turning point. For the past two years I had given almost all my energy to my legal case and OPCR, but in the back of my mind, I still believed I would eventually resume my business interests. Now I knew my life was taking a new path and I would not rest until stories like mine and Rick's no longer happened. I also knew I couldn't live forever on the handouts of others. For the first time since OPCR's founding, I turned my attention to how we were going to fund our ongoing activities.

We began organizing carwashes and other activities every few weeks to raise money. Between these and a few government-sponsored projects that enabled us to hire people on a temporary basis to further our research, we scraped together enough money for an operating budget of just over $16,000 in 1986. "To think that not long ago, I had been dealing in projects worth millions of dollars", I told myself. Even if it wasn't much, it was a start.

From my early contacts with influential people, I had also quickly learned the impact of professional and academic credentials. While people sympathized with my position, they tended to regard it as being atypical of the majority of divorce and custody cases, and asked for studies to back up my conviction that countless children were actually suffering the costly repercussions of the way custody cases were handled in the courts.

That realization led to the creation of OPCR's first scientific committee. Through a mutual acquaintance, I had met Dr. Jean-François Saucier, a noted Montreal child psychiatrist and member of the University of Montreal's Faculty of Medicine.

Dr. Saucier had long studied the effects of divorce on children. His research had shown that children of divorced parents suffered from even greater stress than those who had lived through the death of a parent. According to Saucier, it was ongoing conflict between divorced parents that most negatively affected a child's long-term development.[18]

He consented to be a founding member of our scientific committee, and with his help, it soon expanded to include several other respected professionals who daily saw the effects of divorce on children. Among them were psychologist Dr. Liliane Spector-Dunsky, social worker and mediator Dominic D'Abate, and social worker Lorraine Filion, a pioneer in what would become the family mediation service of the Quebec Superior Court.

Over the next year and a half, we developed a program for an international conference whose theme was to be "Children and Divorce: How to intervene before, during and after?" We recruited speakers and undertook the extensive legwork that would result in the conference becoming a reality two years later.

In the meantime, OPCR also needed strong support from highly credible individuals in both law and education if we were to accomplish the extent of reform we believed necessary. The problem was how did we go about getting that support?

Happily for the organization, a daring but offbeat idea worked. I placed an ad in the Quebec Bar Association's monthly newspaper announcing that OPCR was looking to expand its legal committee and was seeking the services of interested members of the profession who would be willing to volunteer their time. The ad included the date and location of the "next" meeting.

At the appointed hour, six individuals turned up, among them family lawyers Philip Shaposnik, Marcel Tremblay, Hugues Létourneau, and Yves Baron. The latter was then chairman of the Quebec Association of Family Lawyers.

As I introduced myself and began to talk about the organization, Marcel Tremblay interrupted to ask where was the rest of the committee.

— "Actually there is no committee – yet", I had to confess. "I was hoping this group would consider helping me create one".

I held my breath during the pause that followed. Marcel Tremblay was the first to respond.

— "Are there any other surprises?"

— "No, that's the only one."

To my delight and great relief, they took my unorthodox methods in their stride and several members of that initial gathering have continued to share their expertise with OPCR for many years.

Shortly afterwards, we used a similar method to set up an education committee, attracting among others, Dr. Helen Amoriggi of McGill University's Faculty of Education. Over time, the three separate committees were amalgamated into one scientific committee that remains an invaluable source of guidance and inspiration to this day.

******

In the midst of these efforts to set OPCR on sound footing, I learned the decision of the B.C. Appeal Court. On March 26, 1986, it ruled in my favor and upheld my right to contest my son's adoption and testify during an open hearing in court!

Only a few months earlier, the B.C. Adoption Act had been amended to stipulate that, in the case of unmarried parents, only the mother's consent was necessary for an adoption to take place. I had feared that this change would weigh heavily against me.

Yet, on behalf of the Appeal Court, the Honorable Mr. Justice Seaton argued otherwise: "Any person who has a sufficient tie with a child ought to be heard before an order is made under the Adoption Act," he wrote in his ruling.

He went on to say that even if the Act didn't require a natural father's consent, it didn't follow that I should not receive notice of an adoption hearing. "I conclude that a person with rights of access should have notice," wrote Seaton. "I also conclude that a father who has ties with his child, such as this father has, is a necessary party to proceedings to determine what is in the best interests of the child..."[19]

Mr. Justice Seaton also pondered whether an access order could survive an adoption order. After citing conflicting rulings from previous judgments, he determined: "Generally there should be a complete break and all former access terminated, but there will be cases where that should not be so." In effect, he maintained that a judge granting an adoption could, taking into account the child's best interests, rule that an existing access order remain in force or make a new access order.[20]

After this Appeal Court decision, the B.C. Adoption Act was again amended, this time to require the consent of a natural father. The ruling lifted an enormous weight off my shoulders. If Peggy and Jack persisted in their attempt to adopt Rick, I would, at least, have the right to oppose the adoption in court. There was also some small comfort in knowing that my access need not necessarily cease should the adoption ever go through. That said, I still found repugnant the idea that my son could be adopted against both his and my wishes. Nevertheless, it was a fact with which both of us would eventually have to come to terms.

For the moment, I had even more immediate worries where Rick was concerned. I hadn't seen him since Easter of the previous year. Ever since the Alberta court had turned over my $7,500 bond to Margaret Turfus' legal firm, I had been unable to raise any more money. In the spring of 1986, I once again asked the Alberta Court of Queen's Bench to forego the bond requirement. For several years I had shown my good faith by complying with all court orders and I argued that my conduct was such that a bond was no longer necessary. Lack of money was the only thing keeping Rick and me apart.

I still don't understand how not seeing the father who loved him could be judged in my son's best interests, yet, in early June, my request was denied.

A few days later, I received a phone call from an individual who introduced himself as Marcel Corbeil and explained that he was a local businessman.

— "Hello, Mr. Di Done, how are you today?" he said, as I picked up the phone.

— "I'm fantastic," I responded cheerfully, as I always did, regardless of how I really felt.

— "Are you sure?" he pursued.

— "Of course."

Then he told me he had followed the media coverage of my hunger strike and had heard me interviewed again recently.

— "What about your son?" he continued. "I thought you hadn't been able to see him for over a year."

— "Oh, that's a different story."

— "Maybe I can help," he continued. "What would it take to bring your son to Montreal?"

— "There's a bond condition," I explained, hardly daring to acknowledge the faint spark of hope that began to rise within me. "I have to deposit $7,500 each time I see my son and I don't have the money."

—"That's not a problem," he responded. "Consider it taken care of. What else do you need?"

I paused just long enough to catch a deep breath, before continuing:

— "There's also the air fare to go pick him up. But it's not that simple. First I have to fly to Calgary, then rent a car to drive to Revelstoke where my son lives, drive back to Calgary with him and then board a flight for Montreal together. Then when it's time for his return, we have to do it all over again in reverse. It's only when he comes here that his grandparents and the rest of the family have a chance to see him," I added. "We're a close family and we all miss him very much."

— "Give me the dates you want to go and I'll arrange everything," said the voice on the other end of the phone line. "Bring your son to Montreal and have a good time together."

I was stunned. I felt like someone trapped in a relentless whirlpool who suddenly finds a lifeline fast within his grip. Marcel and I met a few days later when he brought me a cheque to cover the bond money and travel expenses. By the end of June, $7,500 was deposited at the Courthouse in Edmonton. It wasn't until a long time after, that Marcel, who was close to me in age, mentioned that he, too, had children he could rarely see because of a divorce.

I telegrammed Peggy immediately to advise her the bond money was in place and that I would be able to bring Rick to Montreal for the month of July. I can only imagine her lack of enthusiasm, but she did nothing to prevent the visit.

Rick and I spent a few days catching up together in the West, before flying to Montreal where he would meet Brigitte for the first time and be swept up in reunions with family and friends. One evening we were having dinner with some friends in a Calgary restaurant when Rick suddenly asked, "Is everyone here Italian?" When I said, yes, as a matter of fact, we were, he responded with a huge grin, "Good! I love Italians!"

Throughout this and other visits, I consciously avoided any reference to the upcoming adoption hearing and all the other legal proceedings that his mother and I were engaged in. He had enough to deal with in his young life. This was supposed to be a holiday and I meant for us all to have a good time.

Rick accepted Brigitte as another member of the family and she was sensitive enough to give us the space we needed. He loved to swim and the three of us passed many days with my parents and my aunt Toni and uncle Richard at the lake in the Laurentians.

Rick and I also liked to visit a small Italian café just across the street from our Place Robert apartment. Like most kids his age, my son had discovered video games, and Pac Man was at the height of its popularity. The café's manager, Vallerio Maggiore, had a soft spot for Rick, and every so often passed him a roll of quarters to keep the Pac Man game going. He also refused to accept any money for the juices and ice creams my son ordered during his stay.

Vallerio Maggiore was also extremely good to me. Over the years, on those dreaded days when Rick and I had to catch an early morning return flight to B.C., he would open his café at 5:00 a.m. just to accommodate me. Along with the special cappuccino he knew I liked, he offered many a comforting word.

In late July, as the day approached for the trip back to Revelstoke, Rick withdrew into himself. I promised him I would do everything I could to see him again soon, but neither of us could be sure whether "soon" meant two months or two years. Marcel Corbeil's generosity had brought us together completely unexpectedly, but how many times does one receive a gift like that?

Something my son said on the drive back to Revelstoke was a heart-rending reminder of how much he was being affected by the strife that surrounded him. "Papa," he began, "if it's OK with you, can I hug you goodbye before we get to Revelstoke?"

I looked at him inquiringly.

— "I don't want to upset Mom and Jack," he added, his expression confused.

— "No problem – whatever feels better is all right with me," I said, struggling to keep my expression even.

This conversation would come back to me a few months later when Peggy submitted in Court another psychological report from Jim Fornelli in support of her and Jack's adoption bid. The report, which had been prepared before this latest trip to Montreal, stated that Rick "clearly has not suffered from not seeing his father . . .and it can be speculated that not seeing his natural father has contributed to his wholesome development." Fornelli quoted Rick as saying: "I don't miss Ricaardoe very much, but I am not going to tell him that. He will get mad . . ."

If Rick had said that, I didn't for a minute believe he meant it. If so, why did his eyes light up whenever we met? And why did all the photos of our times together show a happy, smiling boy who spontaneously reached for me and looked genuinely at ease in his surroundings? Why, too, every time I had to take him back to Revelstoke, was my son so vocal about not wanting to leave me? When he was much older, Rick himself shed some light on how a young child learns to submerge his own feelings in order to cope with such a constant tug-of-war on his emotions: "I told them all what I thought they wanted to hear."

Each year, as he grew more aware of the conflict between Peggy and me, he faced ever different and conflicting messages. I remember one evening when he was nine or ten, he telephoned me and, out of the blue, asked, "Is it true, Papa, that I'm a bastard? Because Jack and Mom say that's why they want to adopt me – so we can be a real family." He started to cry.

"Hey," I said. "Who told you that? You're a fine boy, a great boy. You have a real mom and a real dad and you have grandparents and aunts and uncles and cousins and we all love you very much. You're not a bastard and whoever told you that is one himself."

That was exactly how I felt and I was straight with my son. But what else was he hearing from others? He was now very aware that the adoption was a distinct possibility, and sometimes I would lie awake at night, tears streaming down my face, agonizing over what he had been told and how he was interpreting it.

Of one thing I could be sure: my version of reality, and Peggy's version of reality, were not one and the same.

Everyone creates his or her own version of reality, according to Aldo Morrone, a Montreal social worker and internationally recognized expert on mediation. (I first met Aldo when I took a course on mediation that he was giving jointly with Justin Lévesque, another respected authority on mediation who has published a book on the subject and trained mediators in a number of different countries. Ever since that course, I have been fortunate to count both men among my friends). Aldo also says that problems between couples arise when either person or both believe that their version of reality is the only version.

I can only assume that in Peggy's version of reality, she was acting in Rick's best interests, even as she sought to exclude me from his life. How she justified this when she knew how attached Rick was to me and I to him – I will never know. But for years she maintained that Rick needed a secure family life, that she and Jack were the ones best positioned to give this to him, and that I was a constant threat to the stability of their home.

At one point, in the spring of 1986, she had written to me suggesting that if I truly cared for our son, I wouldn't be trying to break down "the fabric of the family that is his basic security and support."

— "For a situation to have become bitter," her letter continued, "there must have been opposition along the line, and had one of us voluntarily backed off, then certainly life would have been more peaceful . . . In determining who should have made the exit, I submit that I, who bore Branden and raised him properly, without assistance for the most part and never complaining about my choice, should undoubtedly have the first priority to continue nurturing him."[21]

Certainly her view wasn't uncommon. Aldo Morrone explains that many psychologists and social therapists in the 1960's and 70's supported the idea that one parent naturally had a closer psychological bond to the child than the other. And he maintains that such thinking gave rise to the notion of the single-parent family – a notion which, though well-intentioned, is in his view, "testimony to the unfortunate way that divorce has been handled over the years. There is no such thing as a single-parent family," he says. "By definition, there have to be two parents."[22]

In two different perceptions of reality lay the crux of the strife between Peggy and me. She believed that she was the one who could best provide Rick with the stable family life that he desperately needed, whereas I refused to argue over who was the best parent or the one most suited to raising our son. We were both his parents and he needed what each of us could offer him in love, guidance and emotional and physical care.

That's the real tragedy of our story: both of us wanted the best for their child, but with differing viewpoints we were incapable of finding common ground – at least not without help from someone trained to lead us through our different versions of reality. And at the time we most needed it, that help was nowhere to be found – least of all in the legal system to which we had entrusted the best interests of our son.

******

And so it continued. At the end of September 1986, Marcel Corbeil contacted me and asked me once again if the bond money on deposit in Alberta since June had been returned. I explained that I had not yet received the money and that this was another lingering source of frustration. Even though I had returned Rick to his mother on time, it often took months for the bond to be reimbursed.

Marcel said there was no rush; he was only asking because he needed someone to represent his ski accessory company at a trade show in Calgary in mid-October. He had business obligations elsewhere and had thought of me.

"You'll be doing me a favor," he said. And since the bond is still with the Court, you could take a few extra days to see your son."

"I'd be more than happy to go," I said, "but the ski show is on a weekend. Outside of Christmas, Easter and summer vacation, the only time I can have access to my son is on a weekend. It would mean staying an entire extra week to be able to see him."

"Don't worry about that," he answered. "I want you to go and I can take care of any extra expenses."

I jumped at his offer and telegrammed Peggy immediately asking whether there would be a problem about arranging a visit with Rick for the weekend of October 24. When Rick called me shortly after, I mentioned there was a good chance I would be coming to see him and we began making plans.

A couple of days later I had still heard nothing from Peggy. Then Rick called back to say he couldn't see me after all because the whole family was going out of town. When I asked to speak to his mom, he said she wasn't there. When I called back a little later, Peggy answered, but hung up as soon as she heard my voice. On my next try, Jack answered and slammed down the phone.

I then wrote to the Amicus, Sandy Hogan, explaining what had happened and confirming my intention to spend time with Rick. "Since I cannot make any arrangement over the phone or in any other way, I will be there on October 24 at 7:00 p.m." I sent similar letters to Peggy, her Edmonton lawyer, and my lawyer. Only after my letters were already on their way did I receive a typed half-page letter from Peggy stating that Rick had an out-of-town doctor's appointment that would keep the family away the entire weekend of the twenty-fourth. The terse message concluded: "We have pre-arranged appointments and plans involving Branden on all other weekends in October as well."

There I was with a non-refundable airline ticket that expired October 28 and Peggy saying she could not find any time convenient for my visit. Once again, I had to ask the Court in Alberta to enforce my visiting rights. Finally, through our respective lawyers, Peggy agreed that I could see Rick for at least part of the weekend in question.

As wrenching as these negotiations with Peggy were, there was one bright side to this whole incident that touched me deeply. On the second day of the ski show, I was amazed to see Marcel Corbeil himself walk up to the booth where I was working. He said he had completed his other business earlier than anticipated and had decided to attend the show after all. Something about the way he looked left me wondering since, whether he had concocted his story as a means of allowing me to see my son.

During the interval between the ski show and my visit with Rick, I drove to Edmonton to spend some time with Walter Morandini. Walter's family, like mine, had originated from the north of Italy and we had met several years before when he had done some renovations on one of the properties in which I was then a partner. Since then we had become friends. He had spent much of his childhood in an Italian orphanage and it had not been a happy experience. He was always concerned about how my son was doing.

I had made an appointment to meet with Sandy Hogan to discuss my latest difficulties in obtaining access to Rick, and to sound out his opinion on the adoption question. Walter volunteered to come with me.

He was as shocked as me about how that conversation with Sandy Hogan unfolded. After I had brought him up to date on recent events, the Amicus remarked: "Why do you want your son with you so much? If my wife had ever left me with our children, I wouldn't have known where to begin."

"I'm sorry you feel like that," I responded. "But I have no problem caring for my son."

Then he really floored us with a comment to the effect that it was well known that Italian husbands treated their wives like slaves.

"Actually, Italian women have a lot of courage," I said. "They work very hard for their families just as Italian men do."

Walter and I left in disgust. Either Sandy Hogan was completely immersed in stereotypes and outdated thinking, or he was deliberately trying to provoke me to show how "unstable" I was.

A similar incident occurred when I brought Rick back after our brief visit the following weekend. Walter had accompanied me on the drive to Revelstoke and he, Rick and I had had a pleasant time together. However, the mood changed dramatically when the three of us encountered Jack in the doorway of the Frontier Restaurant – our usual meeting spot. Before I realized what was happening, Jack made a grab for my wrist with enough force that my watch came off in his hands. He threw it on the pavement angrily and told me if I knew what was best for me, I'd never come back. "The boy has a father and mother and I'm the father here," he said angrily. "We don't need another father."

Then he turned to Walter: "And you, yeah you – what's your name?" When Walter said he was a friend, Jack countered: "You'd better not come back here either."

At that point the restaurant owner intervened and within a few minutes, the RCMP arrived and took my complaint. All the while, Rick just stood there in disbelief and frustration, not knowing where to look or who to turn to.

Over the next few months, there were also incidents involving my scheduled twice-weekly phone calls with Rick. If too many days went by without a call, I would telephone him person-to-person. On one such occasion, Jack answered. When the operator asked for Branden (I had purposefully said "Branden" so as not to cause any unnecessary problems), Jack asked her to hold on and called out in a loud voice: "Anyone here by the name of Branden?" A few seconds later, he came back on the line and said there was no Branden there. The next time we saw each other, Rick mentioned that he had overheard the whole incident.[23]

At other times, the line would suddenly disconnect without notice in the middle of our conversation.

As Rick grew older, his own exasperation with the situation began to show more often. One day he told me outright he was tired of having to call me like clockwork twice a week.

— "Why can't I just call you when I feel like it? he asked sharply.

— "Well, I wouldn't have a problem with that," I answered. "You're absolutely right. You should be able to call me whenever you feel like it. Just like I should be able to call you whenever I feel like it. And Grandma and Grandpa and aunt Toni and the rest of the family should be able to call you whenever they feel like it. But under the circumstances, that isn't possible. So don't you think we should live with what we have and make the best of it."

— "Yeah, you're right," he said with a long sigh.

That Christmas, I was again able to bring him to Montreal, thanks once more to the generosity of Marcel Corbeil. On the surface everything went well, but both Brigitte and I noticed a growing restlessness in Rick and he complained of frequent stomach aches.

Not long after the holidays were over, Marcel called again. This time he let me know that due to a business commitment, he needed me to return the money he had loaned me for the bond. "I'm still waiting for it," I said, recounting how after each visit, my lawyer had to obtain formal confirmation from Peggy's lawyer that Rick had been safely returned to his mother. Only once this confirmation had been received, would the Court in Edmonton begin the process to release the money.

— "Even here you can work the system if you're so inclined," I added. "It's easy for people to drag their feet and cause delays. But you have my word I'll do whatever I can to get the money back to you as quickly as possible."

— "I have some contacts in the Quebec Justice department," responded Marcel Corbeil. "If you don't mind, I'll give them a call. Maybe they can help."

— "Of course I don't mind," I said. "Do whatever you can. You've already been more generous than I could have ever imagined."

Soon after, I, too, called the office of Herbert Marx, the Minister of Justice of Quebec. I was put through to one of his advisors. Tony Manglaviti listened as I explained my problems with bond money and access. Based on his own experience as a lawyer, he thought that returning the bond money should be a routine matter and was surprised at the difficulties I had described. He offered to make inquiries about my case with the Alberta Attorney General's office.

A short time later, the bond money was returned and I was able to reimburse Marcel Corbeil in full.

But as for any future visits with my son, I was back to square one: scraping together the bond money through loans and handouts from my father, other family members and a number of loyal and very patient friends. My father wasn't a rich man by any means, but he made many a sacrifice on my behalf. So, too, did several other family members.

And there were many friends who supported me, time and again, because they were touched by my steadfast resolve to maintain my relationship with my son. One such person was Charles Caruana. I met him originally through his wife, who worked at the local municipal office, and who asked me about OPCR and if we needed volunteers. She also mentioned that her husband was studying for his chartered accountant's license.

Not long after, during a fundraising carwash that we organized in the neighborhood, a car drove up and a pleasant-faced man rolled down his window. "I'm the husband of the woman you spoke to at the municipal office," he said, having seen all the OPCR signs. "My wife told me about you and she mentioned you might need help with your accounting. If you like, I can see what I can do."

A few days later he came by the OPCR office, which was still housed in our basement apartment. "I felt sorry for you," he confessed many years later. "You had no staff on the payroll; you were undernourished and you looked like you weren't getting enough sleep. You had one good suit that grew more and more threadbare the longer I got to know you. Yet as far as your son was concerned, you had to be the most determined person I have ever met."

Now he jokes about the way I was living, but it was no joke at the time. During that first meeting, I had nothing in the fridge to offer him except some water I had boiled up with dandelion greens – an herbal tonic I used to take at that time.

"Bitter herbs", Charles reminds me today. "They were truly your bitter herbs".

For several years thereafter, Charles kept OPCR's books for free and he is still involved in the organization. Soon after our meeting, he also arranged for OPCR to move into our first real office space. He and some associates had some unused space they offered us rent-free – an arrangement that persisted for some time.

Charles also introduced me to Vincent Chiara, a lawyer who would donate many hours of legal services to OPCR and to my personal legal struggle for my son.

They were just two of many people whose generosity enabled me to make regular trips to see Rick. When I desperately needed cash for the bond, they would say: "Try to raise as much as you can on your own, and we'll make up the difference." Often the difference would add up to several thousand dollars, and even though it would take ages to repay them, they never pressured me for the money.

Sometimes an airline would give me a free pass when I explained how OPCR was working to reform the custody laws so that other parents and children would be spared what my son and I were going through. And on numerous occasions, a local service club paid for my flights west. Then Vincent Chiara introduced me to a sympathetic travel agent who went out of his way to help me keep costs down whenever I traveled to see my son.

All these people made a huge difference in helping Rick and I overcome the more than 4,000 kilometers that separated us. Even so, that vast physical distance was only one of our problems. Parental alienation was a far more dangerous and insidious foe. During Rick's next visit to Montreal at Easter of 1987, I learned first-hand how children can be manipulated by one parent to turn against the other.

There had been yet more friction over the arrangements for this visit. Once again I had tried to have the bond condition eliminated to no avail. Then to reduce travel costs, I asked the Court if Peggy could put Rick (who was now nine) on a plane in Calgary and I would meet him at the airport in Montreal. (I knew Peggy was planning a trip to Alberta around Easter. Two months before, she had given birth to her second child – Rick's brother Jason – and

Rick had mentioned that the family was planning a visit to the Tokens to introduce them to their newest grandchild. I reasoned they would be passing through Calgary on the way.)

Peggy responded with another petition seeking to further restrict my access. In her affidavit, she said she didn't approve of Rick traveling alone at his age. She also said that the twice-weekly phone calls were a major source of stress and suggested they be eliminated, and that the frequency of my access be reduced. She also wanted to prevent me from leaving B.C. with Rick – which would effectively have prevented any contact with his grandparents and other relatives in Montreal.

To support her case, she submitted another recent psychological evaluation of Rick, this one from a Vernon psychologist named Martin K. Impey.

Impey's report was based on interviews with Peggy, Jack and Rick, and referred to several other previous evaluations that Peggy had obtained. But glaring in their omission were any of the evaluations that I had submitted over the years, attesting to the good relationship my son and I enjoyed. I could only surmise that Impey had never seen these. What really disturbed me was his conclusion that Rick was actually afraid of me.

He referred to some drawings he had asked Rick to do, immediately after he had encouraged my son, with little success, to talk about me. According to Impey, the drawings were ostensibly about an animal going on a trip.

Rick's drawings showed two animals: one quite a bit smaller than the other. In Impey's interpretation, the small animal initially looked pleased when it encountered the larger one. But after the larger "dangerous animal with long fangs and an angry look" threatened, "You're not going to get away!", the smaller one said, "Oh, yes, I am, I hope," and made its escape. According to Impey, the small animal was Rick and the dangerous one me. He fully supported Rick's adoption and counseled Peggy to seek a court order to prevent any further contact between the two of us.

How he could come to such a damning conclusion without ever having met or talked to me was beyond my comprehension.

This is why many concerned social workers, psychologists and other professionals called upon to act as expert witnesses in custody and access cases are themselves calling for the creation of professional standards in this field. For several years, OPCR has benefited from the counsel of Dr. William Rowe, Director of McGill University's School of Social Work. He believes that anyone who wants to practice in the delicate area of custody and access evaluations should first be required to follow a certified training program that demonstrates their competence and ensures their continued involvement as the family environment changes. He is also in favor of setting up a formal complaint procedure to review assessments whose quality is in doubt.

Otherwise, as he puts it, there is a constant danger that battling parents will take the attitude: Smile while you're talking to the assessor, present your best face, get through the day and you'll get the best deal. And the assessment is reduced to one more way of getting back at an ex-spouse, rather than a useful tool for discovering what is truly in the children's best interests.

Impey's recommendations notwithstanding, an Alberta court order in April 1987 upheld my access rights unchanged and I was able to bring Rick to Montreal for a week. Exactly how great a toll the constant bickering and legal squabbling were having on him I would soon discover.

Part way through his stay, I had arranged for him to meet with Dr. Liliane Spector-Dunsky, a psychologist with the Jewish General Hospital's Institute of Community and Family Psychiatry in Montreal. For over a year, we had been working together on OPCR's scientific committee, and she was familiar with the pending adoption hearing. She offered to meet with Rick and give me her own professional opinion about his state of mind.

The meeting lasted only a few minutes. Rick made it abundantly clear that he was fed up with being dragged from one psychologist or psychiatrist to the next and being put through test after test. In a subsequent report, Dr. Dunsky commented on his sadness and suffering: "He wishes someone could take a decision, whatever it may be, as long as the ongoing tension ends…" He wants "to be able to see and be in contact with both his biological parents."

She painted a picture of a confused, pained, puzzled child with an understandable lack of trust in the adults who, at this point in his life, were most important to him. "Alternatively and under the right conditions," she added, "he could also be allowed to recover some inner peace and devote his energies to pursuing his growth."

The evening of that interview, Rick and I were lounging around, watching television. There were just the two of us, as Brigitte was still working evenings. Rick showed me a large wart on the underside of his foot for which he was being treated.

A while into the TV program, I felt his foot pressed against my leg. I moved my leg away slightly, but a few minutes later, the same thing happened. Then I realized he was deliberately pressing the foot with the wart against my skin. When I turned to look at him, he quickly pulled away.

"Hey," I said, "you're doing that on purpose. I think you want me to catch it."

I was completely unprepared for what came next.

— "I do – because I don't want to see you anymore." He almost spit the words out. "My name isn't Ricaardoe Di Done, it's Branden," his voice rose in pitch. "You only want to see me to make trouble for my mom. You're not my father – my father is Jack!"

I stared at him in disbelief. Stay calm, I told myself. Otherwise, you're history.

"I am your father and I can prove it to you," I said, keeping my voice as matter-of-fact as possible. Then I went to a drawer and, fumbling through a stack of papers, pulled out my copy of his original birth certificate that gave his name as Ricaardoe Branden Di Done and listed me as his father. Then I found the Court order of Justice Dea that had reinstated my visiting rights.

Finally I said, " I have something I want you to watch". For over half an hour, we sat side by side glued to the video of Marilyn Weston's *As It Is* show that documented my relationship with Peggy. Our struggle over Rick's custody, the three years I had been unable to see him, and all the legal and financial hardships I had endured in order to maintain my access to him, including reversing the initial adoption. When the video was over, tears were streaking down his face. He leaned over and hugged me. "I'm sorry", he said, "I just don't know whom to believe anymore."

"I'm going to call your mother right now", I told him. "You can pick up the extension and listen yourself to what she has to say."

I put the call through and was never so glad to hear Peggy's voice on the other end of the line. "Hi", I said, "I just wanted you to know that Rick is fine and his visit is going well."

Then I steered the conversation around to future access visits, without mentioning that our son was listening. "Why don't we try to reach some agreement so that our son can see both of us freely. You know how much these visits mean to me. You know how much I love him." Then she responded, "Ricaardoe, I know you're a good father and that you love him a great deal ...," and she added something about how it would still be better for Rick if I stopped seeing him until he was older and able to make his own decisions.

I can't recall how the conversation ended. All I cared about was that Rick had heard those magic words. Afterwards, he and I sat down and really talked things out. I told him the whole story from my point of view, stressing over and over that I had fought all these years not to prevent him from enjoying his mother's care and affection, but to ensure that he grew up knowing the love of both his parents and his entire family.

That confrontation brought us closer than ever, but it made me keenly aware of just how vulnerable he was.

The next day, OPCR held its first annual Easter party for underprivileged children, many of whom were victims of family breakdown and no strangers to the economic hardships and other social problems that all too frequently followed. I asked Rick and my father if they'd like to come along. After the emotional grind we'd been through the day before, it was so good to see him with the other kids, laughing with his grandfather, eyes wide as he took in a room full of brightly colored balloons, crazy-costumed clowns, black-caped magicians and a seemingly endless supply of chocolate.

*****

Within a day of Rick's return to Revelstoke, I got a letter from a Kamloops lawyer named Kristian Jensen. He was informing me that he had just taken on Peggy and Jack as clients and that they intended to proceed with the adoption petition as quickly as possible. He also noted that they would seek to have any access on my part denied if the adoption order was successful. Of all Peggy's lawyers, he was the only one I can say I truly disliked.

At the time, I no longer had a lawyer in B.C. representing me who was familiar with the case. Cheryl Hass had since left Kamloops and was living in another province. For more than a year, I had been trying to get myself approved for legal aid as my financial situation was as precarious as ever. My legal bills, expert witness reports and court-related travel costs since the start of the original custody hearing had now reached more than $200,000. In addition, the outstanding balance on my credit cards was in the thousands of dollars. On top of this, my family and friends had already given me some $40,000 over the years to help me out.

To qualify for legal aid in B.C., my application first had to be approved by the corresponding authorities in Quebec. An initial application made in the fall of 1986 had been turned down and it was only after I appealed this decision and appeared in person to explain exactly how I had reached my present circumstances, that the review board finally approved my eligibility.

I was still waiting for legal aid in B.C. to appoint me a lawyer, when I received another notification in June 1987 – this time from Peggy's Edmonton lawyer. Briefly, it stated that Peggy was applying to have the jurisdiction for everything related to Rick's custody transferred from Alberta to British Columbia.

Peggy insisted that this had nothing to do with trying to circumvent my access rights. She argued that neither she nor I retained any strong ties in Alberta and that continued litigation in that province was proving a real financial hardship for her and Jack. Furthermore, she noted that the Amicus in Alberta supported the transfer of jurisdiction because Rick had now resided in B.C. for several years and the best evidence related to any custody issue would be found in that province. The Amicus also noted that funding restrictions prevented his office from conducting investigations outside the province of Alberta and, as a consequence, its ability to obtain unbiased information in Rick's case was greatly hampered.

I didn't see things in quite the same light. I had little confidence in the Amicus, who from my point of view, had always been biased in favor of the mother. Moreover, the undertakings had restricted both Peggy's and my ability to successfully initiate changes to the original custody order in another province (though both of us had tried). This was critical because it eliminated the problem of conflicting orders.

There was a consistency to be gained by remaining under Alberta law. Its courts had long recognized my status as Rick's father and, on several occasions, had enforced my access rights when Peggy tried to do away with them. The thought of starting all over in a new jurisdiction, with differing laws and legal interpretations, was too much.

Quite frankly, I believed that Peggy's real reason for wanting the jurisdiction transferred was to smooth the way for the adoption and what she hoped would be the eventual elimination of my access rights. I consulted with another lawyer at Freeland Royal McCrum who agreed to contest the jurisdiction transfer on my behalf. By now, I was also receiving legal aid in Alberta.

Against this unfolding background, I brought Rick to Montreal for our annual month-long July visit. We were both anxious about this latest twist in his mother and Jack's push for adoption, but avoided any discussion of it. We wanted to enjoy our holiday together and any mention of the strife between Peggy and me only caused Rick more pain. Then I learned that the hearing on the jurisdiction transfer was scheduled for July 31 in Edmonton, the very day Rick and I would be making the return trip west.

I called my Edmonton lawyer in a panic. "There's no way I can be in court that day," I said, worried this might be some new tactic to thwart me. "They know that's the day I have to bring Rick back." My lawyer wasn't overly concerned. She said Peggy wouldn't be there either and the case would simply proceed on the basis of our affidavits.

Before leaving Montreal I also talked to Tony Manglaviti to see whether he thought the date of the hearing was cause for alarm. He believed it very unlikely that an Alberta Court would release us from our long-standing undertaking to use that jurisdiction. "After

Grandfather Theodore Di Done, Ricaardoe Jr. and Grandmother Francesca Di Done: Reunion after having been separated for one year and a half, Montreal, Quebec, July, 1986.

Ricaardoe Jr. and author: Montreal, Quebec, Summer 1986.

Author and Ricaardoe Jr.: Ste Lucie des Laurentides, Quebec, Easter 1987.

Author and Ricaardoe Jr.: Ste Lucie des Laurentides, Quebec, Summer 1988.

**Author, Aunt Toni, Brigitte Jalbert, Odette Landry, Ricaardoe Jr.,
Grandfather Di Done, Denis Landry, Diane Landry: Gathering at chalet of
Grandfather Di Done, Ste Lucie des Laurentides, Quebec, Summer 1988.**

Author and Ricaardoe Jr.: Jr. quietly resting on father at Denis Landry's
residence prior to departure for British Columbia, Laval, Quebec, Summer
1988.

THE ADOPTION

Rick and I had barely landed at Calgary airport when I learned of the fateful Alberta judgment that would start the slow but unstoppable march towards my son's adoption. Like the foothills of the vast continent-dividing Rockies just visible in the distance through the airport terminal windows, the real threat of his adoption was still only a faint rising on the horizon. But deep within me, I knew the landscape that lay ahead, as surely as if I had mapped it. And it formed a seemingly impenetrable wall between my son and myself.

My fingers had trembled as I dialed the offices of Freeland, Royal and McCrum from a phone booth in the airport.

"I'm sorry, Ricaardoe, but the news isn't good," said Marusia Petryshyn – the lawyer who was then representing me – as she came on the line. "I just got back from the court-house a few minutes ago. The judge has granted the mother's petition and the Alberta court-has relinquished its jurisdiction. Neither of you is bound any longer by your former undertakings. The jurisdiction for your son's custody and access is now in B.C."

Suddenly I was oblivious to the rush of people and luggage around me and for a few split seconds nothing existed but some huge unseen vacuum that was sucking away at my insides.

— "I don't believe it", I gasped finally, absorbing the shock. "This is crazy! How can they do this? They're trying to totally erase me from my son's life… First it's the jurisdiction. Then it'll be the adoption. And then they'll cancel my visiting rights. I can see it all happening." I was struggling to keep back the tears.

"There is always the possibility of making an appeal," my lawyer said. "It's something you need to think about. Though personally I wouldn't hold out much hope on that score. I suspect that most Appeal Court judges will give considerable weight to the fact that your son has now been living the better part of his life in B.C. and uphold the decision."

— "This is too much", I answered. "I'll have to call you back. I don't know what I'm going to do and right now I've still got to get my son back to Revelstoke."

— "I'll expect your call. Once again – I am sorry. This has taken us all by surprise."

As I hung up the receiver, I looked over at Rick who was sitting nearby drawing with the crayons he had brought from Montreal. We only had a few hours left together and I didn't want him to know how distraught I was. I took a deep breath and walked over to him. "C'mon", I said, taking his hand in mine, but avoiding his eyes. "We have to find Vile'm and Jake. They're going to meet us here and then we'll all drive to Revelstoke together."

The previous day, I had phoned both Vile'm Weber and Jake Vanderschaaf. They knew how despondent I became at the end of every access visit and were always ready with a compassionate ear. Whenever I was in Alberta, we would get together and often one or the other would come along for moral support on the trips to and from Revelstoke. This time, they had both offered to drive Rick and me.

On our way to retrieve our baggage, I told Rick I needed to stop at the washroom. Locked in the privacy of a cubicle, I fought to regain my composure, but instead the tears came in huge soundless sobs that exploded inside my rib cage. "What's next?" I kept asking myself. "Everyone keeps telling me it's not possible - she will never succeed and then the impossible happens." I was as close to despair in that airport washroom as I've ever been.

It was only when Rick called out, "Papa, what's taking you so long?" that I pulled myself together and quickly dried my eyes. "I'm coming, I'm coming," I said, as I emerged and made a beeline for the sink to wash my face and hands. He couldn't help but notice my red-rimmed eyes, but didn't say anything. He didn't have to. With our inevitable separation drawing closer, we each knew how badly the other felt.

The minutes passed as we waited restlessly for Vile'm and Jake. After an hour, I knew something was wrong. They were both usually punctual. There was no answer at Vile'm's home in

Edmonton. Then I tried Jake. After several rings, I heard his characteristic Dutch accent on the other end:

— "There's been a tornado here, Ricaardoe. It wiped out a trailer park on the outskirts of town. It's very serious. I'm sorry, but there's no way either Vile'm or I can get down to Calgary – the roads are a mess."

— "Don't worry about it", I answered. "It sounds like you've got more than enough to deal with there. I'll be passing through Edmonton on my way back. I'll see you then."

As I replaced the receiver, I turned to Rick and briefly explained about the tornado. "It looks like we're going to be renting a car after all."

All I had in my pocket was a dollar bill, some loose change and Brigitte's credit card that she had given me early that morning in case we ran into any difficulties. My own credit cards were useless, having long ago reached their maximum. It didn't occur to me that I would have trouble using Brigitte's card. However, when the rental-car clerk saw that the card and my license were under two different names, she refused to take it.

"Don't you have any other way to pay for the car?" she inquired.

I explained how the tornado had altered our original plans, and that I didn't have any other cards or cash on me. "We're really stuck", I said. "and I have to get my son back to B.C. Is there any way you could possibly make an exception to help us out?"

The clerk looked from my son to me and something in our expression must have touched a chord. She offered to see what she could do. She made several phone calls explaining our situation to whatever authorities she reported to, but to no avail. "I'm very sorry," she said, shaking her head sympathetically as she hung up the last time. "But I just can't make an exception. We've had too many problems with this kind of thing."

"Well, you did what you could and I really appreciate that", I responded as I reached for Rick's hand, and started to turn away. Then, on an impulse, I took my last dollar out of my pocket and gave it to her. "This is for you – for being so helpful. You're a very nice person and I wish you a most beautiful day."

Before Rick and I had gone 10 steps, she called out, "Wait! Come back. I shouldn't do this, but what the heck. You look so honest. I'm going to give you the car anyway". She took the imprint of Brigitte's card and handed me a set of keys.

Rick and I never did make it to Revelstoke that day. The more I thought about the jurisdiction transfer, the more worried and outraged I became. Finally, I could no longer concentrate on the road. We had only been driving for about half-an-hour and had just reached the outskirts of Calgary when I pulled the car over onto the safety of the shoulder. I didn't tell my son I was too distracted to drive. I simply asked him: "Rick, what do you think? Would you rather go back to Revelstoke today or do you want to wait until tomorrow?"

"If we go back tomorrow, we could have one more day together," he answered. "That's what I'd like, but I'm sure not going to be the one to tell Mom."

"That settles it," I said. "We'll go back tomorrow. And we have a good excuse. I'll send a telegram saying the tornado delayed us."

The next day Rick and I left very early in the morning and before long we were well into the Rockies. Already the road was lined with tourists in cars and camper vans stopping every few kilometers to revel at the breathtaking views of those towering peaks. But the beauty of our surroundings was lost on us.

Each time we passed over this same stretch of highway, it seemed to get harder and harder. Rick resisted the feeble attempts I made to cheer him up. "What's the use?" his eyes would glower at me. "It's not going to change anything." He was right. No amount of words could take away the helplessness we both felt.

Only after many hours in the car, when we were finally approaching Revelstoke, would his look soften. Then he would lean over and touch my hand lightly. "So I guess I'll talk to you next week," he'd say awkwardly. "You bet we will," I would answer. "No matter what happens, you're my son, I love you and I'll always be there for you."

" I know, Papa," and a fleeting smile would at last cross his face.

After Rick had left, I would go into the restaurant, order a meal and try to work up my courage for the long, lonely journey back through the mountains. If a friend like Jake or Vile'm had come along, it wasn't quite so bad. They did their best to raise my spirits and we would take turns at the wheel. But how I hated those drives when I was alone.

With each new wrenching experience, the pain of our separations worsened. Sometimes I would point the car east and then turn back after half an hour because I couldn't see the road through my tears. On one occasion, I managed more than a hundred kilometers before I gave up and turned the car around.

Back in Revelstoke, I'd check into a hotel and then head for the bar. I consumed a lot of Brazilian coffees in those days. Thankfully, over time, I also made friends in that town and their friendly greetings and sympathetic gestures would help me through those mind-numbing hours that inevitably followed Rick's departure. Occasionally, my stays stretched into days and I would drop by the Chamber of Commerce to inquire about real estate. In the back of my mind, I was even considering a move to Revelstoke.

Leaving Rick on that first day of August, immediately following the jurisdiction transfer, was especially hard. Not only were we both reeling from the hurt of another separation, I now had to brace myself for the very real threat that a B.C. Court might eventually cancel my visiting rights – the same visiting rights I had just spent eight years of my life fighting to preserve in another court in another province.

*****

My frustration with the legal system hit a new high when I learned a few days later in Edmonton that the judge who had dismissed our undertakings was a former attorney of the Token family. Moreover, for a very brief period at the start of the whole custody dispute, he had even represented Peggy.

After so many futile attempts to have the undertakings revoked, Peggy had finally succeeded with a judge who happened to be a family acquaintance. I was back in Montreal in late summer when Freeland, Royal & McCrum appealed the ruling on my behalf.

Then, within days of launching my appeal, Freeland, Royal and McCrum notified the Alberta Court that they would no longer be acting as my legal counsel. This was not a case that could be handled on legal aid and the firm had already made it clear I had little chance of winning the appeal. Even if I had the money to pursue this, I wondered where I would find a lawyer willing to pit him or herself against a judge in a case with potential conflict-of-interest overtones.

In the aftermath of these events, I wasn't informed when my appeal came up for a preliminary hearing that fall, and no one appeared in court on my behalf. The court officials in Edmonton claimed they didn't know how to reach me, even though they managed to contact me months later with a notice that my appeal had been dismissed.

When I questioned this through the Alberta Legal Aid Society and two other law firms, I was advised that even if I applied to reopen the case, there was little chance of success. Rick was clearly a B.C. resident and would therefore naturally fall under the jurisdiction of the B.C. Courts. To continue the process would have cost me a minimum retainer fee of $5,000 and I was forced to let the matter drop.

About the same time that Freeland, Royal and McCrum ceased to act for me in Edmonton, the B.C. Legal Aid Society was arranging for Kamloops lawyer Peter Allik-Petersenn to represent me in the upcoming adoption trial in B.C. Neither of us knew that Peggy had already contacted the legal aid authorities in both B.C. and Quebec and would maintain a regular correspondence with them over the coming months. Alleging that my financial situation wasn't nearly as desperate as I made it out to be, she was questioning my eligibility to receive legal aid.

Although, none of her allegations were substantiated with proof, an internal investigation was already under way. But it would be almost two years before anyone confronted me directly with the content of her accusations.

In the meantime, my legal aid continued uninterrupted and Peter took on the case.

He represented me throughout the adoption trial and later became the B.C. director of OPCR and a very good friend. Then as now, Peter lives and works in Kamloops where the adoption hearing was to be held. As part of his general legal practice, he regularly accepts legal aid clients and has increasingly specialized in family law. He is a strong proponent of alternate dispute resolution (mediation) and is himself a trained mediator.

Our initial contact was always by phone or letter. Peter had asked for a delay to familiarize himself with the case, and as yet, no new hearing date had been set. From the outset, he warned me there was a strong likelihood that the adoption would go through and that the most I could hope for was to have my visiting rights maintained. This alone would be highly unusual, he said. Normally an adoption would automatically cancel any existing access arrangements, and we had already been advised by Peggy and Jack's lawyer, Kristian Jensen, that this is exactly what they were seeking.

Peter suggested that if I wanted to prevent the adoption altogether, my best and only real chance lay in obtaining a custody order in another province. We both felt it would be useless to try this in B.C. where the adoption petition was already in motion. Furthermore, in cases where a child's parents had never been married, the general legal opinion in that province held that adoption orders were routinely granted to the mother and her new husband.[24]

Instead, we agreed that I should apply in Quebec for either joint or full custody of Rick. Quebec law differed significantly from B.C. law as far as adoptions were concerned, and I had been assured by Tony Manglaviti, Vincent Chiara and several other lawyers that in my home province, an adoption would not be allowed in a case like Rick's where, regardless of marital status, I had always acknowledged my son, showed real concern for his well being, and benefited from court-ordered visiting rights. Given this prevailing attitude, there was a very small chance that the Quebec Superior Court might look favorably on my request for custody precisely because of the likelihood that B.C. would allow the adoption.

To prepare for both a custody petition in Quebec and the adoption hearing in B.C., Peter advised me to obtain an up-to-date psychological evaluation of Rick that he anticipated would counter the expert reports Peggy already had supporting the adoption.

However, in her role as Rick's custodial parent, Peggy had recently informed me in writing that he was not to be examined by any psychologist or physician without her permission. When Peter sought permission through her lawyer, we received no response. Only when he said he would petition the B.C. Supreme Court to allow Rick to be examined by a psychologist of my choosing, did she give her approval.

Everyone agreed it would be easiest for Rick if the evaluation were to take place during our upcoming summer vacation together in 1988. This caused another delay in the adoption proceedings. I also had to justify to my son why he was to be subjected to yet another psychological examination. His initial reaction was far from positive.

— "You know your mother and Jack want to proceed with the adoption," I told him. "Without these doctors' reports, I don't stand a chance of stopping them. That means that one day you could be cut off from me and from all your friends and family in Montreal. And from everything you've told me, that's not what you want to happen."

— "I don't, Papa. I want to be able to be with you. I'm just so fed up going to see all these doctors. The whole thing's so stupid."

— "You're right," I said. "But what other choice do we have?"

Grudgingly he agreed to my making an appointment with Dr. Arthur Neumann, an Edmonton-based psychologist whom Peter Allik-Petersenn knew and highly recommended.

Raising the money needed to bring Rick to Montreal that July was another story. By the last week of June I still didn't have sufficient cash for either the bond or the airfare. In desperation I called Gilles Proulx, the host of a popular open-line radio show who was familiar with my plight from previous interviews. I had this gut feeling that if I called his show, somehow the money would materialize.

The capacity of strangers to respond to another human being in times of crisis has never ceased to move me. Gilles Proulx put me on the air and within the space of a few minutes, two local businessmen had called in and offered to lend me the bond money. Then a local service club donated airline tickets for both Rick and me. As I voiced my gratitude to Gilles Proulx and my new anonymous benefactors, I also silently thanked whatever inner force had urged me to make the call.

On the way back to Revelstoke after spending a month in Montreal, Rick and I stopped in Calgary to keep our appointment with Dr. Neumann. To save us additional travel costs and inconvenience, he had generously offered to make the trip from his home in Edmonton to Calgary at his own expense. We arranged to meet at the home of Walter Morandini, where Rick and I were guests.

In the report he submitted a short time later, Dr. Neumann commented on the open affection that existed between Rick and me and the fact that we were clearly comfortable in each other's presence. But he also noted a tendency to insecurity and high anxiety in Rick. In one test he gave my son, Rick wrote that he "was not living a normal life" and that it was "stupid to have these court cases and adoptions," Rick added that his greatest worry was being adopted and his greatest fear was "not to see either side of my family any more," Dr. Neumann concluded that it was definitely in my son's best interests that he be permitted to continue regular contact with me and the rest of his paternal family.

In fact, Rick's family in Montreal was about to expand. Brigitte was expecting our first child in October. When we told Rick during his summer visit, his eyes lit up and he was genuinely excited. He often spoke of his brother Jason and how much fun it was to have a baby in the house. Now he could look forward to another baby brother or sister. When he returned to Revelstoke at the end of July, I made sure he had some gifts tucked away in his suitcase for Jason.

The preoccupations of two major legal cases ongoing simultaneously in two different provinces, seldom left me. But fortunately during that late summer and early fall of 1988, I was also caught up in other much happier events that demanded my full attention and energy.

Brigitte's pregnancy was rapidly coming to term. She was doing very well and we were both thrilled at the thought of having our first child together. The baby was due the second week of October and I was convinced the newborn would arrive on October 8 – my own father's birthday. "You wait and see," I kept telling him. "You're going to have the best gift you could ever want – a new grandchild born on your birthday."

My instincts must have been working overtime. On October 8, Brigitte gave birth to our beautiful eldest daughter, Alexandra, and my father got his birthday present. Alexandra was a happy, healthy baby and we considered ourselves very blessed. Nevertheless, a new baby meant additional financial responsibilities and a move out of the dingy basement apartment into a larger residence. OPCR's finances were still sufficiently shaky, and I had yet to draw a salary. So we were still very dependent on Brigitte's income and the maternity allowance she received for the first few months following Alexandra's birth.

Even as Brigitte and I brought our new daughter home, I was also working feverishly with OPCR's small, but now permanent staff, to complete the last-minute preparations for our first international conference – a three-day event that took place at the end of October.

The conference dealt with the effects of divorce on children and how essential it was to consider their needs at every step of the process – from the most basic "How do you tell your kids you are going to divorce?" to "How do you help them adjust to a completely new, and from their point of view, unwanted family situation?"

Under the leadership of Dr. Saucier, our scientific committee had attracted several leading psychologists, mediators and other professionals who were at the forefront of research into the effects of divorce on children.

Among them was Dr. Neil Kalter, widely recognized for his work at the University of Michigan's Center for the Child and the Family. He noted that even a decade earlier, a conference like ours would have been unheard of.

This was because it was still thought uncertain that divorce had any significant negative effects on children. The prevailing thinking just a few years ago had viewed divorce's effect as something akin to a head cold: uncomfortable, but … not serious, something that would go away, whether you did anything about it or not.

Dr. Joan Kelly, then head of the Northern California Mediation Center, shared her pioneering work on mediation. Among its most important benefits, she said, it "contained or diminished, rather than escalated, parental conflict regarding children." Her findings also revealed that it wasn't "just the easier, friendlier divorces" that could be handled effectively through mediation.

Another speaker who greatly influenced OPCR's development was Mr. Justice Alvin C. Hamilton. In October 1988, he was the Associate Chief Justice of the family division of the Manitoba Court of Queen's Bench, and one of the early promoters of family mediation in Canada.

I had met Judge Hamilton at a conference a couple of years before and was excited and encouraged by the advances in family law he was spearheading in Manitoba. A rare voice within the legal system of his day, he had the courage and sensitivity to question whether existing divorce laws weren't more concerned with protecting the rights of adults – even to the detriment of their children. In his speech to conference delegates, Judge Hamilton reflected on what a Charter of Children's Rights might contain. Would it include, he asked:

- The right to a loving parent?
- The right to two loving parents?
- The right to have two parents to love?
- The right to enjoy grandparents?
- The right to be fed, clothed and housed?
- The right to an education?
- The right to be respected as a person?
- The right to be free from sexual abuse?
- The right to be protected from emotional harm?

And, in the unhappy event that the child's parents should separate, would it also include…

- The right not to carry the blame?
- The right to continued financial support?
- The right to be insulated from the dispute?
- The right to continue to have two parents?
- The right to retain grandparents?

- The right to love?

- The right to happiness?[25]

Judge Hamilton related how Manitoba had recently established the specialized family division court of which he was Associate Chief Justice. In that court, he explained, judges heard only family law cases – a significant breakthrough in his opinion. "The resolution of family disputes is so important and yet so difficult, that it requires the undivided attention of judges committed to that task," he told conference participants.

Previous to the creation of the family division, he had personally been called upon to judge a disparate range of cases from contract and labor disputes to injury, rape and murder trials. Interspersed with these, he had also heard family law cases, with all their knotted complexities of human emotions and relationships. As he put it, he was always grateful when these cases were over and "I could return to a nice clear-cut civil or criminal case."

All that changed with his appointment to the new family division. "I devoted more energy and patience to that task and found the law and the personal problems of the litigants of such interest and importance that I was quite content to spend all my time in family law," he told us.[26] He stressed that, in addition to their knowledge of the law, judges in a specialized family court must have a particular sensitivity for the children, the unseen witnesses and oft-times, victims of these cases.

Judge Hamilton also described the central role played by mediation in such a court. The Manitoba Court he had helped create included a team of social workers who practiced mediation. The court also oversaw and followed up on all support payments. Mediation was obligatory for any couple involved in a custody or access-related dispute and a resounding 60 per cent of cases were resolved at this stage.

In the other 40 per cent, the couple and their lawyers were required to attend a pre-trial conference before a judge (other than the one who would preside over an eventual trial). Here the parties had a chance to state their respective positions in an informal and confidential atmosphere. (Pre-trial discussions could not be referred to in any subsequent trial.) Judge Hamilton noted that he himself used the pre-trial conference to encourage the couple to work out their own solution for themselves and their children, rather than suffer the costly and bitter exercise that would further damage their relationship and ability to act as responsible parents.

He suggested cooperation and compromise as a safer alternative and would tell the parents that they were better positioned to work out a solution that would fit their family circumstances than a judge who didn't know them, their children or the options available to them.

The fact that the divorcing spouses' lawyers could not get a date for trial until after the pre-trial conference was concluded added to the latter's effectiveness, according to Judge Hamilton.

Four hundred people attended OPCR's first international conference, which proved an unqualified professional and financial success for a fledgling five-year-old organization. Following the conference, we drew up a list of recommendations calling for the establishment of dedicated family courts and a mandatory mediation process, which we sent to every member of Parliament across Canada. We also began planning for a second international conference to take place in four years' time.

The euphoria of Alexandra's birth and the conference quickly burst when Peter informed me that the adoption trial might take place as early as that November. In the end, it was delayed until the following March due to a surplus of cases on the court roster.

That delay gave me a faint window of hope. By now I had proceeded with my custody application in Quebec with prominent local lawyer, Julius Grey. Vincent Chiara advised me not to spend the money - "You don't have a chance, Ricaardoe", he said. But Julius Grey, known for his difficult and high profile cases, thought it was worth a try. Peter Allik-Petersenn believed it might buy us some time. Rick was almost 11; by the age of 12, B.C. law stipulated that he would have to give his written consent to any adoption.

In the interim, he worried constantly about his future. He would call and ask me, "Papa, did you get custody yet?" Then my heart would break as he begged me to do something to stop the adoption. "You can't let it happen", he repeated every time I talked to him. "You've got to stop it."

Knowing how strongly he felt, I considered any chance, no matter how slim, worth pursuing.

Rick was in Montreal for the Christmas holidays when I was called to appear in Quebec Superior Court for a hearing on December 22. Then, at the last minute, while I waited with Julius Grey for our case to be called, the hearing was postponed.

To avoid raising false hopes, I hadn't told Rick about the hearing, and was very grateful that his attention was distracted by the excitement and anticipation of Christmas preparations. He was also looking forward to Alexandra's christening, which we had deliberately planned for the end of December so he would be able to attend. He was genuinely fond of this new little sister and pleased when she responded to his attention. But throughout the holidays, his mind often seemed to wander. Several times during that visit, he took me aside. "If the adoption does go through Papa", he asked, "will we still be able to see each other?"

During Rick's stay, we went to see Dr. Abe Worenklein, a Montreal psychologist, who had done considerable research on children. A second report by an expert-witness would strengthen our case against adoption. From the very beginning, Dr. Worenklein was concerned about Rick who, he said, "seemed to be programmed to make statements about how great life was in B.C." Yet questioning "revealed a great deal of ambivalence about his step-father and mother."

Rick eventually confided that his mother had cautioned him about speaking with any doctors. He also seemed very confused about his "dad". According to Dr. Worenklein, Rick spoke of having two fathers and "was unsure of the difference between the two. He also contradicted himself about whether he was allowed to mention me at home, adding that he did call me from a public phone booth. He wasn't clear why he didn't use the phone at home. All through the interview, Rick was extremely anxious about how any information he supplied would be used and he openly expressed his dislike of doctors.

In the midst of Rick's confusion, Dr. Worenklein noted a clear and strong attachment to me, as well as marked concern that an adoption could sever our tie and be "the beginning of the end" of his relationship with me. Rick was "quite anxious about this possibility and was clear in saying that he worried about this" remarked Dr. Worenklein.

The psychologist concluded that he himself was "extremely concerned about the adoption", adding that it shouldn't be allowed due to the child's apprehensions, his confusion over his identity, and the history of the mother's attempts "to deny the child a close and loving relationship with his father."

Every professional I consulted stated that an adoption was not in the best interests of my son. My son himself kept saying he didn't want it. And yet we moved closer and closer to its becoming a fact. One thinks this kind of thing can't happen. But it can and it did.

Peggy and Jack must have realized that any psychological evaluation I presented in court would support my son's right – and need – to continue his relationship with me. Perhaps Rick himself said something to them. Whatever their reasoning, they softened their stand and made it known that they would no longer oppose my continued access if I would agree to the adoption.

At one point, Peggy even proposed that a representative of the B.C. Attorney General's department mediate an agreement between us. But when I spoke to the woman whom Peggy suggested, the first thing she wanted to know was why I was so opposed to an adoption. "Don't you think it would be better for your son's stability and security?" she asked. This didn't strike me as the line of questioning an impartial mediator would take, and I refused to be part of what appeared to me a biased process.

There was simply too much history in this whole unhappy affair for me to accept Peggy and Jack at their word. Then, an incident in January 1989 – just two months before the adoption hearing – fuelled my conviction that they would persevere in their efforts to alienate Rick from me.

It happened the day I returned Rick to Revelstoke shortly after New Year's. Ever since the scene at the Frontier Restaurant the previous year when Jack had grabbed my arm and broken my watchstrap, neither he nor Peggy came to meet us when Rick and I arrived. Instead they sent a friend named Norma, who had always been pleasant to me.

There had already been problems over the date I was to return Rick. In the weeks before Christmas, I had asked Peggy to let me know exactly when he resumed school after the holidays so I could take advantage of an advance reservation discount that would cut travel costs in half. She never got back to me. Eventually I took a chance and booked a flight on January 4, the earliest return date available. The reservations were non-refundable and, as it turned out, Rick was late getting back for school. (I had figured on the Quebec school system whose Christmas break was longer than the one in B.C.). To complicate matters further, on our arrival in Calgary, a major snowstorm and dangerous road conditions prevented us from leaving for Revelstoke until early the next morning. Peggy saw this as a deliberate abuse of my access and she and Jack later laid a contempt of court charge against me.

When Rick and I did reach Revelstoke before noon on January 5, we called Norma to let her know we had arrived. About half an hour later, she pulled into the parking lot and hurried over to us. Usually she would take time to ask us how we were and how the trip had been. But this time she appeared extremely nervous and on the brink of tears.

"Is something the matter?" I asked her immediately.

Her voice wavered as she looked straight at Rick: "How could you say you didn't want to come back here because you were afraid Jack would beat the 'shit' out of you? "

Before Rick could even reply, I interrupted: "He never said that."

"Well, why did you write that in your affidavit then?" she said, turning to me.

"I never put any such thing in any affidavit", I responded.

"Well, I don't know who's lying here…" she broke off.

After an awkward moment, I gave Rick a goodbye hug.

"What's Norma talking about?" he asked, before he got into her car.

"I really don't know", I answered. "Don't worry about it. There must be some misunderstanding. I love you and we'll talk soon".

Back on the highway, I puzzled over Norma's strange accusation. Furthermore, her distress had seemed very real. Did she think my son was making up stories? Was she genuinely concerned about his safety? Or was she part of some new scheme intended to suggest that I was making false accusations behind Rick's back about his being afraid to come home?

The more I thought about what had happened, the more concerned I grew. I had known for years that Jack had a quick temper. Once before he had deliberately applied a hot match to my son's hand, causing a scar the size of a pencil-end that had remained visible for several years. He had caught Rick playing with matches and it was his method of disciplining him. Were there other incidents I wasn't aware of?

By the time I reached Lake Louise, my imagination was running wild. I stopped to call Peter Allik-Petersenn and seek his advice. He suggested I call the Social Services department in Revelstoke and ask them to check on my son. A few days later, one of their staff reported back to me that she had indeed dropped by Rick's school to see if he was all right and had found no reason whatsoever for concern. This made me all the more wary that the whole incident might have been staged to make me look bad in front of my son.

*****

In the weeks to come, Peter and I were in frequent contact. After two years and a series of delays, the adoption hearing was finally scheduled for March 8-10, 1989 in Kamloops. We had desperately hoped that my Quebec custody case would be heard before the adoption, but this wasn't to be. The Montreal hearing took place the week following the adoption.

I had sufficient experience inside a courtroom that neither its stiff atmosphere nor the tactics of an opposing lawyer could any longer intimidate me. But I was very anxious. I remember discussing the possibility of my son's being adopted with OPCR's legal committee and hearing every member tell me, he or she would be astounded if the adoption went through. I wish I could have had their confidence. Their experience revolved largely around Quebec law, but by now I was all too conscious of how significantly adoption laws varied from province to province.

I firmly believe that this lack of standardized family law from one province to the next only encourages people to jurisdiction shop, lengthening an already painful process and increasing the hurt that children and the whole extended family must endure after divorce. Standardization of family law across the country was then, and remains, a major goal of OPCR.

I arrived in Kamloops a few days before the trial to review with Peter, how we planned to proceed. I was painfully aware that our chances of preventing the adoption were small, and Peter cautioned me again when we met. But this didn't lessen his personal concern for my son or his indignation at what he considered a totally inappropriate adoption. He worked tirelessly to assemble a convincing argument that we hoped would, at the least, safeguard my visiting rights.

Even before the hearing began, we had one strike against us. Peter had already informed Kristian Jensen that he would be submitting Dr. Worenklein's expert report as evidence. Jensen had responded that he wanted the opportunity to cross-examine the psychologist in court. Both Peter and I had already spoken on several occasions with Dr. Worenklein who indicated his willingness to testify on my behalf, as long as he had sufficient notice. I, too, was anxious that he appear as a witness because his report came down so strongly against the adoption.

But up until a very short time before the trial, we couldn't get any confirmation from Jensen as to which day our witness would be needed. This was critical information for me. I was already facing a bill of several thousand dollars to cover Dr. Worenklein's fees; and every additional day we required his presence would increase that amount considerably. As a legal aid recipient, I couldn't afford to err on the side of caution and bring him to Kamloops any longer than was necessary.

When Peter was finally able to determine the exact date he would be required, we came up against a schedule conflict. The doctor was already booked to testify at another trial in Montreal. On top of this, we had only obtained his final report towards the end of February – and for evidence to be accepted, we should normally have submitted it 30 days prior to the hearing's start. It would be up to the judge to determine whether or not he would accept the report as evidence.

Days later when Peter raised the issue in court and asked for an adjournment so that Dr. Worenklein could be present, the judge – at the urging of Peggy's lawyer – refused on the grounds that Rick's best interests lay in resolving this case as soon as possible. After all the delays that had already occurred in this one case, we found it very strange that a few extra days could not be allowed to enable Dr. Worenklein to testify. As a result, his report was never admitted as evidence.

At any trial, so much depends on the presiding judge, and it didn't take more than a few minutes before Mr. Justice Finch, for both Peter and I to realize we were facing an uphill battle. In the first few minutes of the trial, he asked Peter bluntly: "What is there in the case that's going to show that it would be bad for this child for an adoption order to be made?"

By placing the onus on us to show why an adoption should *not* happen, his personal bias seemed clear. That, at least, was our perception – and it was hardly an encouraging start.

From Justice Finch's perspective, the hearing must answer three key questions: did Peggy and Jack have the ability to bring up, maintain and educate Rick properly? Was the adoption in the best interests of the child (and of his parents, including myself)? And could my consent be dispensed with?

Throughout the hearing, Kristian Jensen argued that the adoption was the best way to end the ongoing litigation that had dominated all our lives for far too long and had caused such stress and insecurity for Rick. Adoption would make him an indisputable part of Peggy and Jack's family unit and give him the same legitimacy and stability that his younger brother had enjoyed from birth.

He noted that should the adoption be granted, his clients were willing to allow my continued access to Rick; however, he also made it clear they considered the existing access conditions overly generous. They also wanted Rick to have more say in the actual arrangements: for instance, if he preferred to spend only two weeks with me in the summer rather than a month, he should be free to make this decision. Or if he didn't feel like phoning me twice a week, he shouldn't have to.

"Funny how they always assume he wants to spend less time with me," I thought to myself. "Would they be so quick to support his decision if he wanted to spend the entire summer with me?"

In theory, it only made sense that Rick should become more involved in the decisions that affected him directly. Yet, he was still a highly impressionable 11-year-old and I had already witnessed how Peggy and Jack had tried to turn him against me. How they would seek to influence him in future, remained my greatest worry. In their eyes, I didn't have the legitimacy of a real parent. They saw me as a constant irritant – something to be endured, even tolerated – but not at all encouraged. An adoption would only solidify their position.

That sentiment was further reinforced when Peter Allik-Petersenn asked Jack if he considered me to be part of Rick's family. "Perhaps in the back of my mind, I do," Jack responded. "But not deep in my heart."

Peter contended that the adoption was decidedly not in Rick's best interest. The child already had a father who loved him and was eager to share in his care. How could adoption by a third person – and yet another name change (this would be number six) – secure his sense of identity? And what if, in the future, problems were to arise between Peggy and Jack and they went their separate ways? What identity would that leave my son?

Positive, open and ongoing communication with both his natural parents was what Rick most wanted, and needed, to secure his sense of self. That wasn't simply my own belief, I told the court when my turn came to testify. It was also the opinion of many experts in child psychology who had participated in OPCR's international conference.

If the adoption went through, what confidence could I have that Rick would be encouraged to maintain open and loving communication with me – no matter how many court orders enshrined my visiting rights? Legally, I would no longer be his father.

Should access be prevented, what recourse would I have other than continued and painful litigation? When was this whole process supposed to halt?

Peter reminded the court of the many difficulties I had already experienced over the years enforcing my visiting rights, the series of name changes that had been made without advising me or the court, the cheques I had sent to help support Rick that had never been cashed, the first adoption in 1983 for which the only "notice" sent to me was delivered care of the Token's clinic, the problems with phone calls, the letters sent to Rick that were returned unopened and so on.

"Nothing happens in a vacuum," said Peter. "There has been a long history of animosity and that history of animosity is likely to continue. For that reason an adoption order is not going to assist this child."

If past history is an indication of things to come, Peter continued, how would an adoption put an end to further litigation? Would it not only aggravate the situation further? Contrary to Peggy and Jack's implication that I had instigated the lion's share of the 21 court orders that already littered this case, he pointed out that most of those rulings had defended my continued access in the face of their ongoing campaign to curtail it. Even now, he said, they had an outstanding contempt charge against me because I had brought Rick back three days late after Christmas.

Justice Finch was openly impatient with accounts of past problems between Peggy, Jack and myself. He questioned how events going back several years were pertinent to the immediate decision before him. As he constantly reminded both Peter and Kristian Jensen, he was interested only in what was relevant to whether or not the adoption order should be made. "I would have thought that had to do with fitness, the parents, and the welfare of the child," he said.[27]

He also refused to admit Marilyn Weston's *As it is* video as evidence. Despite its having been made under international broadcast regulations, Kristian Jensen vehemently objected to it as "pure propaganda." His reaction wasn't unexpected. That video was a powerful demonstration of the bond that existed between Rick and me since his earliest years. It contradicted Peggy and Jack's frequent contention that our relationship was relatively superficial.

Our inability to use this video in court was another frustrating example of the rigidity of the legal system in dealing with the very blurred reality of human emotions. Peter and I didn't have the luxury of time and money that would have been required to track down and bring the producer to Kamloops for cross-examination.

Therefore, in the court's eyes, the video may as well not have existed.

In limiting his interest to the fitness of the adopted parents, I believe Justice Finch overlooked the importance of the extended family in connecting the child to something larger than himself. Seen in this light, adoption was, in fact, an amputation, since an adopted Rick would no longer be legally recognized as a member of the Di Done family. And who, in future, would guarantee his right to benefit from the love of that larger family? Would he still have the opportunity to share experiences with its members, learn from them, and hear their stories and the stories of those who preceded them? Or would he simply be cut off from these roots that could so enrich his distinct sense of identity and self-worth?

However, those weren't the questions Justice Finch was asking. He wanted to know why the adoption order should not be made; and he apparently never got what he considered a convincing answer. On Friday, March 10, he ruled the adoption should go ahead. With that decision, the child who had been born Ricaardoe Branden Di Done, and had grown up as Branden Token in B.C. and Ricaardoe Di Done Jr. in Quebec, became officially known as Branden Roaff.

As part of his ruling, Justice Finch granted me, with a few minor changes, the same access to Rick that I had had through the Alberta order. Peter Allik-Petersenn believed that the report of Dr. Neumann – which had been accepted uncontested – was an important factor in preserving my access.

To allow the adoption to proceed, Justice Finch had to dispense with my consent. He suggested that one rationale for doing this was my "persistent neglect" to contribute to my son's support. (That I regularly outfitted my son with new clothes and sent him gifts of toys and money had made little impression on the judge.) Financial support was not, however, the deciding factor for Justice Finch.

His written judgment cited the best interests of Rick and of everyone else concerned as sufficient reason for foregoing with my consent.

"It is in everyone's interest for this continuing litigation to be brought to an end. An adoption order will be a step in that direction. It will bring some greater certainty into Branden's life.

He will know that further battles for his custody are over. He will know that the petitioners are his legal parents. He will also know that he need no longer be subjected to examinations by psychologists, psychiatrists or other consultants for the purposes of the continuing litigation. All of this will be to his benefit and to the benefit of his parents as well.

I do not see any harm in this from the respondent's standpoint. He is Branden's natural father and Branden knows it. They have a loving relationship, which will be permitted to continue. The petitioners do not oppose continued access by the respondent; and in any event, I would on the evidence have been disposed to grant continuing access in the circumstances. The adoption order will mean that the respondent need no longer devote the time, energy and money to these continuing legal battles. He will be able to devote himself to more constructive pursuits including the development of his relationship with Branden during his access visits. So, for those two reasons I consider this to be a proper case in which to dispense with the consent of the respondent, the natural father ... "[28]

The fact that the B.C. Supreme Court had ruled exactly as Peter had predicted did nothing to diminish the anger and frustration I felt towards a system that would allow an adoption under such circumstances. Nor could I understand the motivation of a lawyer like Kristian Jensen who, knowing that my son and I loved each other and were opposed to the adoption, still continued to push for it.

Before leaving the courthouse, I approached Jensen, unable to contain my feelings: "How could you do this? You know my son loves me and this isn't what he wants." "I'm here to represent my clients," Jensen responded. That's my role as a lawyer." "Even when you know what you're doing is hurting a child?" I asked, turning away in disgust.

With the calm of hindsight, one might say that Justice Finch's decision sought to cement a compromise that would, above all, put an end to the endless litigation over Rick. What the decision didn't consider was how Rick himself would react.

Rick had just recently celebrated his eleventh birthday. Had he turned 12 before the trial took place, his written consent would have been required. Even though evidence had been given that he was opposed to the adoption, the judge never took the opportunity to talk to him directly and learn first-hand how Rick felt about a decision that would forever affect his life. (Today, the B.C. adoption law has been changed to reflect a child's right to have a say in determining his or her own future. While it still only insists on the written consent of children 12 and over, judges must now consider the views of those between seven and 12, regardless of whether their consent is required.)

Rick and I spent the weekend immediately following the trial, together. Unsure of what Peggy and Jack had told him about the adoption ruling, I played it cautiously when we first met and tried to be upbeat.

— "Hi, how are you?" I asked him, smiling as if nothing had happened.

— "Give me a break," he said. He wasn't smiling and his voice bordered between anger and dejection.

— "What do you mean?"

— "The adoption," he answered. He looked at me like I had just landed from another planet. "Mom says Jack is now my legal father and you're not."

It wasn't an easy morsel to digest for a kid already confused about his true identity. His downcast eyes said it all. He didn't care about the niceties of the legal system. As far as he was concerned, both his mother and I had failed him.

"Listen," I said, "We still have our visiting rights. And I'm going to appeal. If it's what you want, we're going to find some way to cancel that adoption. I don't know how yet, but sooner or later, we're going to cancel it."

Rick's reaction helped me shake off my own despondency. That relations between his mother and I could degenerate to this point was unacceptable. And the judicial system, dedicated to preserving my son's best interests, was so far off the mark it would have been laughable had I not seen the scars it caused.

You can't enforce a decision involving the lives and feelings of children and families by first pitting them against one another and then expecting them to cooperate in an atmosphere of peace and harmony. In a country as advanced as Canada, we still had a long way to go.

I vowed there and then to continue my efforts to make mediation services widely available to parents in mid-rupture. Somehow we had to move kids far from the epicenter and shield them from the after-shocks.

I also appealed the adoption order through Vancouver lawyer Lawrence Kahn, referred by Peter. Two years and $10,000 in legal fees later, the B.C. Appeal Court upheld the decision of Mr. Justice Finch in a judgment dated June 5, 1991. OPCR paid the $10,000 on my behalf. Apart from the fact that I had worked so long without any salary, its Board of Directors considered my attempt to overturn the adoption an important test case and a potentially powerful catalyst for reform. The organization also covered the expenses for my custody application in Quebec, which was dismissed for lack of jurisdiction shortly after the adoption trial.

After the B.C. Appeal Court decision, Julius Grey and I even attempted to have the adoption overturned by the Supreme Court of Canada. But after evaluating our preliminary submission, that court declined to hear the case. The country's top court does not have to explain why it refuses a case, but I eventually learned that it was considered too isolated an example to sufficiently serve the interests of the Canadian public.

Ten years into the fight to maintain a close and caring relationship with my son, I was running out of options.

Author, Alexandra Di Done, Ricaardoe Jr.: Montreal, Quebec, April 1991.

While in Kelowna, B.C., Jr. announcing his wish to permanently stay in
Montreal, Quebec, 1992.

Alexandra Di Done, author, Ricaardoe Jr.: Ricaardoe Jr.'s permanent stay in Montreal, 1992.

Ricaardoe Jr., Alexandra Di Done, Antoni Di Done, Marina Di Done, Samantha Di Done: Montreal, Quebec, August 26, 1997.

Alexandra Di Done, Ricaardoe Jr., Samantha Di Done, author, Antoni Di Done, Brigitte Jalbert, Marina Di Done: Montreal, Quebec, August 9, 1997.

FULL CIRCLE: SETTING ASIDE THE ADOPTION

The adoption that was supposed to put an end to the years of litigation over Rick never did accomplish that goal.

Two letters, written exactly the same day and dated a mere month after Justice Finch's ruling, illustrated the contradiction between what the judge had hoped his decision would achieve and the additional conflict it actually caused. The first letter, from Peggy to me, was intended as a peace overture. In it, Peggy thanked me for my restrained reaction to the trial and judgment and asserted her hope that we could put our struggle to rest before it consumed all our youth and energy. "We would both have more to offer Branden by concentrating on useful projects," she wrote, suggesting that if I abstained from any further resistance, she and Jack would also be easy to deal with.

The second letter, addressed to Peter Allik-Petersenn, came from Peggy's lawyer. He noted that his client would be willing to accept a lump sum payment of $2,800 to settle the outstanding contempt charge she had laid against me shortly before the adoption trial. He added that even if these contempt proceedings were dismissed by the B.C. courts, his client was prepared to make a claim against the $7,500 bond that was still on deposit in Alberta.

I refused to pay and the charges were eventually withdrawn. But it had given me my first post-adoption taste of how "easy" dealing with them would be. If they would take that kind of legal action because Rick was a couple of days late returning from his Christmas holiday, what else were we to expect?

For more than two years now, Peggy had also been protesting my eligibility for legal aid with the authorities in both Quebec and British Columbia. She claimed that my access to legal aid was threatening her family unit and our son's stability by enabling me to "force" them into court on a regular basis. She refrained from mentioning that my initial application for legal aid had resulted directly from her and Jack's desire to adopt Rick and cancel my visitation rights.

When she learned that I would be appealing the adoption, she renewed her efforts to have me cut off from legal aid. Citing testimony I had given before Justice Finch, she said I had refused a regular salary from OPCR. In fact, I had said that the organization's Board of Directors agreed that I should draw a regular salary but that so far I had been unable to do so because our revenues weren't sufficiently high.

That I still drove a "late model" Lincoln Continental (actually, twelve years old) and wore expensive clothes (rather threadbare), were offered as evidence of my supposedly lavish lifestyle.

My first indication of real trouble came in mid-1989 when I received a letter from the Quebec legal aid service saying that my right to receive legal aid had been contested and was being suspended.

I appealed and was called to a hearing before a committee in October, where, only then, did I get detailed information about the nature of the accusations against me. Among other things, I was told that it was common knowledge that my family had money.

"To everyone but us!" I answered. "My family has done their best to help me, but they certainly aren't rich".

The list of accusations went on. Peggy complained that I only used legal aid for minor cases, but seemed able to hire "high-priced lawyers" when I felt it worth my while. She didn't say whether she considered the adoption trial – for which Peter was paid by legal aid – a minor case.

After that session before the investigating committee, I was given so many days to produce a stack of additional information in my defense. In the end, I decided it wasn't worth the paperwork, time and physical resources that would be required. I also suspected that my years of outspoken criticism of the legal system were catching up with me.

Out of principle, I wrote a long letter to the head of the committee, refuting the accusations that had been made against me. But I was well past the deadline and my legal aid had already been cancelled.

The most disturbing part of this whole episode was that the legal aid authorities had based their decision on often-erroneous evidence and unsubstantiated hearsay. Once again, I had the distinct impression that our legal system readily accepted the notion that a mother should fight ceaselessly for the right to be with her children, and at least in Peggy's case, it routinely overlooked or downplayed any transgressions on her part. But it seemed totally unprepared for a father who was equally committed to his children – and my every action was subject to intense scrutiny and faultfinding.

I was especially angered by the appeal committee's suggestion that my family and Brigitte could have been doing more to help me. Even if they had had the financial resources to assume the crushing burden of my legal costs – which they didn't – they were strictly innocent bystanders in my conflict with Peggy. Did they have to keep giving until they put themselves into the poorhouse?

The legal costs exacted by marriage breakdown don't stop at the two individuals immediately concerned. They have repercussions on any subsequent relationships those two people may form and affect not only the children of the initial union, but any others that follow. What purpose does it serve anyone if the financial pressure is so high that the second relationship also collapses?

If the people handing out legal aid doubted my sincerity, there were others in positions of influence and responsibility who strongly supported my efforts and made it possible for me to see my son on an increasingly regular basis. I wrote to politicians, bank presidents, airline companies – anyone who would listen to my story. One bank representative significantly reduced an outstanding debt; rental car magnate Ted Tilden gave me free rental cars for my trips to and from Revelstoke; Air Canada and other airlines and organizations donated free travel passes; a reporter friend in Edmonton arranged complimentary hotel stays.

The problems of families in crisis transcend borders. These were all people who encouraged OPCR in its vision of evolving into a national organization that would push for inter-provincial and even international cooperation in promoting and reinforcing the responsibilities of divorcing parents towards their children.

We began by opening a western Canadian office in Kamloops with Peter Allik-Petersenn as director. In addition, OPCR set up a department permanently dedicated to raising funds for the summer camps, and Christmas and Easter parties we organized regularly for disadvantaged children, as well as for our educational and counseling services that included a grandparents' support group.

*****

With business as well as personal ties in B.C. and a slightly more stable financial situation, I began visiting my son on an almost monthly basis. Rick also took to calling me early in the morning just after his mother and Jack had left for work. He didn't want them to know how frequently he spoke to me.

Sometimes at the conclusion of a weekend access visit, he would ask: "Are you leaving in the morning?" Then he'd add, "If you stay, we could have breakfast together the minute Mom leaves". It didn't take much to persuade me.

On one occasion just over a year after the adoption, this routine of ours created an incident with the police. It was the beginning of August and we had just returned to Revelstoke after a month in Montreal. Neither of us wanted this holiday to end and we quickly invented reasons why I should linger for another couple of days.

Revelstoke is a small town and Peggy and Jack's home was only a few minutes away from the motel where I stayed. Two mornings in a row Rick had joined me for breakfast and a swim in the pool. On the third morning, he called bright and early and asked if he could bring two friends along. I offered to pick them up and we were just sitting at the counter waiting for our breakfasts when an RCMP officer walked into the motel coffee shop.

The color drained from my son's face as he watched the Mountie make eye contact with me. I quickly got up and intercepted the officer.

Apparently one of Peggy's neighbors had seen Rick and his friends drive off with me. Alarmed by the Alberta plates on my rental car, she had alerted Peggy. The Mountie had come prepared to charge me with kidnapping.

— "Just a minute, Officer". I said. "I didn't force my son to come here. He called me up and asked if he and his friends could see me."

— "He's with friends?" his voice showed surprise.

— "Yes," I said. "Ask him yourself."

The Mountie approached Rick. "Is that your dad?"

— "Yes," Rick answered. The Mountie then looked inquiringly at Rick's friends who nodded their heads in agreement.

— "Did you telephone your dad this morning and ask to see him?"

— "Yes," said my son. "We just wanted to go for a swim."

— "If you want to spend time with your dad, why don't you let your mom know? She was worried about you," the Mountie pursued.

— "Because she doesn't want me to see him."

The officer turned back to me and I briefly explained the situation. "I'm sorry about disturbing you like this," he said after a few more minutes. "Obviously there's been a misunderstanding. But I'm still going to have to take your son and his friends home."

— "All right," I said. "But would you do us a favor and let him and his friends drive with me. You can follow right behind us."

Under the Mountie's watchful eye, I drove three disappointed kids back home. That effectively put an end to those few hours of "stolen time" with my son and marked another occasion when almost a full week would pass before I could overcome the crippling sense of loss and leave Revelstoke.

There were other episodes when Rick reached out as if he felt a constant need to set the record straight. Just before Christmas of 1990, we were in the car on our way from Revelstoke to Calgary, when he turned to me and said, "Papa, remember the picture I drew for the psychologist where the monster was chasing the boy and the word 'Helen' was printed on the picture?"

He was referring to the drawing that Martin Impey had used as part of his psychological evaluation. Impey had maintained that the monster represented me and my son was struggling to escape me. I had forgotten about the name Helen on the picture.

"Well, the doctor asked me to draw a boy running away from a monster. There was a little girl in the room with me. I left the picture on the table and she just wrote 'Helen' on it."

The following January when he was back in Revelstoke, he called me one night and told me he didn't want to be Jack's son. He asked me to do everything possible to cancel the adoption.

— "Why don't you write me a letter saying that's how you feel," I suggested.

— "OK," he replied. "But only show it to the judge. Make sure Mom and Jack don't find out."

A couple of weeks later I received an envelope in the mail addressed in his boyish handwriting. Inside was a single loose-leaf sheet that was blank except for four lines in pencil at the top of the page that read:

"Dear Dad,

I don't want to be adopted.

Love,

your son."

*****

About this time, Brigitte and I began seriously discussing the possibility of moving to B.C. The idea had been simmering in my brain for a couple of years as each new separation from Rick became harder to endure. In many ways, the move made sense. It would eliminate the physical distance between Rick and us, allow him to move freely back and forth between both his families and have a normal relationship with all his younger siblings. I told Brigitte I could hire someone to direct the Montreal office of OPCR, while I concentrated on expanding our presence in the West.

Walter Morandini had recently built a home near Kelowna and each time I visited the area, its appeal grew. Kelowna lies in the Okanagan Valley – a beautiful and fertile fruit belt in south-central B.C, famous for its spectacular mountain scenery, lush orchards, and long hours of summer sunshine. Kelowna had the other advantage of being situated barely 200 kilometers from Revelstoke. Furthermore, Rick had told me that his mother and Jack had recently bought land in a town just a few minutes' drive from Kelowna and were eventually planning to move there.

There was also a small but thriving Italian community in Kelowna and I had made friends there easily. Earl's Restaurant – overlooking Okanagan Lake – was a favorite gathering point. The management liked me and would boast to their other clients about their regular customer who traveled more than 4,000 kilometers just to eat at their table.

At the end of June, Brigitte was adamant that we take a family holiday. She had never been to Western Canada and wanted to see for herself if we could make a life there. We flew to Edmonton with Alexandra, who was now 20 months old, and then drove on to Revelstoke where Rick joined us.

As we traveled back through the Rockies, heading for the famous tourist sites of Banff, Lake Louise, Moraine Lake and Jasper, we thought our first real family vacation would be marred by the dark storm clouds that obstinately hovered all around us, obscuring our view of the towering mountains. But luck must have smiled on us.

All the while we were in the car, the rain poured down in sheets, but as soon as we arrived at each day's destination, the clouds thinned and the sun suddenly appeared to salvage our sightseeing. Brigitte and I reveled at the incredible panorama of endless snow-capped rock and turquoise, glacier-fed lakes. Alexandra had a wonderful time playing in all the puddles.

It was fascinating to watch her and Rick together. Despite their age difference – or perhaps because of it – they responded wonderfully to each other. She wanted to follow him everywhere and do everything he did, while he enjoyed the attention and was careful to watch out for her. I took rolls of photographs of the two of them together – both in the Rockies and after the four of us returned to Montreal for Rick's annual summer visit. Looking back at those pictures, they are much more than a record of the happy vacation memories that might fill any family album. They are also a reminder of the emotional upheaval my son experienced each time he had to leave one of his families to be with the other. The big beaming smile that he displayed so readily at the beginning of our trip and during the subsequent weeks we spent together in Montreal faded almost completely in the day or so before our return to Revelstoke.

Brigitte was taken by what she had seen of B.C. and Alberta during our short trip. She had also had the chance to meet many of my friends and they got along well. Towards the end of the summer, she announced she was pregnant again and our second child, Antoni, was born in March of 1991. Brigitte later told me that seeing me play with our newborn son and Alexandra made her realize just how much my children meant to me. That's when she made up her mind that if I really wanted to move West, she would support me. Over the next year, we made our decision. We were going.

In May of 1992 I combined a business trip to OPCR's Kamloops office with a visit with Rick over the long Victoria Day weekend. We had been invited to stay at a friend's ranch just outside Kelowna. Brigitte and I had agreed beforehand that I would tell my son that weekend, of our plans to move.

I waited till our second evening together to break the news. All afternoon we had been out racing an all-terrain vehicle over the mountain trails on our friend's property. The trails were steep and we had ridden dangerously close to the edge on a couple of occasions. We laughed about it that evening, neither of us wanting to acknowledge just how much of an escape valve we found in that recklessness.

There was a lull in our conversation when all at once my son said, "I hate it when you leave."

— "I hate leaving you, too," I answered. "But I have some news for you."

— "What is it?"

— "Well, Brigitte and I have been talking this over and we've reached a decision. We're going to move here to Kelowna so we can be closer to you."

It took a few seconds for this to sink in, then Rick burst out: "What? You'd move all the way here just for me? Brigitte and Alexandra and Antoni, too?"

I nodded my head yes.

— "Wow!" he said. "But, hold on, Papa. Don't do that."

— "What do you mean?"

— "This summer I'm going to come stay with you in Montreal and I'm not going back."

— "Don't be silly," I said. "You stay here. We'll come. Later on when you're older, if you still want to live in Montreal, we can think about moving back."

— "No, Papa," he said, with an air of finality he rarely exhibited. "I'm coming. They're all a bunch of losers here."

I didn't press the matter further. We would see what developed in July. Rick arrived that summer, intent as ever on staying with us. But he hadn't shared his plan with his mother and Jack. At the end of July, he called his mother to tell her he was having a good time and wanted to stay a couple of weeks longer. In mid-August, he told her he'd be coming back at the end of the month, and when the end of the month arrived, he announced that he wanted to start school in Montreal and would return to Revelstoke later that autumn.

"Mom, you always told me I should do what I wanted to do. Well, this is what I want to do," he countered, when Peggy pleaded with him to return. "It's not like they're trying to force me to stay here. I want to stay."

As much as I wished him to stay, I was also very concerned about having another kidnapping charge laid against me. I checked with a number of people including Peter Allik-Petersenn and Vincent Chiara. And I called Brigitte's brother-in-law who was then a senior official with the Quebec provincial police force. They all said the same thing:

"What can they do? You're not keeping him here against his will. It's your son who doesn't want to leave. He's 14 years old – you can't tie the kid down and force him to go back. The worst that might happen is, you'll be arrested, kept for a day and then released."

Peggy was beside herself and tried everything to convince Rick to return. There were constant phone calls back and forth. One day she would berate him that his actions could cause a split between her and Jack and ruin their marriage. A few days later she would reverse her approach completely and even suggest that she might leave Jack if that would make a difference. Rick's response showed his growing maturity, cynicism and concern for his younger brother: "So what are you going to do then – make another kid unhappy?"

There were calls from Peggy's sister, Lydia, as well as from her mother. Each took a turn urging Rick to return. After each of these calls, he would become utterly depressed and shut himself up in his room.

To insist that he wanted to stay with us showed an amazing amount of courage. But his decision was tearing at his insides. While he had never had an easy relationship with Jack, he loved his mother and it was obvious he missed Jason. Often we'd overhear him on the phone talking to his younger brother, asking him about how he liked kindergarten and what was happening with their friends in Revelstoke.

Eventually the pressure from his mother, combined with his growing adolescent need to assert himself, became powerful tinder. "Why can't she just accept that I want to spend some time with you after all these years?" he burst out more than once.

Brigitte and I did our best to ease the tension. "If you feel good about staying, we'd like you to stay," I told him. "If you want to go back, you go back. In any case, your mom is always welcome to visit you here. We'll make sure she has a place to stay. And you can phone her in Revelstoke anytime you want."

After many arguments and extended telephone conversations, Peggy reluctantly accepted his decision to live with us. He enrolled in a local school and gradually settled into a pattern of schoolwork and activities with friends. We lived next door to a family whose children had known and played with Rick ever since he started coming to Montreal. Their friendship helped him to fit into his new life and soon he was part of a group of kids his age who would meet regularly at a nearby park for an informal game of ball or soccer.

In October of that same year, OPCR held its second international conference. Brigitte, too, was now a member of the organizing committee. So it had become a real family affair. Even Rick attended a few of the sessions.

Participants ranged from judges and lawyers to social workers, psychologists, mediators, law enforcement officers and others – most of whom saw, on a daily basis, the direct effects of family breakdown.

Over the three-day conference, experts from several different countries exchanged research findings that focused public attention on what it was like – from a child's point of view – to contend with the burden of abuse, family breakdown, separation from a parent, the remarriage of a parent, adoption, new blended families, and so on. Among its supporters, the conference counted the Honorable Alan B. Gold, then chief justice of the Quebec Superior Court, as well as international representatives of UNICEF, and the heads of Quebec's professional corporations of social workers and psychologists and its chamber of notaries.

The conference not only gave OPCR new contacts in an increasingly connected global network of people working to advance the interests of children, it also validated the soundness of the proposals we had been making all along. Over the coming years, we would continue to build on these foundations, and before the end of the decade, had organized two other international conferences.

Meanwhile, on the home front, our family also continued to expand. With the birth of our daughter, Marina, in May of 1993, the family now consisted of three youngsters under the age of six and one teenager. Rick had adjusted well to life in Montreal and showed no inclination to return permanently to B.C. His marks had improved and he was good with the younger kids. At the end of each school day, they expectantly awaited his return. They were also quick to take his side if he and I should argue.

One day Alexandra made us all laugh. I forget what Rick had done or why I was reprimanding him – I just remember it was a nice day and we were standing near the open front door of our home. My voice directly mirrors my mood, and whenever I get upset or excited, it immediately rises in volume. I calm myself just as quickly, but to a five-year-old, that initial loud blast can be quite daunting.

Before I knew it, Alexandra had marched onto the street and announced to a complete stranger – the first passer-by she saw: "My dad isn't being nice with my brother – he's talking very loud."

For once I was at a loss for words and we all started to laugh. Yet Rick was actually very touched that his little sister would take his interests so much to heart.

That first year Rick lived with us was a happy one indeed. He and I even took singing lessons together. It was a great stress-reliever and sometimes, we would be driving together in the car and spontaneously burst into a verse of "Volare," "La Donna Mobile" or some other stirring Italian melody. During one family trip to Cape Cod, I'll always remember Rick, sitting in the backseat with the younger kids, teaching them the words to a favorite song.

During the summer of 1993, when he was 15, Rick worked at OPCR. Through this involvement in the organization, he became aware that he was far from alone in enduring the kind of family conflict he had known all his life. One day, Claire Harting, a journalist who had been following our story for several years, asked if she could interview the two of us.

It was the first time I heard Rick articulate his feelings to a stranger. As a parent, it was one of those rare moments when you get absolute confirmation from your child that the course of action you chose was right.

"If over all these years my father hadn't fought as long and as hard for me as he did – often without my being aware of it – I wouldn't know him today," he told Claire Harting. "I wouldn't even know that he is my father or that he gave me his name. Most fathers would have given up the fight long ago. I owe him a lot."

"The whole thing is horrible," he added. "It doesn't make any sense that a kid who has a father and mother who love him and who loves them can have another name and another father imposed on him by a court. There are laws that need to be changed in this country".

That summer Rick remained frequently in touch with his mother. He had been back to B.C. to see her earlier in the year and he made another trip just before school resumed in the fall. We had given him his own phone so he could talk to her whenever he wanted. He knew, too, that the door was always open should she wish to come to see him.

Things were going well, and he seemed content.

Then shortly before Christmas, he called me from school, completely distraught and in tears. "They want to change my name," he said, his voice breaking as he tried to get the words out. "The principal says I'm not really Ricaardoe Di Done – that I have to be Branden Roaff. I don't want to be Branden Roaff – my name's Ricaardoe."

He only calmed down somewhat when I promised to talk to the principal right away. The problem had to do with his eligibility for English schooling in primarily French Quebec.

To protect the future of the French language in a province surrounded by a vast and predominantly English-speaking North

American continent, most children are required to enroll in the French system, unless they are considered eligible for English schooling. Eligibility depends on their having done a large part of their education in English elsewhere in Canada; or having a parent who did his or her elementary education in English anywhere in Canada (I had attended French school and because of the adoption, was no longer legally his parent); or having a sibling in the English system.

When Rick first came to live in Montreal, we had enrolled him in the English system on the basis of his English schooling in B.C. We had also enrolled him as Ricaardoe Branden Di Done – the name he had used since birth in Montreal and the name he wanted to go by.

It was when the Provincial Education Ministry studied his records and realized that, in actual fact, it was Branden Roaff who had attended school in B.C. and not Ricaardoe Di Done, Jr. that the problems arose. The only way he could legally remain in English school in Quebec was if he was registered under the name Branden Roaff.

This is what his principal had tried to explain to him. But a 15-year-old doesn't care about legalities. Already struggling to gain confidence in himself, establish his identity and gain the approval of his peers, all Rick could imagine was how "stupid" he would appear to his classmates when he suddenly emerged with a completely different name.

In meetings with the principal and the school board representative involved in his case, I recounted the problems he had had with all his name changes, how proud he had been over the last year that he had resumed his identity of Ricaardoe Di Done and how distressed he was at losing this identity yet again. Both of these school officials showed a great deal of compassion and understanding and we eventually reached a compromise: in school, he would always be known as Ricaardoe Di Done; however, at the ministry his formal records would remain under the name Branden Roaff.

Outwardly, he seemed reconciled to this solution, but from that time forward, his behavior underwent a steady and serious deterioration. The anxiety over his adoption that had been quietly simmering in the background suddenly boiled over in a new rage and rebelliousness. If the first year we had spent together as a family was idyllic, those to come were anything but that.

I knew by heart the statistics about the effects of divorce and family breakdown on children. I spent my working life quoting them as a compelling argument for social change. Still, you're never really prepared when those statistics suddenly take on a life of their own in your own child.

Rick's grades began a sharp descent. Hardly a week passed when I didn't get a call from the school about unexplained absences or unacceptable behavior. At home, he developed a surliness that caused increasing friction between Brigitte and myself. Then there was the money missing from my wallet and the other children's piggy banks as he began experimenting with marijuana and hashish, and fell into a pattern of lies, petty theft and, finally, inevitable confrontations with the police.

At one point, I cut off his allowance completely because I feared he would only spend it on drugs. I called Peggy to alert her to what was happening and to ask her, for his own good, to refrain from sending him any money. "If we're going to help him out of this, we've got to stand together," I said.

A few days later I overheard him talking to his mother on the phone. By this time I was so concerned about his behavior that I quietly picked up the receiver in another room to listen in on the conversation. I couldn't believe what I heard. She was asking him to let her know if he needed money and where she should send it to him.

In the tense and difficult months that followed, what saved my relationship with my son was the line of communication – though badly frayed – that remained open between the two of us.

— "Why didn't you just kidnap me and take me away from all this when I was little," he said to me on more than one occasion. "Then I wouldn't have to deal with all this shit now."

In the midst of these other problems, the adoption festered like an open sore. Rick's frustration was concentrated in the knowledge that it prevented him from legally using his Di Done name.

One day in April of 1994, he had a very long and painful telephone conversation with his mother when he tried to convince her to help him change his name back to Ricaardoe Branden Di Done.

— "Mom, I'm using the name Di Done now. But the school – they want to change it. You've got to see my point, Mom. I don't want to use the name Roaff. I have a real father and his name is Di Done and that's why it should be done."

— "I'm not really keen on Di Done," Peggy responded, suggesting that he wait till he was an adult to change his name if this was what he still wanted later on. "And the name Ricaardoe – I just don't see it. It doesn't suit you — it belongs to him — and it was never meant to be your name in the first place."

— "Mom, over here, everyone knows me as Di Done—if I don't get my name changed legally, they're going to put it to Roaff. Why do you want Roaff? I don't want Roaff—I have a biological father. All you have to do is sign an affidavit or something that says my name is Ricaardoe Branden Di Done."

— "I just wonder what's coming next after this," Peggy continued. "First you change your name, then you lose the adoption, then what? I never see you again?"

—"Why are you talking like that, Mom? Like that's really going to happen!"

The conversation went on, with Peggy convinced that I was behind all this, trying to mould my son in my own image and cut him off from her, while Rick argued that that wasn't the case at all – it was what he himself wanted.

Finally Rick said, "So my whole life, I'm going to have two identities?"

—"I suppose that's the way I see it," Peggy answered him. "I'd hate you to be Ricaardoe Di Done – it does something to me inside that just kills me—and that's all I can tell you. I feel as bad about that as you feel about what you're talking about. You have to try and put yourself in my shoes and see how I feel…I want you to be your own person…but I guess you can't understand that."

—"Mom, you think I want to bring you to court?" Rick asked, by then close to tears. "I don't understand why you can't just turn the page. Don't you see my life's so messed up – everything that happens to me – I graduate, I get married – and you guys are still going to be sitting at separate tables. You don't speak – it's so stupid…and it's all for something that happened 10 years ago."

When they finally hung up, there was still no resolution, and Rick's unhappiness and confusion became all the more evident in the months that followed. Canceling the adoption was the only route remaining – but it left Rick heartsick and openly torn between his desire to please his mother, me and himself.

— "At least one good thing will come of this," I would say, trying to help him channel his frustration into something positive. "No other kid will go through this because we're going to change the laws. And it will all be because of you."

When I spoke like that, his spirits would lift and he would say: "You're right. We've got to cancel it."

We talked frequently with Peter Allik-Petersenn who continued to research the existing B.C. case law to see what precedents existed. I also consulted Montreal lawyer and mediator Philip Shaposnick, who, since our first meeting the day he agreed to be part of OPCR's legal committee, had remained close to the organization. It was he who suggested that he represent Rick and me in another possible option.

In mid-1994, we jointly petitioned the Quebec Court's Youth Tribunal for two things: that I be established as Rick's legal father with all the responsibility that entailed and that he legally be recognized as Ricaardoe Branden Di Done, his original name and the one by which he wanted to be known.

Judge François Godbout heard the case in July. Rick was now 16 and his testimony carried considerable weight. He told the judge that what he really wanted was to have his name changed and for both his mother and I to be considered his legal parents once again.

Judge Godbout listened most sympathetically. Given the circumstances and the close relationship between Rick and me, he called our request "natural, laudable and justifiable" *(translation)*. However, to stay within the constraints of the law, I would have to adopt Rick, and the judge first had to be satisfied that he was legally eligible for adoption.

Under Quebec law, one condition for a child to be adopted was that his parents had not provided for his care and education for a period of longer than six months. Since Peggy and Jack had not contributed to his upbringing for the past two years, we all believed he met this condition. However, when the judge asked him directly if both his mother and his father had ceased to provide for him during that period, it was too much for him. He told the judge that his mom had sent him money and some clothes.

And he was clear that while he did not want to be Jack's son, he loved his mother and did not want to endanger his relationship with her anymore than he had wanted to lose me in the past.

Judge Godbout was faced with an insurmountable legal dilemma. Rick's desire to remain the legal son of one of his existing parents (Peggy) and at the same time be considered eligible for adoption by me, were "two incompatible and opposing objectives," *(translation),* effectively tying his hands.

In the courtroom he went even further in acknowledging the weakness of the judicial system in dealing with family breakdown. "It is clear to me – and especially with Ricaardoe's (Jr.) testimony – that it is in his best interests to live with his natural father . . . . But the point is how to proceed with that legally *because the law, in this case, is in the way.*"

Rick was devastated. In his mind, he had ruined our chance of ever having me as his legal father. I, too, was disappointed, but I couldn't help admire his loyalty to his mother in the face of such a difficult and compromising position.

Later that summer, Peter called me from Kamloops. "I think I might have found something to help us," he said. In reviewing previous adoption cases in British Columbia, he had come across one that was particularly relevant. It involved an application by a now-adult adoptee who had requested that his adoption be set aside. The original adoption order had been made in accordance with the court's inherent power to oversee the welfare of minor children. In this particular case, everyone involved – the adoptee, his adoptive parents and the social services authorities – agreed that the adoption should be set aside. Yet, the court ruled that it could not do this for the pure and simple reason that the petitioner, who was over 19, had reached the age of majority. In essence, the court's authority over adoptions was restricted to minor children and once a person reached adulthood, it no longer had any power to alter an adoption order.

Nonetheless, the ruling also stated that there was nothing explicit in the law that said you could or could not set aside an adoption. In the case in question, the court noted it would have seriously considered the request had the person made his application *before turning 19*.

— "What you're telling me, Peter, is that if Rick applies to have the adoption cancelled before his nineteenth birthday, there is a chance it might work?" I wanted to be absolutely clear on this one. My son had already been disappointed far too many times.

— "Ricaardoe, you know as well as I do that there are never any guarantees," Peter replied. "But if Rick is really serious about having this adoption set aside, one thing is certain. He can't wait till he's a grown man – he has to act now."

What clinched Rick's decision was an episode involving his sister Alexandra's schooling. It hammered home how far ranging the adoption's effects could be on himself and those he cared for.

In September of that same year, Alexandra, who was now turning six, started kindergarten. The school we had chosen for her – which was part of the English system – offered a particularly rich language environment with instruction in English part of the day, and in French the remainder. In addition, the children learned Italian. With our family background, it suited us perfectly.

But once again we were to run into problems with the province's language law.

In September 1994, Alexandra had been accepted into the English system, based on the fact that her older brother was already attending high school in English. She couldn't claim eligibility through Brigitte or I because neither of us had attended English school.

Two months (and a new, nationalist Parti Québecois government later), we received a letter from the Education Ministry revoking her right to English instruction. An appeal to the ministry did no good. Her case was now tied to Rick's and it had since come to the ministry's attention that he was adopted. As one bureaucrat informed me, this meant that Rick was not, in fact, her brother, but the legal equivalent of a "stranger" living in the same house.

I was outraged and Rick was furious that the government was claiming Alexandra wasn't his sister. (The matter was eventually resolved to our satisfaction, but it took media coverage, another year of appeals, the decision of the B.C. Supreme Court setting aside the adoption, and support from an influential PQ cabinet minister, before the Minister of Education intervened personally in the case.)

This controversy was the last straw for Rick. Shortly after we received the initial letter from the ministry, he came to see me one evening.

— "I've made up my mind," he said. "I'm ready to go to court to cancel the adoption. I want to be Ricaardoe Branden Di Done once and for all."

— "Are you sure?" I looked him straight in the eye. "I don't want you to be hurt again if it doesn't work out."

— "I'm positive," he answered. "I'll be 17 in January. Let's do it before it's too late."

Both Peter and I thought it would be a good idea for Rick to have one more talk with Dr. Abe Worenklein. We wanted to make very sure that this was what he wanted and that Peggy and Jack couldn't say he was being pushed into it.

In a letter to Peter following his meeting with Rick, Dr. Worenklein confirmed that he wanted to be known as Ricaardoe Di Done Jr. and not Branden Roaff. He quoted Rick as saying, "I don't love him (Jack) anything close to my real father." Worenklein also substantiated Rick's anger over the adoption and the problems that had resulted with Alexandra's schooling. He concluded that it was Rick's own decision to use the Di Done name and that he was not being badgered into it.

At the end of November 1994, with Peter representing us, we applied to the B.C. Supreme Court to set aside the adoption. The petition, signed by Rick, read in part:

"At the time the Order of Adoption was made, I was just under 12 years of age.

As a result, I am informed, my consent to the adoption was not legally required.

If my consent had been required and/or asked for, I would not have consented to my adoption by Jack Roaff. Jack Roaff and I do not have a good relationship nor have Jack Roaff and I ever had a good relationship. I do not want to be the legal son of Jack Roaff. I wish to have my natural mother and my natural father as my legal parents."

A court date was set for mid-January 1995 in Kamloops. Though our physical presence wasn't strictly necessary, both Rick and I wanted to be there as evidence to the judge of the seriousness of our request.

A week before the hearing, Rick announced that he wanted to leave for B.C. immediately so that he could have a few days alone to talk things over with Peggy and Jack. He was convinced that if he told them face-to-face that it was his wish that the adoption be set aside, he could somehow avoid the ordeal of bringing them to court and restore peace among us all. "If I can just spend a few days with them," he said, "I'm sure I can persuade them to go along with this."

"Ricaardoe," I said, "don't go. You're too young and you're no match for them if they decide to try to change your mind. Remember all the things they told you about me that weren't true – that I wasn't there when you were born and I wasn't your real father? What makes you think they are going to act differently now?"

"Papa, I want to do this. It's the best thing for everyone and it's important to me."

I hated the idea of his going alone – now – just days before the court case. But his eyes begged me not to intervene and their message was clear: "This family has had too many arguments for too long." His mind made up, he set off for B.C. confident that he could make a difference.

I prepared to join him a few days later. At 11 p.m. the night before I was to fly out, the telephone rang. It was Rick with the call I had been both dreading and expecting.

— "There's no point coming tomorrow," he said. "I'm not going to court after all."

— "What do you mean you're not going to court?   What's happened?"

I could only imagine the arguments, negotiations, and alienating tactics that had taken place over the past few days. Rick's voice sounded distant and thoroughly sick of the whole affair. He said he didn't want to talk about it.

— "What did they tell you," I started to ask. He cut me off.

— "Mom says if my name goes back to being Ricaardoe, every time she calls me by my name she'll think of you and she hates you."

— "Well, then you can be Branden Di Done," I said.

— "No, the Di Done is a problem, too …" he went on. "I've been thinking – maybe it's not such a big deal if I'm adopted. After all, we know better. That's what matters…"

— "Rick, your mother is playing games with you," I exploded. "It is a big deal – look at what's happened with Alexandra. Look, it's up to you – Ricaardoe Di Done or Branden Roaff, I don't care. But for God's sake, make up your mind. Enough is enough!"

I banged down the phone. Just as quickly I regretted my outburst and tried to call back, but the line was now busy. I called Peter and related what had just occurred. He advised me to go ahead with my plan to leave in the morning. "Who knows what his mother and Jack are telling him. The sooner you can talk to him and get to the bottom of this, the better for everyone. If worse comes to worse," he added, "we'll go to court anyway and tell the judge exactly what happened."

The next morning I flew to Kelowna, where I had arranged to stay with Walter Morandini. Peggy and Jack had since moved to their new home and were living just a few kilometers away.

I called Rick as soon as I arrived.

— "We need to talk," I said. "I need you to tell me what's been going on?"

— "Why don't you talk to Mom," he said and handed the phone to Peggy.

She said she and Jack didn't understand why we were in such a big hurry to have the adoption set aside. "It's not that Jack is so opposed to canceling it, but he feels you're pushing Branden into it – that it's your idea and not Branden's. Why can't this wait till he's a little older and we can all be sure that this is what he really wants."

— "Peggy," I said, "he has a natural mother and a natural father who love him. This adoption never made sense. If something happened to you tomorrow, where would he be? I'd have absolutely no say over what happens to our son."

— "It always comes down to what you want," she answered. "You always want things your way."

— "Yes, I want this, but so does our son, and that's what counts. Ever since the adoption took place, he's been asking me to do something to cancel it. He's proud of his Di Done name and he wants to keep it. You're the ones who keep putting doubts in his mind and you know very well that he and Jack have never been that close."

After many phone calls back and forth and many similar conversations in the next 24 hours, Rick finally agreed to see me. The sun was just going down when Peggy dropped Rick off a short walk from Earl's. I saw him coming along the sidewalk and hurried to meet him. He didn't say a word – he just came up and gave me a hug. Although he was almost as tall as me, at that moment he reminded me so much of the little boy who used to run up, throw his arms around me and say, "Papa, I love you this much all the way around."

Then he pulled away. "Do you mind if I go down to the water – I just want to walk by myself for a bit," he said.

— "Not at all," I said. "I'll wait inside. But don't be too long – you don't want them to run out of that rigatoni and spicy sausage you like so much."

A few minutes later, when he still hadn't returned, I set off anxiously to look for him. I found him standing motionless on a deserted wharf, staring blankly down as the cold water lapped against the pilings.

"Are you all right?" I said, putting an arm on his shoulder. He looked at me, we hugged once more, and tears started falling.

— "Let's go in," I said, breaking the silence. "No matter what happens tomorrow, you have a real mom and a real dad and we both love you."

— "I've made up my mind," he said. "I'm going to court with you."

— "Good! This adoption has to go."

We stayed at Walter's that night and the next day drove together to Kamloops where the hearing was to take place.

Neither Peggy nor Jack appeared in court. In the small, 20-odd seat courtroom, there were just Rick, Peter, myself, Kristian Jensen and the Honorable Mr. Justice Robinson. I hadn't seen Kristian Jensen for almost six years – since the day the adoption was granted in this same building.

In my eyes, he had come to personify everything that was wrong with the legal system. "You knew perfectly well all along that my son never wanted this adoption," I confronted him outside the courthouse, just before the session began. "Well, we're back again today and this time we're going to set it aside. Do you know how much suffering that adoption has caused my son? Is that what you believe the best interest of the child is all about?"

The whole process took little more than an hour. Peter read affidavits from Rick, myself and Dr. Worenklein supporting our petition. Kristian Jensen rarely intervened, offering only that his clients were quite willing to support Rick's decision if, at age 19, this was what he still wanted.

That was the opening Peter was waiting for. Our whole case turned on Rick's making his request before his nineteenth birthday.

"My Lord," Peter began, "we cannot wait until the petitioner is 19 to make this request. The Court can only set the adoption aside while he is still considered a minor." Thereupon he proceeded to summarize the earlier case he had researched.

Mr. Justice Robinson produced a compromise. On January 16, 1995, he set aside the adoption, ruling that the order should take effect no earlier than six months before Rick's nineteenth birthday, and on the condition that Rick confirmed in writing at that time that this was what he truly wanted. Notice was to be given to Kristian Jensen, who agreed on Peggy and Jack's behalf, that they would not oppose

Rick's wishes, once that notice was given. The judge had given Rick another year-and-a-half's leeway to make his final decision.

Rick was buoyant as we left the courthouse. At long last the years of litigation were over and his mother and I could once again be both his natural and legal parents. On paper it all looked so neat and simple. In the precise and colorless language of the law, sixteen agonizing years of struggle and heartbreak – an entire childhood – were compressed into a two-page ruling.

But outside the courtroom, life never stands still. The year following the hearing wasn't an easy one for my son. As the months passed and his nineteenth birthday drew nearer, the pressure mounted on his mother's side not to sign the document that would cause the court order to take effect.

To be truthful, my own patience was running thin. I had given all my youth to the fight to maintain my parental responsibility and we were still dithering to the end. Trapped in the middle between two parents with completely opposing visions, Rick vacillated from one day to the next about whether he should sign. "Ricaardoe," I said, at the end of my rope, "Make whatever decision you must, but make a decision. Then I don't want to hear about it anymore. It's time for all of us to get on with our lives."

In July of 1996, Rick signed the affidavit, confirming he wanted the adoption set aside. With much effort and encouragement, he also pulled himself together and proudly graduated from high school. Since then, he has been working at odd jobs, unsure of what his future course should be. Just recently he has come up with a plan that makes sense and he is optimistic that he's on the right track. I will do whatever I can to support him, as my family has always supported me.

But who can say what scars he will carry as he journeys through life? Or how what has happened to him will influence his own beliefs and future relationships. When I think of the pain he has suffered, my eyes still well up with tears.

What saves me – as it continues to help him – is the knowledge that this story must never be repeated. Only when I can be sure of that will I be able to rest content.

April 29, 2000 in Montreal, Alexandra Di Done's confirmation
(From L to R): **Marina, Rick, Antoni, Alexandra, Brigitte, Samantha and the author.**

September 2000, an evening in the backyard of the Di Done household.
(From L to R): Samantha, Marina, Ricaardoe, Antoni, Alexandra and Rick
(Photo: Brigitte Jalbert)

Some of the Pioneers of Family Mediation involved with the O.P.C.R. *(From L to R)*:
Aldo Morrone, B.A., Family Mediator, Family Mediation Service of Youth Centers of
Montreal, Philip Shaposnick, B.A., B.C.L., Lawyer and Family Mediator, Interlex
Group of Canada, Ricaardoe Di Done, Dominic D'Abate, Ph.D. Accredited Family
Mediator, director, Consensus Mediation Center.   (Photo: Ricaardoe Jr.)

(From L to R): Ricaardoe Di Done, Hon. Sheila Finestone, Canadian
Senator, Rashmi Mayur, Ph.D., President, OPCR India, William Spears,
M.B.A., Project Coordinator, OPCR.   (Photo: Ricaardoe Jr.)

POSTSCRIPT

Much has changed in the three decades that have passed since this story began. The traditionally clear-cut and separate parental roles that society formerly ascribed to mothers and fathers have blurred and evolved. The nurturing and care taking of children is no longer perceived as the exclusive domain of mothers, just as financial support of families is no longer restricted to fathers.

From the perspective of children caught in the middle of their parents' break-up, however, some things never change. Rick is now in his early twenties; yet his struggle to deal with his conflicting emotions towards his mother and myself goes on. Always there are reminders. Not long ago, his mother paid his airfare so that he could spend some time with her and the rest of his family in B.C. The ticket was issued in the name of Branden Roaff.

Court decisions and rulings have no jurisdiction over the human heart. Rick has coped with two separate identities all his life, and it is a lingering reality that he must continue to deal with. For the children of family breakdown, there are many such lifetime issues.

This is not to undermine the important breakthroughs that have taken place. Although there is still no superhighway, leading people straight to a saner and more humane way of dealing with family breakdown, at least roads are opening in this direction.

On January 1, 1981, California became the first U.S. state to pass legislation requiring all parents to enter mediation *before* petitioning a Court for custody or access of their children. Recently, there were as many as 33 U.S. states where at least one jurisdiction had a mandatory mediation program.[29]

In Quebec, before a couple with children can file in court for a divorce, a 1997 law requires that they attend a free group information session about the mediation process and its benefits. (They do not have to attend this session together.) Should they then decide to proceed with mediation, they are entitled to five additional publicly funded 75-minute sessions with a mediator.

In other Canadian provinces, mediation is also making headway, free in some jurisdictions, with fees calculated on the couple's ability to pay, in others. Some provinces are testing the effectiveness of mandatory information sessions, similar to those given in Quebec.[30]

Elsewhere in the world, including Australia, Britain, the U.S., France, Italy, Spain, Belgium and Switzerland, to name just a few, mediation is becoming increasingly popular as an effective means of reaching parenting agreements after divorce or separation.

There is also growing emphasis on the need for education and information programs to sensitize parents to the needs of their children during and after separation, and to equip them with communication and dispute resolution skills to help them in their new co-parenting arrangements. Some provinces, like Saskatchewan and Manitoba, have programs directed specifically at children to help them cope with family breakdown, and some provinces are recognizing the need for children to have a voice in their future and are appointing children's lawyers.[31]

Important developments have also occurred on other fronts. In December 1998, a special Canadian parliamentary committee on child custody and access released its recommendations for reform of the Divorce Act, following a year-long study that included public hearings and testimony from some 500 parents, children, judges, lawyers, mediators, psychologists, and other groups such as OPCR. Among the committee's extensive list of 48 recommendations were several ideas that OPCR has been actively promoting since its creation.

The report, entitled "For the Sake of the Children," recognizes the principle that divorced parents and their children are entitled to "a close and continuous relationship with one another." It recommends that the terms "custody" and "access" be replaced by "shared parenting," and that both parents share responsibility for their children's welfare. Among other proposals are the following:

- Development of a parenting plan by divorcing parents that would clearly outline each person's responsibilities for the care of their children;

- Attendance by divorcing parents at an education program aimed at improving their understanding of the impact of divorce on children;

- Participation by parents in at least one mediation session to help them develop a parenting plan;

- Equal access for both parents to their children's school and medical records so they can take part in key decisions;

- Expansion of unified family courts across Canada, that in addition to their judicial functions, would include a broad range of support services such as family and child counseling, mediation, and follow-up services to monitor the implementation of shared parenting orders;

- Maintenance of children's relationships with grandparents, siblings and other family members, where this is in the children's best interests, by incorporating provisions to this effect in parenting plans.

As yet, these proposals have not been implemented and the federal government has said it will take three years to study them. Should the government change in that period, who knows what will become of them?

Meanwhile, children and their families wait for the benefits of such reforms, and until they become law, so much still depends on the goodwill of the separating parents. Where that goodwill does not exist, I have no doubt that a story like Rick's could repeat itself even today.

In part, this is because we still have a long way to go before we move away from what Quebec lawyer and mediator Philip Shaposnick calls our " conflict culture." Not that conflict is unusual or even necessarily bad; as long as there is life, people will hold different opinions about the best course of action to take in any given situation. What is noteworthy is how we resolve that conflict.

A few years ago, in the midst of a discussion with several family lawyers about the devastating effects of a long drawn-out divorce and custody struggle, I mentioned my conviction that our adversarial legal system only further embitters already fragile relationships.

— "Well, what do you expect us to do?" one of the lawyers responded. "We don't start the fights. Our job is to serve our clients

– and if our clients insist on attacking each other, the conflict will escalate…"

—"Exactly my point." I said. "If you can't do anything, why don't you stand aside and let someone trained to reduce conflict step in."

In a conflict culture, the automatic response is to call in a lawyer. The tougher and more outspoken our lawyer, the better we think our chances of "winning" the conflict. We have been conditioned to win conflicts, not to resolve them through compromise and consensus building. If our lawyer does try to reason with us, and looks objectively at what would be the best outcome for all concerned, chances are we'll say, "You're not tough enough. I need a real street fighter."

So the system feeds upon itself. Highly combative parents seek out highly aggressive divorce lawyers, who, in turn, draw on an arsenal of tactics to "get" the other party and cast them in the most villainous light possible. The children become the forgotten casualties.

Not every family conflict descends to the sickening depths that Peggy's and mine did. But what if one parent is prepared to compromise – and the other refuses to do so? What recourse does the first parent have – especially if he is a father in a system where many of the judges, lawyers and others who will ultimately decide his fate have grown up in homes where child-raising was primarily the mother's responsibility? It is hardly surprising that the conflict grows ever more intense.

Peggy and I were perfect examples. Back in 1981, I would have gladly accepted the compromise of having joint custody of our son. The response from every lawyer I talked to was: "It's pointless to ask for that. The mother doesn't want it, so you'll never get it." Instead we engaged in sixteen years of legal warfare. When I knew she wanted our son adopted, I countered with a petition for custody. When she got one expert report, I would get two or three. There was no check on the number of petitions we could file, no limit on the number of delays our lawyers could obtain, no mechanism to halt the escalating conflict.

In reality, custody and access have become a thriving industry that supports a whole battery of professionals including family lawyers, psychologists, and social workers, in addition to the judges and other staff members who keep the wheels of our courts turning.

The greater the conflict, the greater the cost to both the family – and to society. Every day, medical professionals treat the emotional and physical after-effects of destroyed relationships. Teachers struggle to share knowledge with youngsters whose attention is focused on family problems – not on their studies. Police and other public security officials are confronted daily with the actions of distraught, despairing parents and of emotionally messed-up kids.

Divorce is not going to go away. Furthermore, divorce statistics don't even take into account the increase in common-law relationships, which, in Canada alone, have tripled since the early 1980's.[32] We are only starting to gather information about the frequency of break-ups among these unions.

When a couple falls "out of love," only time can lessen the heartbreak of a failed relationship. But, as a society, we can implement better solutions for managing the separation process and containing the hurt. We owe it to our children. This is why I believe so strongly that mediation services should be both free and mandatory.

Had Peggy and I been obliged to follow a process of mediation, chances are we would have arrived at an agreement that was more flexible and better suited to our needs than anything a judge – however fair and objective – could have decided. No one could know our personal situations – and our son's needs – better than ourselves.

After everything that happened, it is only natural to wonder whether we would have ever been capable of the honest, open discussion necessary to reach such an agreement. Certainly the chances diminished greatly with each new legal action. A skilled mediator right from the start, would have made all the difference, steering us through the minefield of mistrust we both erected when we knew our relationship was over and each of us was terrified at the thought of losing Rick. A realization that we both shared the same fear might have opened a path for discussion, in all frankness; how we could live separate lives and yet still ensure that our son enjoyed the love of both his parents and their families.

Peggy and I were not unique. Every week, mediators deal with couples who would prefer never to be in the same room together. Philip Shaposnick and his co-mediator and social worker wife, Bernice, have adopted a collaborative, problem-solving approach to handling the situation. The mediation takes place in the calming atmosphere of their pleasantly decorated office, in a portion of the room furnished with a two-seater couch and two chairs. As mediators, he and his wife each take one of the chairs and invite the couple to sit together on the two-seater. The idea is not to inflict more discomfort on them, but to emphasize that even as their conjugal relationship is ending, they must still work together as parents. Ultimately, they must come to some understanding and move forward.

The mediator is not there to tell the couple what to do – but to help them come to their own decisions. Justin Lévesque, respected Quebec author, teacher and mediation pioneer, suggests that a mediator's power is almost magical in its ability to enable two people – who have come to see each other as rivals and sworn enemies – to believe that a solution is possible. "The magic works by focusing attention away from the conflict and the source of division and onto what the couple still has in common....The mediator frames the situation in a different light and offers the parties points of view that they haven't yet considered."[33]

We know that mediation is far less costly than litigation and that mediated agreements are also reached must faster. There is also mounting evidence that divorcing couples who use mediation to reach a settlement comply with it more readily than they would a ruling handed down by a judge. In our case, this could have eliminated years of legal battles and further alienation.

Why, then, isn't use of mediation more widespread? Certainly in cases of severe domestic violence and abuse, mediation may not be possible or even desirable, and these should be treated separately. But on the whole, the benefits of mediation are well documented.

Some opponents argue that since the vast majority of divorce settlements in Canada are reached out of court, there is little need for mandatory mediation. Yet, how many couples actually comply with these settlements six months, one year, three years after they are reached? And why, if these agreements are working, is there such growing concern about the financial well being of children in separated families? And why is collection of support payments still such an issue?

An out-of-court settlement is primarily an agreement reached between lawyers in an adversarial process. Unlike mediation, it does not encourage the couple to sit down together and actively participate in working out their own differences. As a result, it is not likely to help them gain the cooperative, problem-solving and conflict resolution skills they will need to successfully implement their agreement and raise their children in peace.

In my personal experience, opposition to mediation is particularly strong among lawyers. At a meeting of some 150 family lawyers in Montreal a couple of years ago, only one lone voice was in favor of making it mandatory for couples to attend even an information session on mediation. It is tempting to attribute this to a fear of lost business income – and I suspect this is a contributing factor – but this would also be a serious oversimplification.

For the legal profession, mediation – particularly mandatory mediation – represents a revolutionary and unfamiliar means of managing the divorce process. For years, lawyers have been trained to defend what they see as their clients' rights. Their goal is to win the case for their client and they are highly skilled in diverse methods of argument and attack to achieve this goal. If their client is undergoing a divorce or separation, winning the case becomes synonymous with "winning" the children, the greatest share of the property, the best possible (or least damaging) financial settlement and so on. Good lawyers put their heart and soul into their work. But, as mediator Aldo Morrone asks, where families are concerned, is it the right work?

Not long ago, some representatives of OPCR were discussing the subject of mediation with the head of the family division of the American Bar Association. The individual in question congratulated us on our efforts to promote mediation, but in the same breath noted that even in mediation, it was essential that both parties retain their lawyers.

Precisely because the language and spirit of mediation represents such a dramatic change from traditional litigation, it has been my personal experience – and that of OPCR – that Bar Associations in Canada and elsewhere have been slow to promote it. Since lawyers tend to dominate the ranks of elected officials, it is not surprising that legislators, too, have been slow to act.

I am also convinced that it is essential that professionals such as social workers be very involved in the mediation process. These are people who are trained to help others resolve their problems in a positive way that takes into account everyone's concerns. In my view, it would be cause for grave concern if the legal profession, with its deep adversarial roots, ever attempted to become the sole watchdog over the mediation process.

The tragedy that my son, his mother, myself and both our families endured, has made me a strong proponent of free and mandatory mediation. This being said, I don't believe mediation alone will cure all the ailments facing families today. Mediation is but one tool in a whole social support system that should include education, counseling, specialized family courts, family-friendly terminology and a formal complaint mechanism in the event that either spouse neglects his or her responsibilities following a split.

Prevention of family breakdown starts with education. Why then don't we routinely train people to become good parents – starting in elementary school? A recent comment by Eugenia Repetur Moreno, the Executive Director of the Canadian Association of Social Workers, noted that "we teach young people about birth control and the need for safe sex, but we never tell them there's a point where it's all right to have children…or explain to them their future responsibilities as parents."

When couples do encounter marital problems, they are often unsure where to get the counseling that could help them restore their relationship. Or they feel there is a stigma attached to this kind of professional help, or that they can't afford it. Making these services highly visible and widely accessible could eliminate much of the human suffering and the social, legal and medical costs that follow so often on the heels of family breakdown.

When reconciliation is clearly out of the question, any couple with children who wish to file for divorce should first be obliged to meet with a mediator. However, I also understand that you can't force people to cooperate with each other. Some people will automatically opt for mediation because it offers the least painful route out of a distressing situation. But others – out of fear, a history of an abusive relationship or an overwhelming desire to lash out at what has hurt them – will find themselves incapable of cooperating with a former spouse.

That's when a specialized family law court is needed, with judges trained in the psychology of human relationships and child development, as well as the intricacies of family law. These specialized judges would not have to divide their attention between a family law case one day and one involving corporate or criminal law the next.

Judges might begin by asking both parties why mediation failed in an effort to determine the underlying motives of each spouse. Were there very legitimate reasons for their inability to cooperate, or has one or both simply been operating out of their own self-interest, regardless of the serious and lasting repercussions on the lives of their children and other family members? The flexibility each spouse is willing to show in encouraging the other person to continue to fulfill his or her parental role would then become an important factor in the judge's eventual decision.

A major complaint about the current system is the length of time it takes to resolve family conflicts, which must vie for court time with a host of other types of cases. At very best, a settlement in a contested divorce takes one-to-two years. But, as we have seen, cases like mine can drag much longer. By concentrating on fewer cases, judges in specialized family courts would make their rulings sooner. Meanwhile, parents and kids could get on with the process of healing.

Lastly, even the best mediated agreements or court decisions should be reviewed every so often to ensure that they are still serving the interests of all concerned. The circumstances that lead to divorce and family break-up do not usually develop overnight. They are an accumulation of actions and behaviors over an extended period. In the same way, parents' emotional, financial and social situations continue to evolve after a break-up and their children's interests and needs change and mature.

Agreements about where the kids will live, how both parents will maintain their involvement and what financial support is required are really the beginning of a process – not the end. How well both parents are upholding the agreement and whether changing circumstances warrant adjustments, should be the subject of periodic reviews by an objective third party – in much the same way that patients who have undergone surgery or other treatment are encouraged to have regular medical check-ups. When problems or disagreements arise, there must also be a mechanism to hear and address complaints.

*****

I have traveled a long and difficult road since that day, as a young man, when I first stepped off the plane in Edmonton. During that time I have learned many hard lessons. Foremost among them is that parents have a sacred trust. We are responsible for the happiness and well being of our children and that responsibility to cooperate for the good of our children never ceases, even if our spousal relationship ends.

For the vast majority of separations and divorces, fighting it out in court is not the solution. Peggy and I did that for sixteen years. Nothing was achieved and so much of our lives was lost. Only by putting aside our own differences and cooperating for the sake of our son, could we have really accomplished something worthwhile.

We needed tools to do this – and at the time they simply weren't available. By allowing us to escalate our conflict, the system pushed us further and further away from resolution.

People often ask me what I would do if I were suddenly transported back twenty years. Would I make the same decisions I did then? Frankly, I don't know.

I do know that I would never abandon my son. My life to date includes its full share of mistakes, but my insistence on remaining a central presence in my son's life, on letting him know how proud I am to be his father and how much I love him, is not one of them.

All the same, the means I had to take – sixteen years of legal battles – were extremely painful, destructive and costly in every way and for everyone involved.

When I think of the broadened view society now holds of the role of fathers and mothers, and of the increasing interest in mediation and other positive family interventions, I am heartened that my persistence is helping to bring about change. But when I remember the lost time that Rick and I can never regain and the scars that he will carry all his life, I am not nearly so confident.

This book began by describing a decision that my son should never have had to make to cancel his adoption. It ends with a plea against perpetuating an adversarial system that drives so many separating parents to engage in actions that they realize too late are ruinous to their own children.

Rick, like hundreds of thousands of kids like him, wanted only to have both his parents beside him as he matured into adulthood. How long will it take our society to grasp what every child instinctively knows? How long will it take us to act accordingly? The opportunity is there before us. I pray that we don't waste it.

Ricaardoe Jr., Alexandra Di Done, Antoni Di Done, Samantha Di Done, the author, Aunt Toni and Marina Di Done at the author's residence, Father's Day, summer 2003   (Photo: Brigitte Jalbert)

The author, Ricaardoe Jr. & Dr. Rashmi Mayur at the author's residence, summer 2002. (Photo: Brigitte Jalbert)

The author and Ricaardoe Jr. in front of the Canadian parliament for a press conference on Bill C-22 (Divorce Act) at the National Press Gallery in Ottawa, June 2003. (Photo: Brigitte Jalbert)

The Honorable Lise Thibault, Lieutenant-governor for the province of Quebec, Me Peter Allik-Petersenn, Mr. Peter B. Yeomans, President of public security, city of Montreal, the author, Professor Richard Cloutier, School of Psychology, Laval University, at the OPCR's 5th International Conference on the Child, May 2002.   (Photo: Ricaardoe Jr.)

Ms. Roshni Udyavar, OPCR Director for India, Me Peter Allik-Petersenn, OPCR Director in B.C., the author, Mr. Denis Landry, Professor Garfield A. Brown, OPCR Director for South Africa, Dr. Sadig Rasheed, Director, Program division, UNICEF, at the 5th International Conference on the Child, May 2002. (Photo: Ricaardoe Jr.)

The author at one of the OPCR's yearly Christmas celebrations for underprivileged children in Montreal, December 2002.

The author visits a BMW S.E.E.D. project school while participating at the Civil Society Global Forum at the U.N. World Summit on Sustainable Development in Johannesburg South Africa, August 2002.

APPENDIX I

CONSEQUENCES OF SEPARATION AND/OR DIVORCE

There are revealing studies that have been conducted on the effects of a separation or divorce on children :

- Most children of divorce have great difficulties in school and in personal and social relationships. There is also a noticeable increase in drug and alcohol use and a higher rate of delinquency.[34]

- Divorce has a number of negative consequences on the quality of life in adulthood. There are physical health problems, depression, and low educational attainment.[35]

- Several studies have demonstrated that parents who are separated are at a higher risk of experiencing stressful events (accidents, loss of employment, sickness, etc.) than parents of intact families. The separation seems to reduce the capability of individuals to effectively deal with the troubles of life.[36]

- Children from reconstituted families represent 30% of the school population in urban centers. They constitute 60% of the students who have difficulties or behavioral problems at school.[37]

- The suicide rates for divorced Quebec men and women are five times higher than those of married people.[38]

- Children and parents of broken families have six times more mental and physical health problems than the children and parents of intact families.[39]

- The standard of living of the whole family is dramatically reduced when there is a divorce. There are less financial resources available and less human resources available since the parents are preoccupied with dealing with their own emotional upheavals and stresses.

OUR RECOMMENDATIONS

We have enumerated a few of the problems that the break–up of the family can have on children, parents and other family members. The negative consequences of separation or divorce on the development of children can be reduced. We must bring an awareness of the different types of problems. We therefore propose the following:

- Create courses at the elementary and secondary level in order to educate and sensitize students about parental responsibilities.

- Create a system of family reconciliation, which is available at all times for couples and families in crisis.

- Put into place family mediation services that are free, mandatory, and non-judicial, for all couples experiencing marital difficulties or going through divorce proceedings.

- Eliminate terms that create friction between the parties. For instance, replace the expressions "legal custody" by "parental responsibilities" and "support orders" by "financial responsibilities of parents".

- Create a court specializing in family matters where judges have an extensive background in family law as well as in psychosocial matters.

- Create an office of formal complaints where one spouse can file an official complaint in the event that the other spouse does not respect his/her financial or other responsibilities.

The above-mentioned recommendations are further elaborated upon in the brief presented to the Joint Committee on Custody and Access that is found in Appendix II.

Parents and children should have access to preventive social services and professional help in order to avoid an escalation of crises and difficulties. Parental involvement must be encouraged and reinforced through services that will help them. Parents cease to be spouses or partners after a separation or divorce, but they do not cease to be parents. Parenthood must continue to be exercised in an atmosphere of harmony after a break-up.

APPENDIX II

FAMILY MEDIATION:
A PROCEDURE THAT BENEFITS EVERYONE

Brief

Presented to the Special Joint Committee
On Child Custody and Access

By the
Organization for the Protection of Children's Rights

Researched and written by:
Riccardo Di Done, Founding President and Project
Manager
Ms. Angela Ficca, LL.M., Lawyer
Claudia Bragaglia, Psychosociology Student
Submitted in Montreal
Friday, 3 April, 1998

TABLE OF CONTENTS   PAGES

INTRODUCTION

The Organization for the Protection of Children's Rights (OPCR), which was founded in 1983, is a non-profit organization whose mission is to protect and defend the rights of children and adolescents. More particularly, the OPCR's purpose is to help those who are experiencing difficult situations relating to the break-up of the family, as well as physical and psychological violence, school drop-outs, juvenile delinquency, suicide, alcohol and drug abuse and so on. With the support of its multidisciplinary team of professionals, the OPCR provides assistance to people in difficulty and helps minimize the problems experienced by children, adolescents, parents and grandparents involved in family conflicts.

The outcome of the current debate over child custody and access will definitely have a direct impact on the lives of many children, but also on our society in general.

From a socio-economic standpoint, it is essential to address the problem comprehensively, rather than to limit ourselves to a single aspect of the issue that may serve the interests of one small group. It even appears to be beneficial to do so and this is precisely what this brief will attempt to show.

With the aid of this brief, our organization hopes to demonstrate that automatically resorting to mediation in family conflicts is a legitimate measure.

Apart from mediation as a way of solving problems, the Organization also suggests preventive measures for enabling families to avoid the trauma of a break-up. These recommendations are set out below together with their benefits. We begin with a brief historical look of family mediation in Quebec since 1981, then we outline our organization's position on the issue. The repercussions of divorce on adults and children are then described, thus explaining the reasons for our organization's position and its recommendations.

BACKGROUND

Sudden developments in the issue of family mediation are not recent phenomenon. Mediation has followed a long and tortuous path, one that has thrown up increasing difficulties to slow, if not stop, its progress.

In 1981, the Quebec Department of Health and Social Services introduced a family mediation pilot project at the Superior Court in Montreal. In 1984, however, despite the program's undeniable success, the Government of Quebec was still reluctant to extend it to the rest of the province. It cited as a reason the fact that it was awaiting the findings of a research project conducted by the Department of Justice Canada on mediation services in four Canadian cities, including Montreal. However, rumor circulating at the time held that the Minister of Justice was stonewalling because he wanted mediation to come under his department's jurisdiction.

In August 1987, while the debate on the issue followed its course, the Department of Health and Social Services refused to waste any more time and asked the Cabinet to allocate nearly $1 million to expand family mediation services to the rest of Quebec. It also insisted that the entire system be managed from the province's Social Services Centers.

The Richardson study, which was conducted for the Department of Justice Canada, was ultimately published in February 1998. The very high marks it gave to the Montreal mediation program surprised no one, since information to that effect had been leaked some time earlier. However, publication of the findings merely reconfirmed the benefits of mediation for families. While some observers saw the findings as grounds to proceed in this matter, others continued to dispute control over the system. And while some fought for control, others conducted more studies and presented numerous briefs to almost as many commissions. Thus, the Standing Committee of the Department of Cultural and Social Affairs, the briefs by the Treasury Board and the Association of Social Services Centers and the study by the Quebec Department of Justice saw the light of day.

The conclusions of the last study included the statement that family mediation services should be taken over by the Quebec Department of Justice rather than the Department of Health and Social Services. With this statement, the Department of Justice appeared to consider family mediation as a "support to the Court", whereas it should be perceived as a "psychosocial service" assisting spouses in resolving their conflicts by inducing them to admit that there is an interpersonal relationship problem. This is why the issue must be viewed comprehensively as a component of family policy.

During this time, senior officials from the various departments continued to debate the issue. However, it appears that the stumbling blocks to their efforts were funding and the issue of whether family mediation should be free or fee-based.

In 1989, the Organization for the Protection of Children's Rights (OPCR) formed a coalition with the Fédération des Associations des familles monoparentales du Québec [Federation of Associations of Single-Parent Families of Quebec], the Fédération des Unions de familles [Federation of Family Unions], and the Association des Centres de Services sociaux du Québec [Association of Social Service Centers of Quebec]. When the issue reached an impasse, these groups asked the Premier of Quebec to intervene in the debate and decide the question.

In 1993, the government ultimately tabled Bill 14, *An Act to Amend the Code of Civil Procedure Respecting Family Mediation,* which would have enabled the Court to adjourn and to refer the parties to family mediation. Bill 14 had one weakness because, in our view, when parties appear in Court, it is already too late to refer them to mediation. Family mediation should be mandatory before separation or divorce proceedings are instituted. The sections of the Act relating to the adjournment by the court to refer the parties to family mediation, came into force.

On September 1, 1997, the Government of Quebec enacted Bill 65, requiring all couples with children to attend a mandatory information session explaining family mediation before the parties are heard in Court. In this way, when a couple, whether they are married or not, is in conflict over child custody and support, family assets or any other property right resulting from the marriage or the support of one of the parties, they must attend an information session before appearing in Court.

OPCR'S POSITION

As a non-profit organization concerned with the welfare of children and families, the Organization of the Protection of Children's Rights (OPCR) has, since its inception in 1983, fervently demanded that a free and non-legal system of mandatory family mediation be introduced. However, we wish to provide you with our recommendations to make mediation as effective as possible.

As an organization that works with victims of family conflict and break-up of the family, we try to provide those people with the tools they need to cope more effectively with their problems.

We believe in the validity of mediation within our social system. In our view, resorting to mediation makes it possible to settle family disputes using a much more moderate method, which markedly reduces the heartbreak of family break-ups.

Based on this same reasoning, the OPCR recommends that the Special Joint Committee currently reviewing the possibility of amending the provisions of the *Divorce Act* concerning child custody and access, help couples to develop a parental plan following separation or divorce. This plan would place emphasis on the responsibilities and duties of each parent. Parents could share responsibility for all activities and problems affecting their children, including recreational activities (sports, leisure, etc.), doctor's appointments and parent-teacher meetings. A schedule could also be established for the entire year.

This plan is an important procedure in countering certain consequences of the legal battles between couples in the midst of divorce proceedings. All too often, the parent who has legal custody of the children is perceived as the winner and the parent with access as the loser. The term "legal custody" is not conducive to a spirit of cooperation between parents. We feel that cooperation is important so that children can continue to feel loved by both parents.

Another recommendation by the **OPCR** is precisely that certain terms that polarize the two parents and suggest images of winners and losers should be avoided. It is important to consider that, at this stage, there is no longer any question of deciding who is the better parent, but rather of determining what action plan should be used to ensure the healthy and balanced growth of the children involved. This approach is fundamentally important since it focuses on the contribution of each parent to the welfare of the children.

It is understood that this involves a change of attitude and behavior on the part of each parent. Although it may be difficult to deal with the past, both parents must take themselves in hand to provide a more harmonious future for their children.

It is absolutely necessary to make parents aware of, and to provide them with, effective tools so that they can adequately discharge their responsibilities toward their children. Family mediation affords families this opportunity.

THE STICKING POINT : THE NOTION OF "OBLIGATION"

Children need the love and security of both their parents in order to grow in a well-balanced way. For this reason, we feel that mediation is so important that it should be mandatory.

Yet the term seems to be the sticking point for the opponents of mediation. They feel it will compromise the spouses' free choice as to whether they will rely on mediation to resolve their situation. We believe this choice is not violated, but more informed by mandatory mediation. The spouses will have an alternative, a choice to manage their conflict themselves. Others even add that mediation should not be mandatory since 80 per cent of cases involving corollary relief (custody, access, support and the division of property) are settled before trial. We feel that this statement disregards the actual situation that spouses experience after the settlement. Although it is true that 80 per cent of cases are settled out of Court, it is also true that many of those agreements are not complied with by the parties. The proof of this resides in the fact that the National Assembly has had to legislate to ensure that alimony is paid *(Act Facilitating the Payment of Alimony)*.

Family mediation should therefore be mandatory before separation or divorce actions are even filed. From the moment the parties have consulted a lawyer to prepare for divorce proceedings, their perception of the system is one of confrontation. The parties have had to prepare for proceedings in which it often appears to be necessary to present their respective versions of the facts, with each party trying to gain the upper hand. They feel they have no other choice but to fight for what they want. Consequently, if the first mandatory step is to consult a mediator and then to seek legal information from an expert, the outcome will definitely be different.

Quebec would not be the first jurisdiction to make mediation mandatory. On January 1st, 1981, **California became the first state to pass legislation requiring all parents to enter mediation before petitioning a Court for custody and access.**[40] Since then, all divorcing couples with children in this jurisdiction have first had to enter mediation. Only afterwards are they directed to petition the Court for custody and access. In Los Angeles, where nearly 500 couples a month seek access or custody, 55 per cent of that number have managed to obtain consent through mediation.[41]

Other data gathered in Los Angeles show that a 75 per cent reduction in the number of custody cases is attributable to the implementation of a family mediation program.[42] According to one Los Angeles Superior Court justice, the daily number of such cases fell from 15 to three or five in the year after mediation legislation went into effect.

Consequently, there are now 33 U.S. states where at least one jurisdiction has a mandatory mediation program: Alabama, Alaska, Arizona, California, Colorado, Delaware, Florida, Georgia, Hawaii, Idaho, Indiana, Iowa, Kansas, Louisiana, Maine, Massachusetts, Michigan, Minnesota, Missouri, Nebraska, Nevada, New Jersey, New Mexico, New York, North Carolina, North Dakota, Oregon, Pennsylvania, Texas, Utah, Virginia, Washington and Wisconsin.[43]

However, we need not cite examples so far afield. The city of Winnipeg, in Manitoba, is also a good basis for comparison. When mediation was introduced here by the Honorable A.C. Hamilton, Associate Chief Justice of Family Division, approximately 60% of the cases settle during, or just prior to the Pre-trial Conference. Another 30% or more settle between the Pre-trial Conference and the trial date. During this meeting, the judge tells the spouses about the negative effects that a legal approach will have on their relationship and the relationship they have with their children. The Honorable A.C. Hamilton explains the negative effects of a trial in the following manner:

"I explain the damaging effect of a trial if children are involved;

explain that they will say things at a trial that are bitter and brutal, that the lawyers will examine and cross-examine them to explore their every fault, their weakness as a mother or father. I tell them a trial will further damage their relationship, will probably involve the children further in their fight and will certainly be costly. They are told that one of them will likely win and one will likely lose, based solely upon the reaction of a judge to the evidence, as it comes out in court."

Up until recently, in another Canadian province, Saskatchewan, when a family action was filed, a "pre-mediation" session was mandatory before the legal process could continue. The purpose of this session was to explain to the parties the mediation process and its many benefits and to determine whether they wished to come to an out-of–court settlement. Following the session, the parties could then decide whether or not to enter mediation. The law was repealed because the Bar Association was against the mandatory pre-mediation session. It is truly unfortunate that that province had to take that step backward.

It is interesting that, in its 1988 report, the Department of Justice, Canada underscored *the positive effects of mandatory mediation,* adding that a number of couples who had been required to enter mediation would never have considered that option if they had not been induced to use it. It appears that there is no negative effect in at least requiring the parties to attend one mediation session.

In the process currently under way, it is essential to understand that mediation makes it possible to assess the attitude of both parties. During the first meeting, the mediator, who has been trained for this purpose can first explain to the spouses how mediation works to ensure they clearly understand the alternatives this option offers. In addition to increasing their awareness, this meeting also reveals to what extent the individuals have been affected by their separation and how capable they are of making decisions. In conducting the process, the mediator takes the time to outline the effects that divorce will have on the conflicting spouses and their children. He will also have the opportunity to determine whether the couple was able to reach agreements while they lived together.

The mediator clearly acts as a moderating factor. The purpose of his role is mainly to temper the behavior and speech of the parties to the conflict in order to keep the discussion on track. By making the former spouses understand that the purpose of the exercise is not to designate a winner and a loser, but rather to reach an agreement that is satisfactory for everyone, while not losing sight of the best interest of the children involved, the mediator can readily manage to limit spousal outbursts and establish good cooperation.

Once the former spouses have fully understood that the agreement reached through mediation will be based on their own decisions and not on a judgment imposed on them by a third person, it becomes even easier to secure their participation. In addition, the informal nature of mediation fosters a more relaxed climate that subsequently reduces tension between the parties.

It should nevertheless be borne in mind that a Court action, in addition to promoting confrontation, could kill any healthy components of a relationship that has gone bad.

Individuals Who Resist Mediation

We understand that it is not necessarily easy for people in the midst of divorce proceedings to sit down together and discuss their problems. This is beyond a doubt the greatest barrier to initiating the mediation process. Knowing perfectly well that angry human beings do not necessarily make the right decisions instinctively, we think it is essential that couples be guided through the separation process so that they can subsequently make an informed choice as to the type of settlement they wish to reach. Even if it is only out of basic consideration for this reality and out of respect for human kind, family mediation should be made mandatory.

We are aware, however, that some individuals will resist mediation and others will commit unpardonable acts (incest, spousal abuse, etc.) which will result in their being arrested and tried. However, prudence is the watchword in both cases because, in some instances, all it takes to aggravate the situation or manipulate the system is one party's ill will or a false accusation.

It is precisely to detect false statements and to limit abuses of the system that we need to establish a special court whose judges have been thoroughly trained in family issues. By combining psychosocial knowledge with their legal expertise, judges will be in a better position to act as moderators.

SOCIAL IMPLICATIONS OF DIVORCE

It is universally known and admitted that divorce has a negative impact on the individuals involved. There is also agreement that these kinds of conflicts affect the families of those individuals and their immediate circle (family, friends and co-workers). And in fact, we have observed that more people than we would originally have suspected are affected by divorce in various ways.

If, to put matters into perspective, we consider that half of Quebec couples (including common law unions) will break up[44], And we add to that the fact that "45 per cent of families break up before the child has reached the age of six, and 25 per cent when the child is an adolescent"[45], we get a fairly clear idea of the picture developing before our eyes.

Repercussions of Divorce

Whether people are directly or indirectly affected by a break-up does not change the repercussions of the break-up itself. The multiplier effect of its impact is felt well beyond the family unit in the various spheres of social life. But let us focus specifically on the parents and children affected by this change in the family fabric because, as may be seen from research conducted by a number of experts, divorce-related problems have much more impact than anyone would dare believe. It is therefore important to make parents aware of the importance of staying involved with their children psychologically, physically, and financially.

In its 1988 report, the Department of Justice Canada states at page 7 that parents tend to underestimate the effects of divorce on their children, mentioning three factors that would help children adjust to their new situation : (1) liberal access and constant relations with the non-custodial parent; (2) a post-divorce relationship between mother and father that is as conflict-free as possible and (3) the restoration of settled and comforting domestic habits.

Every divorce results in observable behavioral changes in the people involved. Whether the feelings it causes are repressed or openly expressed, is of little importance since they eventually come out in one way or another. Very often, these changes are hardest on the most vulnerable people in these situations. A number of individuals seriously affected by their conflicts come to the point where they neglect their children and their spouses, or are physically and/or psychologically violent toward them, or abuse them. In some cases, the injured party even goes so far as to kidnap the children or even kill them and then commit suicide.

(a) Academic Problems

The negative consequences of divorce often result in drug and/or alcohol abuse, juvenile delinquency, dropping out of school and suicide. A study by McLanahan[46] shows that the children of divorced and separated families are three times as likely to drop out of school as the children of intact families. This fact was observed in middle-class families. In addition, children who have lived through their parents' separation or divorce complete fewer years of school than the children of intact families. In 1993, De Sève reviewed the findings of a study by the department of Education and observed that young dropouts most often came from single-parent families, unlike children who continued their education.

Ambert and Saucier (1984) observed that the academic performances of children from broken homes were significantly lower than those of intact families. Using a sample of Montreal Island high school students, they showed that adolescents in separated and divorced families had lower grades, liked school less and expected to leave school sooner than the children of couples who were living together.

A recent study conducted by Rousseau and Leblanc (1991) in Quebec reveals that the children of single-parent and reconstituted families have a higher early dropout rate (this indicator measures the potential to leave the school system) than those of two-parent families.

(b) Suicide

In some instances, individuals have such a profound feeling of helplessness that they commit suicide to put an end to their torment. A number of studies appear to have established a parallel between these two phenomena since their findings associate an increase in the suicide rate with the divorce rate. This observation was made in Canada (Trovato, 1987), the United States,[47] 9 Denmark (1990), Norway (1989), and Finland (1992). Furthermore, according to Fortier, Wilkins, Mao and Wigle (1989), the divorce rate and suicide rate in Quebec followed similar curves from 1951 to 1986.

In 1983, M.F. Charron reported that the Quebec suicide rates for divorced men and women were five times higher than those for married individuals.

Canadian studies have established a link between suicidal behavior in young people (attempted suicide, suicidal ideation) and the separation of their parents. One study conducted in Montreal[48] reported that 43 per cent of adolescents whose parents were no longer living together had thoughts about suicide, compared to 13 per cent of those whose parents were still together.

We think it is important to describe the typical family life profile of suicidal young people developed by Michel Tousignant, as described in Le Devoir in 1993 : *"The typical family life profile of suicidal young people in the case of separation : a separation in which the father leaves the home when the child is around six and a half years old, a new union by the mother when the child is approximately eight, and a new separation around age 10. This creates a high degree of instability before the child's identity has been consolidated, which occurs in early adolescence."* With the aid of this profile, we can form a clearer picture of the state of destabilization that strikes young people in family conflicts.

Divorce and Health

Divorce has such a psychological impact on people that many ultimately develop health problems. In fact, it appears that individuals affected by separation or divorce are six times as likely to develop physical or mental health problems as the rest of the population. One study by Statistics Canada revealed that, in 1991, 56 per cent of children of single-parent families had experienced at least one health problem during the year, compared to less than nine per cent of children in intact families.

Tait made a similar observation in 1992, when he was studying sleep disorders. His reported findings indicate that 27 per cent of adolescents 15 to 24 years of age and living with only one parent had trouble sleeping, compared to 18 per cent of those living with both parents. In their 1986 study, Saucier and Ambert observed that the children of broken families had poorer physical and emotional health, were less optimistic about the future and tended to adopt risky behavior such as smoking.

Similar data are available on the health problems caused by the break-up of the family unit. It is important that parents respect children's vested rights as they could have major psychological problems that, in many cases, will not surface until five or 10 years later. It should not be forgotten that these years of stress can damage the child's physical health.

Economic Effects of Divorce

The number of divorced couples has risen sharply since the *Divorce Act* was passed in 1968. Whereas divorce was almost exceptional at the time, it has become quite common today, and the result has been an incredible increase in the number of single-parent families formed for reasons other than a death.

The study, *"Children's Progress in Canada 1996"*, recently published by the Canadian Council on Social Development, reports that there were more than one million single-parent families in Canada in 1995 (p.10). This 60% increase in the number of single-parent families since 1981 was attributable in large part to separations and divorces.

The population grew poorer over the same period. According to the same study (p. 21), 56 per cent of single-parent families were living under the poverty line in 1994, which represented 1.4 million children, one in every five children in Canada. It is important to note that the poverty line at that time corresponded to an annual income of $15,900.

According to Cloutier and Drolet[49] there is a significant discrepancy in Quebec between separated families, which are mainly headed by mothers, and intact families: single-parent families are characterized by less wealth, less education, poorer health, precarious psychological adjustment and a less satisfactory social life.

It seems important to emphasize that high economic status does not necessarily guarantee that children will succeed in life. From early childhood, children need special care, attention and a great deal of love. If well-to-do parents only give their children independence and financial security, without concerning themselves with their emotional needs, children run the risk of developing emotional deficiencies that can result in serious problems. Consequently, finances are only one aspect of the problem.

And that aspect is not a negligible one since it does not just concern couples coping with divorce, but extends to the labor market which involves thousands of workers who are experiencing family problems. All these people affected by their personal conflicts have difficulty concentrating, lose interest in what they are doing, find themselves demotivated and ultimately are no longer able to function socially.

The result is an increase in the number of depressions, burnouts and illnesses of all kinds. Businesses are thus facing an enormous loss of productivity that results in a decline in profits. To this extent, we can say that the community at large stands to lose a great deal as a result of family conflict.

OPCR'S RECOMMENDATIONS

1. Create courses at the elementary and secondary level in order to educate and sensitize students about parental responsibilities. The goal is to ensure that the next generation may adequately understand and assume its role as parents;

2. Create a system of family reconciliation, which is available at all times for couples and families in crisis;

3. Put into place family mediation services that are free, mandatory, and non-judicial, for all couples experiencing marital difficulties or going through divorce proceedings. Such services should also be available for grandparents and other family members in crisis;

4. Eliminate terms that create friction between the parties. For instance, replace the expressions "legal custody" by "parental responsibilities" and "support orders" by "financial responsibilities of parents";

5. Create a court specializing in family matters where judges have an extensive background in family law as well as in psychosocial matters;

6. Create an office of formal complaints where one spouse can file an official complaint in the event that the other spouse does not respect his/her financial or other responsibilities. The official taking the complaint would first discuss the problem with the complainant and then would speak with the other spouse in order to sensitize the latter to the importance of maintaining his/her obligations and responsibilities. In the event that the

spouse fails to respect his/her obligations and responsibilities, then draconian measures could be taken.

Integrating parental responsibilities into the education system

Parents' understanding of their responsibilities toward their children and the fact that they belong in their lives both financially and emotionally, begins at birth.

It follows the individual's development from childhood to adulthood and is influenced by personal experiences and the models from the individual's environment. Parental responsibilities should therefore be promoted well before separation occurs. A prevention plan could help make more thorough changes in the short and long term.

The first plan would deal with a Parental Responsibilities Training Program for school age children. This would be adapted to the children's development and would progress throughout their primary and secondary education. The program would be made a part of the existing system and would be delivered during courses and discussions related to the family. As a result, the next generation would be in a better position to understand its commitments and assume parenting roles.

Making the present generation aware of the fact that they must uphold their parental responsibilities following a separation or divorce would have an immediate and lasting impact. By attacking the problem at its source, we would be leading people in the right direction.

Reconciliation and prevention system for couples and families in difficulty

In our approach to establishing a mechanism that would be more responsive to the parties' needs, it is important to offer a reconciliation system to couples that are hesitating between working on their marital relationship and instituting separation proceedings.

The family must be recognized as a fundamental collective value. We must continue our efforts to ensure a certain stability for the family and in particular provide parents with the necessary assistance to uphold their responsibilities toward their children.

The Conseil de la famille has published a guide for public and private stakeholders entitled "PENSER ET AGIR FAMILLE" [50] It was thought that there was a need for a well-established family policy. The idea conveyed was an excellent one, as expressed in page 12 of their document : "*A small effort when prevention is still possible will avoid major intervention in a crisis.*" The family assistance information sector must be expanded.

Family mediation

Mediation is defined in many ways depending also on the person who describes it. Despite the diversity of meanings, however, the definitions all state that mediation is a conflict settlement procedure that benefits every person involved. The objective of mediation is thus to find an effective way to settle conflicts and disputes between individuals who must remain in continuous and extended contact.

Family mediation offers many benefits. It promotes discussion in more relaxed setting. The parties themselves work on their own draft agreement; they feel more involved and thus comply with their agreements to a much higher degree. And the atmosphere of cooperation produces benefits later on when it is time to revise the terms of the agreement following a change in the parties' situation.

Unlike a Superior Court Hearing, the family mediation process does not permit the spouses to list their criticisms of each other. The purpose of mediation, which is far from being an adversarial process, is to reduce tension and frustration. To do this, the accent must be placed on possible alternatives for satisfying the entire family, especially the children.

The Cabinet brief raises the question of the place of psychosocial issues in family matters. Children are often most affected during separation proceedings. On page 64, the brief states that: "*45 per cent of families break up before the child reaches six years of age, 25 per cent when the child is in adolescence*".

A couple experiencing a crisis obviously needs help, advice and support, and by placing them in a confrontational system, we take away the energy that parents could use to take care of their children.

The time allocated for mediation sessions should not be limited to only a few hours. Instead, we feel that 12 hours of mediation would enable the mediator to address all the aspects of the break-up.

(a) Benefits of Mediation

We are in favor of family mediation because it has long since proven itself. According to a study conducted by the Department of Justice, Canada, agreed-upon support payment amounts are 12 to 20 per cent higher as a result of mediation. Furthermore, the support payment rate is greater among people who have undergone mediation than among other couples.

The principal strength of mediation lies in the fact that the parties involved in the conflict participate directly in the settlement process to reach a suitable agreement. As a result, they do not have the unpleasant feeling of having to submit to a judgment rendered by a third person, and the agreement reached is not in the interests of any one individual, but rather of all those concerned by the problem. The result is a higher degree of satisfaction in each of the parties, as they are not left with the impression they have lost something. While family mediation does not result in gains for a particular spouse, it does not result in losses for the other either.

Hence the sense of satisfaction felt by those who undergo mediation. By not promoting confrontation, the mediator focuses discussion on the real interests. The difficulties of families must be addressed in a more humane way, focusing in particular on the welfare of the children involved and not losing sight of this aspect, in the process leading to an agreement.

Another point that should encourage the government to expand the concept of mediation is the amount of time and money saved. According to the family mediation pilot project submitted by Ellis Research Associates of Ontario, **total per-hour court costs including the judge, clerk and court reporters is $466.29, whereas the total cost for mediation is $96.30, including the secretary's time.**

Another surprising fact is provided in the Cabinet brief submitted by Mr. Gilles Rémillard (Minister of Justice), Mr. Marc-Yvan Côté (Minister of Health) and Ms. Violette Trépanier (Minister Responsible for the Family) on January 31, 1992 : **"Ten percent of cases heard by the Superior Court are family cases, but the Court allocates 86 per cent of its total hearing time to these cases."** Family mediation would relieve the courts of these cases, while building longer-lasting agreements and reducing the number of applications for amendments to the initial agreement.

A mediation pioneer, Mr. Justin Lévesque, professor of the School of Social Work at the University of Montreal, has described the benefits of the mediation process in his articles. We summarize them below. According to Mr. Lévesque, mediation :

- is an alternative to the interminable quarrels that can result from a break-up;
- goes beyond conflict and terminates the marital relationship with dignity;
- permits dialogue that fosters better communication between former spouses;
- permits more flexibility than the Court as regards the terms of an agreement (example, shared custody on a monthly rather than weekly basis);
- is more economical;
- takes less time;
- does not seek a guilty party;
- involves fathers to a greater degree;
- encourages greater compliance with agreements than in the case of court judgments;
- promotes more regular payment of support;
- enables the parties to learn conflict-resolution skills that can be used in other areas of life (educational aspect of mediation);
- promotes greater acceptance of the conclusions of divorce;
- enables parents to remain parents.

Family mediation offers the advantage of addressing separation in a much more therapeutic way, co-operative rather than destructive. The success of mediation is also directly related to the parties' motivation to settle their dispute. Family ties must be restructured in an entirely different context.

The findings of a study on the cost effectiveness of mediation were published in April 1989 in a comparative report by the Family Mediation Department of the Metropolitan Montreal Social Services Center (MMSSC). According to that report, it is clear that "mediation and the legal process would undoubtedly strike a greater balance in the division of property between husband and wife." In other words, mediation does not reinforce the inequality of powers within the couple; on the contrary, it requires both parties to cooperate in an honest and frank way.

Throughout the mediation process, the emphasis will be placed on negotiations based on the individuals' values and needs rather than on positions that do not always take into account the mutual interests of the spouses and children. Since the agreement is thus structured by the individuals to suit themselves, the chances that they will comply with it are that much greater.

Above all, family mediation fosters greater parental involvement with the children. The study on alimony collection by the Quebec Council on Status of Women states (p.33) that one of the reasons alimony debtors do not pay is that they have lost motivation for personal reasons. Those reasons include the fact that they are no longer taking part in the everyday activities of their children.

Some definitions of family mediation describe a process of assistance in negotiating in a suitable way. Unlike the method of representation by a lawyer, in which the parties leave all the work to their representatives, mediation requires much greater efforts by the couple. The parties must seek out a range of solutions before making a decision. In the end, they very often produce different results from those that would be obtained in court. For example, in a judgment, the non-custodial parent is often granted access every other weekend. However, through mediation, an attempt is made to maximize the presence of both parents with their children, while creating a certain stability for the children themselves.

The relationship between the parties is different with mediation than when there is a Court judgment involved. The Department of Justice writes (p.37), "*63 per cent of women who underwent mediation in Montreal, compared to 32 per cent of those who did not, characterized their relationship with their former spouse as "close."*

The courts acknowledge their limits in family matters. The rules of procedure are clear and the courts do not have time to analyze the parties' emotions, aggressiveness or frustrations. Clients often tell their lawyers in the courthouse corridors that they would like the Court to be told certain facts and the lawyer quite rightly answers that those facts are immaterial as evidence. Family mediation definitely offers more latitude in this regard from the moment the parties avoid criticizing each other.

Lastly, mediation is a conflict-resolution method that can be adapted to today's society. Over the years, we realize that divorce rates have increased greatly; therefore solutions must be found so that these disputes are resolved more quickly and the agreements reached are longer lasting. But above all, we must try to resolve the deadlock between the parties with as few after-effects as possible.

(b) Training for Mediators

The legal system is by nature an adversarial system. Based on their academic and professional training, lawyers try to obtain maximum concessions for their clients. Except for those who practice mediation, lawyers are trained to negotiate, not to mediate. There is a fundamental difference between the two methods of reaching an agreement.

A mediator makes the parents aware that they must consider their children's best interests and needs. He or she should preferably be a psychologist or a social worker, with a concomitant understanding of human nature, awareness of family dynamics and perception of psychological reactions that make that person the most qualified to intervene in these situations.

The mediator's role is to inform parents of the harmful consequences of divorce for their children and to make them aware that their relationship with their children continues even if the couple is no longer together. Specialized family mediators realize that they must keep their knowledge in the field up to date. Thorough training would enable mediators to understand all the subtleties that can arise during the mediation process.

Avoiding terms that antagonize people

The use of certain words necessarily creates winners and losers. Replacing those terms with others that are more motivating for parents is not complicated.

For example, we propose that "legal custody" be replaced by "parental responsibilities" and "alimony" by "family support."

These are only examples based on our line of thinking which would help substitute a social perspective for the adversarial approach. We have even received comments from a few parents who said that the use of the term "single-parent" was not appropriate. The dictionary definition of single-parent states, "where there is only one parent," even though the child still has two parents after separation. All these minor points increase the gap between parents, and disrupt family unity.

Special Court

The Organization for the Protection of Children's Rights recommends that a Special Court be established and presided over by Superior Court justices. It would have full and exclusive authority to hear all family law cases.

Special Court judges would be thoroughly trained in the legal and psychosocial aspects of family issues. Since they would hear only family law cases, they would have the opportunity to develop expertise in this field of law. Family conflict resolution is extremely important and, very difficult, and deserves the special attention of the judges dedicated and committed to it. It is not surprising that, in the performance of his/her duties, a Superior Court judge can hear cases involving Corporate Law, Labor Law, Contractual Liability and so on. His/Her experience may therefore be highly varied and he/she may not have had the opportunity to develop an extensive knowledge of family law. A judge who hears only family law cases could develop that kind of expertise.

In addition to family law experience, special court judges must be sensitive to children, trained in psychology, mediation, child development and interpersonal relations. Among other things, we must promote extensive psychological training so that judges are able to assess the impact of their decisions.

Various approaches may be used with regard to the Special Court. Judges may begin by asking the parties why mediation failed. In this way, they would immediately ascertain the parties' weaknesses and integrate the positive aspects of mediation into the legal system. There would thus be a certain follow-up to our mediation process. Since this would be a Special Court, decisions should be rendered sooner.

It currently takes a year or two on average to settle contested divorces, excluding all the related petitions. Our purpose in proposing a Special Court is to offset all these negative effects.

Formal complaints office

In the same line of thinking and to be as realistic as possible, we believe it would be more appropriate to have a Formal Complaints Office in situations where support (alimony) is not paid or visitation rights are not respected. A Formal Complaints Office would help address these situations.

Our concern once again is to intervene quickly so that children are not harmed by any delays. This service must be effective and simple because default often involves lost time, money, working hours and emotional costs to the alimony creditor. The creditor would report to the Formal Complaints Office and a qualified resource person would prepare the complaint. This would be an out-of-court procedure requiring no professional representation.

Second, this official would meet the debtor to determine the cause of delay in payment of the alimony (support) or denial of access. Some of these problems start with a lack of communication, and a Formal Complaints Office would immediately correct the situation.

It is important that this resource person insist on making the debtor aware of the importance of his or her monetary and emotional contribution to the child. A method such as this one would provide follow-up to our mediation procedure and Special Court. Should this person realize that the situation of the parties has changed, he or she may even induce the parties to return to mediation to update their agreement.

For alimony (support) that is not paid after this process, a collection system could then be implemented. As the percentage of unpaid alimony would decline enormously as a result of all the measures taken, the cost of the collection system would therefore be lower. However, the most desired effect would be a social one. These procedures may call for greater government involvement, but the result will be less suicide, less school dropouts, and less mental and health problems over the long term.

CONCLUSION

WHEREAS, in Quebec, 50 per cent of couples break up and 45 per cent of families do so before the child reaches six years of age, and 25 per cent before the child reaches adolescence;

WHEREAS a large number of children involved in crime (violence, drugs) who are arrested and tried in Youth Court are from broken or single-parent families;

WHEREAS the children and parents of broken families have six times more mental and physical health problems than the children and parents of intact families;

WHEREAS the suicide rates for divorced Quebec men and women are five times higher than those of married people;

WHEREAS contested family cases (10 per cent) occupy 86 per cent of the Superior Court's total hearing time;

AND KNOWING THAT mediation has proven itself as a way of reaching settlements in family disputes through a much less aggressive method;

We recommend that the government introduce mandatory mediation. **For the greater good of children and the family and for a better society, let us give our children the tools they need to grow up as well-balanced individuals.**

Reasons as to why our recommendations may take a long time to be implemented

Research and literature reviews have shown that there are negative consequences on children when there is a separation or divorce. We must ask why the situation has not improved at a more rapid pace. Certain questions remain:

1) Do certain lobby groups have a vested interest in ensuring that things not change?

2) There are changes in government on a regular basis – different priorities come to the foreground and therefore different programs and bills are introduced. While we agree that changes in government are acceptable in a democratic society, we must concentrate on uniting for the well being of

society and our families.

3) The needs of children and the family should transcend partisan party politics and the usual opposition tactics must be put aside in favor of the protection of children's rights. The problems stemming from the break-up of the family should be addressed in an objective, non-partisan manner. Why do we not all work together to find solutions to problems that we all face?

4) Funding for research, in some cases, in Universities is dependent upon the production of results that support a particular view and as such researchers must be able to be more independent so less popular views can be researched and validated.

5) Is it not true that international non-governmental organizations and third sector research often are unable to attract funds for their work because they challenge the established order?

While we speak of the best interests of the child…hundreds of thousands of children are suffering daily.

BIBLIOGRAPHY OF BRIEF

➤ ADAM, K.S., LOHRENZ, J.G., HARPER, D., STREINER, D. (1982): *"Early Parental Loss and Suicidal Ideation in University Students"*, Canadian Journal of Psychiatry, Vol. 27, p. 275-281;

➤ ADAM, O.: *"Les Divorces au Canada, 1988"*, Rapports sur la Santé, Vol. 2, No. 1, p. 57-66;

➤ AMBERT, A.-M., SAUCIER, J.-F. (1984): *"Adolescent' Academic Success and Aspirations by Parental Marital Status"*, Revue Canadienne de Sociologie et d'Anthropologie, Vol. 21, No. 1, p. 62-74;

➤ AMATO, P.-R., KEITH, B. (1991): *"Parental Divorce and the Well-Being of Children: A Meta-Analysis"*, Psychological Bulletin, Vol. 110, No. 1, p. 26-4;

➤ AMATO, P.-R., KEITH, B. (1991): *"Parental Divorce and Adult Well-Being: A Meta-Analysis"*, Journal of Marriage and the Family, p. 53, 43-58;

➤ BLANCHARD, M.-A. (25 avril 1989): *"Rapport corporatif du Service de médiation à la famille du Centre de services sociaux de Montréal métropolitain"*;

➤ *"La médiation des divorces rattachée aux tribunaux dans quatre villes canadiennes"*, Canada, Ministère de la Justice (Février 1988);

➤ CHARRON, M.-F. (1993): *"Le suicide au Québec"*, Ministère des Affaires Sociales, Services des Études Épidémiologiques;

➤ CLOUTIER, R. (1990): *"Avant-propos – Spécial jeunes et nouvelles familles"*, Apprentissage et Socialisation, Vol. 13, No.1;

➤ Code civil de la Californie(1981), Art. 4607;

➤ *"Le Progrès des Enfants au Canada, 1996"*, Conseil canadien de développement social (1996);

➤ *"Études sur la perception des pensions alimentaires"*, Conseil du statut de la femme, Québec (1995);

➤   CONSEIL DE LA FAMILLE (1990): *"Penser et agir famille"*, Avis du Conseil de la Famille à la ministre déléguée à la condition féminine et responsable de la famille, Avis No. 89.2, Gouvernement du Québec;

➤   CONGRÈS 1988: *"Divorce et Enfants : Comment intervenir avant, pendant et après ?"*, Organisation pour la Sauvegarde des Droits des Enfants (O.S.D.E.);

➤   CONGRÈS 1992: *"L'Enfant et les transformations familiales : Vulnérabilité et adaptation"*, Organisation pour la Sauvegarde des Droits des Enfants (O.S.D.E.);

➤   CUMMING, E., LAZER, C. (1981): *"Kinship Structure and Suicide : A Theoretical Link"*, Revue Canadienne de Sociologie et d'Anthropologie, Vol. 18, No. 3, p. 271-282;

➤   DE SÈVE (1993);

➤   ELLIS, D., ELLIS RESEARCH ASSOCIATES (JULY 1994): *"Family Mediation Pilot Project"*, Ministry of the Attorney General, Ontario;

➤   EMERY, R.-E., WYER, M.-M. (1987): *"Divorce Mediation"*, American Psychologist, Vol. 42, No. 2, p. 472-480;

➤   FORTIER, L., WILKINS, K., MAO, Y., WIGLE, D.-T. (1989): *"Le Suicide au Québec, 1951-1986 : Comparaison avec le Canada*, Cahier Québécois de Démographie, Vol. 18, No. 2, p. 393-402;

➤   GUIBAULT, F. (1992): *"Les enfants du divorce : nouveau défi pour les parents, la société et la médiation"*, La médiation familiale, Les Éditions Yvon Blais Inc., p. 159-180;

➤   *"La situation démographique au Québec"*, Les publications du Québec, Édition 1987;

➤   LAURENT-BOYER, L. (1992): *"La médiation familiale : définition, cadre théorique, bienfaits pour la famille et étude de modèles"*, La médiation familiale, Les Éditions Yvon Blais Inc., p. 3-27;

➤ LEBLANC, M., McDUFF, P., TREMBLAY, R. (1991): *"Types de familles, conditions de vie, fonctionnement du système familial et inadaptation sociale au cours de la latence et de l'adolescence dans les milieux défavorisés"*, Santé mentale au Québec, p. 45-75;

➤ LESAGE, R., (1992): *"Déjudiciariser le conflit familial"*, La médiation familiale, Les Éditions Yvon Blais Inc.;

➤ McLANAHAN, The Economist, (20 mars 1993);

➤ MILNE, L., SALEM, P., KOEFFLER, K. (1992): *"When Domestic Abuse Is an Issue"*, Family Advocate, American Family Law Section, Vol. 14, No. 4, p. 34-39;

➤ PROJET DE RECHERCHES (1993): *"Délinquance juvénile, Tribunal de la jeunesse de Montréal"*, Organisation pour la Sauvegarde des Droits des Enfants (O.S.D.E.);

➤ RÉMILLARD, G., CÔTÉ, M.-Y., TRÉPANIER, V. (31 janvier 1992), *"Mémoire au Conseil des Ministres"*, Gouvernement du Québec;

➤ REVUE DE LITTÉRATURE (1993), *"Suicide et divorce"*, Organisation pour la Sauvegarde des Droits des Enfants (O.S.D.E.);

➤ ROUSSEAU et LEBLANC (1991);

➤ SAUCIER, J.M. AMBERT, A.-M. (1986-M.,): *"Adolescents' Perception of Self and of Immediate Environment by Parental Marital Status : A Controlled Study"*, Canadian Journal of Psychiatry, Vol. 31, No. 6, p. 505-512;

➤ STACK, S. (1989): *"The Impact of Divorce on Suicide in Norway, 1951-1980"*, Journal of Marriage and the Family, Vol. 51, p. 229-238;

➤ STACK, S. (1990): *"The Effect of Divorce on Suicide in Denmark : 1951-1980"*, The Sociological Quarterly, Vol. 31, No. 3, p. 359-370;

➤ STACK, S. (1992): *"The Effect of Divorce on Suicide in Finland : A Time Series Analysis"*, Journal of Marriage and the Family, Vol. 54, p. 636-642;

➢   STACK, S., HAAS, A. (1984): *"The Effect of Unemployment Duration on National Suicide Rates : A Time Series Analysis, 1948-1982"*, Sociological Focus, Vol. 17, No. 1, p. 17-29;

➢   TAIT, H. (Winter 1992):*"Sleep Problems : Whom Do They Affect ?"*, Statistics Canada, Canadian Social Trends, p. 8-10;

➢   TROVATO, F. (1987): *"A Longitudinal Analysis of Divorce and Suicide in Canada"*, Journal of Marriage and the Family, Vol. 49, p. 193-203;

➢   TOUSIGNANT, M., BASTIEN, M.-F, HAMEL, S. (1993): *"Suicidal Attempts and Ideations Among Adolescents and Young Adults : The Contribution of the Father's and Mother's Care and of Parental Separation"*, Social Psychiatry and Psychiatric Epidemiology, Vol. 28, p. 256-21.

NOTES

1. Statistics Canada, 1997.

2. *Robert E. Emery, Renegotiating Family Relationships: Divorce, Child Custody and Mediation, American Studies, March 1999; Canada, Ministère de la justice, La médiation des divorces rattachée aux tribunaux dans quatre villes canadiennes", February 1988.*

3. *Source: Divorce: Law and the Family in Canada, McKie, D.C., Prentice, B., and Reed P., Statistics Canada, Ottawa, 1983, p.211.*

4. *Dea transcript, p. 146*

5. *Dea, p. 193*

6. *Source: Divorce: Law and the Family in Canada. Women were only granted co-guardianship of their children in most provinces in 1923.*

7. *Official transcript of Alberta Court of Queen's Bench hearing, April 1, 1981, p.491-493.*

8. *Official transcript of Alberta Court of Queen's Bench hearing, April 1, 1981, p. 496-497.*

9. *Reference: Hannan, Nov. 9, p 26; Parizeau-Popovici examination of affidavit, June 8/83, p.10.*

10. *(Grenier, Feb. 26, 1982, p. 51)*

11. *(Grenier, Feb. 26, 1982, p. 52)*

12. *Translated from Grenier, March 3, 1982, p. 33.*

13. *Affidavit, Peggy Roaff, June 1, 1983.*

14. *Reference: Reasons for Judgment, the Honourable Mr. Justice J.B. Dea, July 29, 1983.*

15. *Gazette, Nov. 5, 1983, p. F-1.*

16. *Freeland, p. 20.*

17. *Reference: House of Commons debates, January 15, 1986.*

18. *Source: Saucier, Jean-François et Ambert, Anne-Marie, "Adaptation des adolescents au décès ou au divorce des parents", Santé Mentale au Québec, 1988, Vol. XIII, 2; also article "Effets du divorce sur l'enfant (résumé") - Jean-François Saucier.*

19. *Seaton, p.6*

20. Seaton, p. 12

21. *Source: letter from Peggy Roaff to Ricaardoe Di Done, March 19, 1986.*

22. *Source: Interview with Aldo Morrone, May 29, 1998.*

23. *Source: Liliane Spector-Dunsky report, April 15, 1987.*

24. *Source: R's affidavit, Dec. 21/88.*

25. *Source: Speech "A little success" given October 27, 1988 during OPCR's first International Conference.*

26. *Speech, p.11.*

27. *Finch, p. 65.*

28. *Finch decision, March 10, 1989, p. 18-19.*

29. Source: *OPCR's Family Mediation: A procedure that benefits everyone,
     April 1998 - presentation to Special Joint Committee on Child Custody
     and Access*

30. Source: *An Inventory of Government-based Services that support the
     Making and Enforcement of Custody and Access Decisions, The Federal-
     Provincial-Territorial Family Law Committee, Department of Justice,
     Canada.*

31. Source: *An Inventory of Government-based Services that support the
     Making and Enforcement of Custody and Access Decisions, The Federal-
     Provincial-Territorial Family Law Committee, Department of Justice,
     Canada.*

32. Source: *The Dynamics of Formation and Dissolution of First Common-
     law unions in Canada, Pierre Turcotte and Alain Bélanger, Statistics
     Canada.*

33. *Unofficial translation from the original French, Méthodologie de la
     Médiation Familiale, Justin Lévesque, Edisem Inc., 1998, p.113.*

34. Judith Wallerstein and Sandra Blakeslee, *Second Chances: Men, Women
     and Children a Decade after Divorce, 1989.*

35. Paul R. Amato and Bruce Keith, "Parental Divorce and Adult Well-Being:
     A Meta-analysis*", Journal of Marriage and the Family*, Vol. 53 (February
     1991), p. 54.

36. E.M. Hetherington, M. Stanley Hagan and E.D. Anderson, "Family
     Transitions: A Child's Perspective" (1989) 44 American Psychologist p.
     303-312 and G.C. Kitson, *Portrait of Divorce: Adjustment to Marital
     Breakdown* New York, Guilford, 1992 cited in Richard Cloutier,
     "Transitions familiales et développement de l'enfant: les enjeux pour
     l'intervention", (1997-98) 28 R.D.U.S. p. 26).

37. (N. Turmel and R. Cloutier, "Séparation parentale et consultation
     psychologique à l'école" (1990) 7 Psychologie Québec, p 8-9 cited in
     Richard Cloutier, "Transitions familiales et développement de l'enfant: les
     enjeux pour l'intervention", (1997-98) 28 R.D.U.S. p. 31).

38. (M.F. Charron, *Le suicide au Québec*, Ministère des affaires sociales,
     Services des études épidémiologiques, 1983)

39. (Statistics Canada)

40. Civil Code of California, art. 4607, 1981).

41. H. McIsaac, cited in Emery and Wyer, 1987.

42. H. McIsaac, cited in Emery and Wyer, 1987.

43. L. Milne, P. Salem, K. Koeffler, 1992.

44. Laurent-Boyer, 1992.

45. Department of Justice document, cited in Rémillard, Côté and Trépanier,
     1992.

46. The Economist, March 20, 1993.

47. Stack and Haas, 1984; Stack, 1989

48. Adam, Lohrenz, Harper and Streiner, 1982.

49. Cited in Le Blanc, McDuff and Tremblay, 1991.

50. Family Thinking and Acting no.89.2

AGMV Marquis

MEMBRE DE SCABRINI MEDIA

Québec, Canada
2003